SEX AND PERSONALITY

Sex and Personality

H. J. Eysenck Ph.D., D.Sc.

University of Texas Press
Austin

International Standard Book Number 0-292-77529-6
Library of Congress Catalog Card Number 76-15479

Printed in England

Contents

The greatness of God is infinite, for while with one die man impresses many coins and they are all alike, the King of Kings, the Holy One, with one die he impresses the same image on all men, yet not one of them is like his companions.

Talmud

Introduction

Psychology holds a central place in our efforts to make sense of the world, and of our place in it; unless we can understand ourselves, and have some firm knowledge of our ways of perceiving, acting and behaving, we are likely to misinterpret the evidence of our senses, and derive entirely false conclusions about our state. It would however be quite wrong to imagine that efforts to place psychology on a scientific footing are likely to receive any wholehearted welcome from most people; quite the opposite is true. Just as humanity resented the efforts of Copernicus and Galileo to displace the earth from its place in the centre of the universe, or the work of Darwin which displaced man from his unique position in the animal kingdom, so nowadays most people resent the psychologist's efforts to replace unreasoned belief by factual demonstration. We are determined to believe certain things about ourselves, and under extreme provocation resort to the famous words of the wartime cartoon: 'Don't confuse me with facts; my mind is made up!' Even suggest that *homo sapiens* may not be as *sapiens* as all that, and all hell breaks loose; we may under duress agree that people who do not share our own political, social, sexual and other views may indeed be misguided, irrational and neurotic; but we would most certainly defend to the death the proposition that our own views are based entirely on sound reasoning, factual research and objective appraisal.

In the sexual field, in particular, there has for centuries (and probably since the beginning of recognisable societies) existed a battle between puritans and libertines, between restrictive tradition and uninhibited permissiveness. Both sides defend their position vociferously, often appealing to such scientific research as may seem to support their point of view and heaping scorn on anything that might seem to go counter to their beliefs; neither side seems willing to realise that perhaps their quarrel may be based on a misunderstanding. When I say that I like strawberries and dislike oysters and you say that you like oysters and dislike strawberries, we are not really taking issue with each other; we are both stating facts that have a personal reference, but no universal validity. The error comes in only when we generalise our own preferences into prescriptive statements, saying that everyone should like strawberries more than oysters (or vice versa). This is too silly for anyone to do in this particular case, but on other issues that is precisely what people do do. Libertines suggest that their way of expressing their sexuality is the only proper way, and that those who disagree with them are neurotic, inhibited and sick. Puritans in their turn believe that their way of expressing their sexuality is the only proper way, and that disagreement indicates possession by the devil, lack of morality and probably mental disorder as well. The implication in such debates always is that there is one and only one proper way of conducting oneself, and that this of course is the way one happens to have chosen oneself. Such beliefs, and such debates, generate more heat than light, and they are likely to lead to intolerance, suppression and persecution of those not sharing one's own views.

This book grew out of the author's feeling that perhaps there was no single, orthodox way to salvation; that perhaps different people are born with different desires, values and attitudes; and that perhaps the desire for a universal *Gleichschaltung* was a piece of authoritarian impudence which had no scientific warrant whatever. Human diversity has always fascinated me, and the belief, inherent in Darwinian evolutionary theories, that such diversity is essential for survival (by allowing pressure of changing conditions to favour now one, now another, form of adjustment, depending on circumstances) seems to me an essential biological underpinning of democratic government. If you find value in diversity you are perhaps less likely to wish to tie everyone on to a Procrustean bed, and if you realise the tremendous pressure exerted by genetic factors in pushing us one way or another in our efforts at adjustment, you are likely to be more modest in your claims for your particular plans of universal salvation, and more desirous of seeing diversity of conduct preserved. It seemed worthwhile, as a first step in the direction of finding out more about the myriad ways in which human beings in our society express their sexual desires, to carry out some empirical investigations, guided by the wish to find out what people were actually thinking and doing, rather than by a desire to tell them what they ought to be thinking and doing.

Scientific studies are seldom of a purely inductive kind, simply gathering facts along Baconian lines; usually there is some more or less explicit theory guiding the collection of data. In this case the theory was quite explicit; it seemed likely to me that people characterised by different personalities would also differ in predictable ways in their sexual conduct, and that such predictions could be tested and would in turn cast some interesting light on the theories of personality that inspired the research. Consequently much of the work reported in this book looks at the interaction between personality on the one hand and sexual attitudes and behaviours on the other. The subjects are very varied, comprising normal adult men and women, students and adolescents, criminals, inmates of Broadmoor Hospital for the criminally insane and so forth. On the whole, results were mostly along the lines anticipated, and this was true regardless of the particular samples studied.

An area of particular interest was that of the differences between males and females. Are the sexual attitudes of men and women in our day and age really as different as tradition has it? Are the relationships between attitudes and personality similar for the two sexes, or are they quite different? These and other similar questions seemed of some interest, and consequently particular attention was paid to the detailed analysis of sex comparisons.

A final item of interest was the question of genetic determination of sexual attitudes and behaviours. It has become fashionable to deny the importance of biological factors in human behaviour, and to attribute all differences that are observed to role-playing generated by environmental pressures. There is too much evidence to the contrary to accept such whole-hogging sociological views in their entirety; there does seem to exist the alternative possibility that some of these roles are enforced by society on men and women, say, because throughout history genetic and other biological factors have exerted pressure in that direction. Without wishing to preempt the discussion, it seemed reasonable to carry out some direct studies of these questions, using our Twin Register; the results would seem to support a view insisting on the complex interaction of genetic and environmental factors in the determination of human conduct, particularly in the sexual sphere.

What do the results of our inquiries have to teach us regarding the general ordering of our affairs in the sexual field? I have tried to indicate the general thrust of the argument in the final chapter, but of course the reader is free to interpret the import of the results in any way he or she chooses. Scientific facts are relevant to ethical, social and legal decisions, but they do not determine them; the facts here brought forward are relevant to such issues as censorship, prostitution, marriage, perverse practices and so forth, but decisions regarding these affairs derive from a wider religious, ideological or political context, and this context will determine to some extent the regard paid to the factual material. My own expertise ends with the presentation of the empirical studies; all I have tried to do is to suggest some practical consequences that seem to me to follow from these. The reader is at liberty to disregard my comments completely; they do not have the same status as experimentally ascertained facts.

I am indebted to many people who helped in the collection of data, too numerous to mention. I also encountered much hostility when approaching vice-chancellors and other eminent academic persons in order to obtain their permission to invite students under their care to take part in the investigation; one of them offered to pray for me in order to make me desist from what he was convinced was not only an impious and odious effort, but was also likely to debauch and corrupt the students involved. Students themselves, as well as the older and more mature men and women who constituted my samples, took a rather more realistic and sensible view of the proceedings; they were interested, helpful and entirely serious in their endeavours to give a realistic picture of their attitudes and practices. Undoubtedly they were not a random sample of the population, but they represented all the diverse ways of looking at sex, indulging or not indulging in sex, and of thinking about sex that one is likely to find in this country at this time. For their wholehearted collaboration in spending countless hours on lengthy and perhaps rather boring questionnaires I wish here to express my heartiest thanks; without their help this book assuredly could not have been written!

H. J. Eysenck Ph.D., D.Sc.
Maudsley Hospital
15 January 1976

4

1

Individual differences in sexual behaviour

The literature on human sexual behaviour is large; even larger is the literature on animal sex. Although there was much interest in the topic prior to Kinsey, it is with his large-scale work that the proper investigation of human sexual behaviour is usually considered to start.(1) Nearly all of this literature has followed Kinsey in being concerned with population parameters; interest centred on such questions as the average number of times men and women had intercourse per week; the percentage of men who had had homosexual experiences, or of women who had Lesbian experiences; the average number of premarital or extra-marital experiences of men and women; or the average age at which men and women had their first intercourse. These are interesting questions, but they are not of very great scientific importance. Nor is it likely that they can be answered with any reasonable degree of accuracy. Kinsey and his followers have proceded in a somewhat Baconian fashion, gathering facts and hoping that later on theories would be developed on the basis of these collections of facts. Unfortunately they disregarded T. H. Huxley's injunction: 'Those who refuse to go beyond fact seldom get as far as fact.'

My belief that these 'facts' are not really very factual is based on the following considerations. In the first place, population parameters cannot be estimated properly except on the basis of reasonably random samples of the population. Now Kinsey was quite well aware of the fact that his samples were by no means random; he tried to compensate for the deficiencies in his samples, but unfortunately this is not possible; his estimates may be near the true values, but it is impossible to know whether this is so, or whether

5

they depart to a considerable extent from these true values. It would be wrong to blame him for not obtaining random, or even quota or stratified, samples; in the nature of things, this would have been impossible when such a very personal thing as 'sexual experience' was being investigated. There is an inevitably high refusal rate for studies of this kind, and no proper replacement can be made for these 'refusees'.

In the second place, Kinsey's interviewers asked for information that is almost impossible to recover, and that in the form asked for probably never existed in the mind of the interviewee. Consider questions regarding frequency of intercourse. Very few people have kept the sort of accurate record of their sexual behaviour that alone could produce a reasonably accurate answer. Guessing how many times one has had intercourse during the past month, or year, or decade is likely to give very erroneous answers; frequencies for many people are so variable (particularly for non-married people), and so subject to illnesses, 'periods' and other disturbing influences, that guesses cannot in the nature of things be at all accurate. Relations between answers given spontaneously to questions of this kind, and records kept afterwards to check on their accuracy, in our experience have not shown a very high degree of agreement.

This is true when the question is purely factual; even greater complications ensue when the answers are value-laden. This is our third point. There is much 'social desirability' in some answers, as compared to others; psychologists have done much work in recent years to demonstrate the importance of such social desirability in shaping responses in questionnaires and interviews. Admittedly Kinsey and his successors attempted to get over this difficulty, but there is no evidence that they were successful in this, or just how successful they were. These three objections are the main ones that have been brought forward; they argue strongly against taking the 'facts' unearthed too seriously.

But even if all the figures given in the literature could be taken as accurate and reliable, it could still be argued that they have little scientific value. Facts in science are important and relevant to the extent that they support or refute a theory; as Darwin pointed out, 'how odd it is that anyone should not see that all observation must be for or against some view if it is to be of any service!' These facts (even assuming them to be such) are quite atheoretical; they neither support nor refute any meaningful scientific theory,

6

and must consequently be judged to be of little systematic importance. This position could of course be altered if the Kinsey studies were to be repeated every ten or twenty years, so that temporal trends could be established (assuming all the difficulties listed above to have been overcome); these trends might be used as evidence for certain psychological or sociological hypotheses regarding changes in sexual mores. But by themselves they are not of great scientific interest or importance.

There is one further objection to the Kinsey-type investigation. Means and averages are meaningful only if there are no great individual differences among the units so averaged. To know that the average number of times people have intercourse is twice a week is meaningful if the numbers averaged vary from 2 to 4, or even from 1 to 5. But in actual fact, when the details are plotted it becomes apparent that many people have intercourse only once a month, or even less frequently, while others have it several times a day. The variability is so extreme that averages tell us little. In line with his intention to provide us with population parameter estimates, Kinsey gives means and variances for most of his tables (or at least these can be estimated from his figures), but all they do is illustrate the extreme degree of variability that is so characteristic of human sexual responses.

Figure 1.1 shows the kind of variability referred to; it gives the distribution of people in the 16–24, 25–34 and 35–54 and 55+ age groups on a scale showing the number of times intercourse took place on the average. The figures are taken from a national sampling survey, and averaged for males and females; within the limitations of accuracy of estimates, limitations of sampling refusals and the other objections noted above, the results should be fairly representative of British men and women in the 1970s. The decline of frequency of intercourse with age is noticeable but hardly surprising; what is interesting in this figure is the great spread, for each age group, of the frequencies. Even in the 55+ group, some have intercourse four to six times a week, others never! This variability makes generalisations pretty meaningless.

Kinsey makes little effort to account for individual differences; he only tries to do so indirectly by reference to sociological variables (like social class) and biological variables (like age). Thus he presents means and variances for different age groups, or different social classes. There is little in the way of psychological theorising,

7

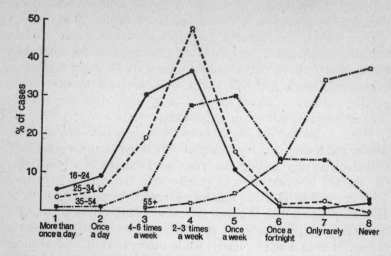

Figure 1.1 *Frequency of intercourse for men and women of four different age groups*

and practically no reference to personality variables, in spite of the fact that such variables are likely to play an important part within age and social class groups. This neglect of individual differences, and this failure to attempt to account for them along psychological lines, is one of the outstanding failures of recent work on human sexual responses.

It might be thought that this stricture does not apply to psycho-analysis; would it not be true to say that psychoanalysts too have criticised Kinsey on similar lines, and have proffered extensive and intricate theories to account for individual differences in this field? I will not here repeat the criticisms I have elsewhere made of psycho-analytic theories, or the failure of these theories to stand up to experimental testing (Eysenck and Wilson 1974); let it suffice to say that 'explanations' given by psychoanalysts of human sexual be-haviour, and individual differences, have no general validity or application. They are usually *ad hoc* applications of arbitrary principles, from which no general deductions can be made, and which therefore cannot be tested scientifically. Psychoanalysis does not enable us to answer the urgent question raised by the existence of very marked individual differences in human sexual behaviour.

It is the purpose of this book to make a beginning in the business of taking a serious look at this vexed question. We will do so, not along Baconian lines, i.e. by arbitrarily relating bits of personality to bits of sexual behaviour, but along the lines of the hypothetico-deductive method, i.e. by trying to make certain predictions from general personality theory (Eysenck 1967) on to selected aspects of sexual behaviour. It is the purpose of this first chapter to outline the major parts of this personality theory, and to suggest how the theory can be used to make predictions in the field of sexual behaviour. It is not expected that these predictions will be verified in their entirety, or even that where they are verified the predicted effects will be very strong. Obviously sexual behaviour is so complex, and determined by so many factors, both systematic and accidental, that no single factor could account for a very large portion of the variance. Nevertheless, it seemed worthwhile to see to what extent predictions from personality theory could be verified, and to obtain a rough idea of the pattern of interrelations that exists in our society. In addition, we were concerned with the possibility of trying to account for sexual behaviour along genetic lines, determining the amount of variance contributed to different types of sexual behaviour by genetic and environmental factors, or by their interaction. This line of thought could obviously be extended to include studies of the degree to which relations between personality and sexual behaviour themselves were determined by genetic and environmental influences. Results of such studies, it was considered, would not answer in any profound sense the questions we were asking; they would form a beginning on which other investigators might build.

One further thought was in our minds. The recurring battles over pornography and censorship, over chastity and premarital intercourse, over marriage and 'living in sin', have usually been waged on the basis that one answer is 'right' and another 'wrong', in some all-embracing, generally valid sense. It seemed worthwhile to investigate people's actual attitudes to these and many other problems in the sexual field, to demonstrate the diversity of answers given, and the complex structure revealed by the analysis of the answers. If the acceptance or rejection of different 'life styles' is regulated to some extent by personality variables, themselves largely determined by genetic factors, then it might have to be concluded that the very notion of 'right' and 'wrong' might have to be given up in relation to these questions, and that what was right for a neurotic introvert

9

might be wrong for a stable extravert. These ideas will be referred to again in the final chapter; here we only intend to mention the wider context in which our investigation is set.

When we turn to the personality side, there is of course a bewildering array of different theories, techniques of measurement and conceptualisations; even the meaning of the term 'personality' is not agreed upon, and the very notion of personality as a persevering and consistent set of behaviour patterns is sometimes doubted (e.g. Mischel 1968). This is not the place to discuss such issues; the theory adopted here to make predictions and to relate personality to sexual behaviour is that which I have presented in some detail in *The Biological Basis of Personality* (Eysenck 1967), and the genesis of which I have described, together with supporting evidence for its meaningfulness, in *The Structure of Human Personality* (Eysenck 1970a). It is open to the reader to argue that other theories might have been adapted for the purpose, and I would be the last to deny that such a possibility cannot be ruled out. Nevertheless, the deed is done, and argument about wisdom of the choice fruitless; the only thing to be determined is the degree of success that this effort has produced. Accordingly a brief outline of the theory will now be presented, together with some of the deductions made from it. It would be pointless to document here what is said about the theory; readers must be referred to the works cited above for detailed information and documentation.

Our personality theory maintains that personality can be described best in terms of a large set of traits (sociability, impulsiveness, activity, moodiness, etc.), and that these traits cohere in certain clusters; these clusters are the empirical basis for higher-order concepts which may be labelled 'types' or, as I would prefer to call them, dimensions of personality. (The term 'type' carries connotations of bimodal distribution or qualitatively different groupings which go counter to empirical fact.) Three main such clusters have been isolated in the very large number of empirical studies carried out during the past seventy years; these have received many different names, but will here be referred to as N (neuroticism), E (extraversion), and P (psychoticism). The methods used for isolating such dimensions, and for identifying the resulting factors, have been discussed in detail in *Personality Structure and Measurement* (Eysenck and Eysenck 1969). These major 'types' or dimensions are conceived as being securely anchored in innate physiological

10

structures, differences in which are responsible, in interaction with environmental determinants, for producing the phenotypic behaviour patterns that we observe, rate and measure; a discussion of the evidence for this genetic hypothesis will be given in a later chapter.

Extraversion is defined in behavioural terms by the various traits that are correlated together to define this factor, traits such as sociability, impulsiveness, activity, carefreeness, liveliness, jocularity and so forth. The physiological basis underlying these and many other traits and behaviour patterns is thought to be low cortical arousal, probably mediated by the reticular formation. The extravert consequently requires greater external stimulation in order to arrive at an optimum level of arousal than the normal (ambivert) person, while the introvert requires less external stimulation than the normal (ambivert) person. This general feature of human behaviour (preferring intermediate degrees of arousal) is shown in diagrammatic form in figure 1.2; the thick curved line indicates the general relation obtaining between level of stimulation and hedonic tone, with intermediate levels of stimulation giving rise to positive hedonic tone, extreme levels of stimulation (pain) or sensory deprivation giving rise to negative hedonic tone. Introverts and extraverts are displaced from this mean in opposite directions, with extraverts having optimum levels of stimulation above (O.L.$_E$), introverts having optimum levels of stimulation below (O.L.$_I$) the optimum level of the average person (O.L.$_P$). It follows that at a given point A which is indifferent to the average person, the level of stimulation would be acceptable to the introvert and mildly pleasant, but unacceptable to the extravert and mildly unpleasant, as lacking in sufficient stimulation. Conversely, at point B, where also the level of stimulation would be giving rise to indifference to the average person, the extravert would be experiencing mildly positive hedonic tone, the introvert mildly negative hedonic tone. The evidence for these generalisations is discussed in Eysenck (1967), and is quite strong.

The prediction from this general formulation would be, in the sexual field, that extraverts would seek for stronger stimulation than ambiverts, ambiverts than introverts. Sexual stimulation being among the strongest sensory experiences commonly encountered, one would conclude from this that introverts would approach it rather more circumspectly, and would shy away from the more stimulating forms of sexual behaviour. Conversely, extraverts would

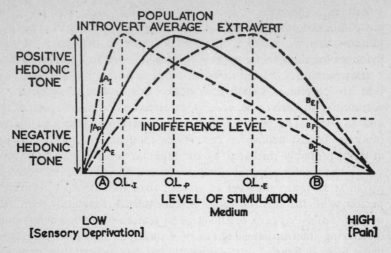

Figure 1.2 *Relation between sensory stimulation and positive or negative hedonic tone for extraverts, ambiverts and introverts respectively*

approach precisely these more stimulating forms of sexual behaviour eagerly and passionately. This prediction is supported by another deduction from the general theory. I have theorised that introverts, because of their higher level of cortical arousal, should form conditioned responses more quickly than extraverts; I have also theorised that socialised behaviour is produced through a process of Pavlovian conditioning, and that consequently extraverts, being poor conditioners, would be likely to show less evidence of socialisation than introverts. The evidence on the whole supports both deductions (Eysenck 1967, Eysenck 1970b). Now much sexual behaviour (perversions, premarital and extra-marital intercourse) is considered to be anti-social, and is consequently more likely to be indulged in by extraverts than by introverts. These two causal chains, through sensation-seeking and through lack of socialisation, should lead to extravert in the same direction, namely greater indulgence in all sorts of sexual behaviour involving persons of the opposite sex; and accordingly the following predictions have been made (Eysenck 1971a):

1 Extraverts will have intercourse *earlier* than introverts
2 Extraverts will have intercourse *more frequently* than introverts

12

3 Extraverts will have intercourse with *more different partners*
4 Extraverts will have intercourse in *more different positions* than introverts
5 Extraverts will indulge in more *varied* sexual behaviour outside intercourse
6 Extraverts will indulge in longer pre-coital love play than introverts

There is one further deduction from general theory that is relevant to these predictions. Extraverts, given their lower level of arousal, would be expected to show greater habituation in experimental situations; i.e., they would react as strongly as introverts to novel stimuli, but would quickly get used to these stimuli and respond less and less, while introverts would keep their original reaction much longer. The evidence supports such a view (Eysenck 1967, Quirion 1970), and we would suggest that the changeableness of the extravert in his sexual behaviour posited above (changes in partner, changes in positions adopted, etc.) might be related to habituation. Clearly habituation to a given stimulus leads to loss of arousal, boredom and disinterest; this in turn would be expected to motivate search for new stimuli. Thus extraverts are genetically predisposed to seek strong stimuli, to get bored by repetition of identical or similar stimuli and to be less likely to be inhibited from searching for such strong and novel stimuli by social taboos. It is this combination of behavioural tendencies on which our predictions are based.

There is some objective evidence that habituation is indeed more pronounced in extraverts in the sexual field. In an unpublished study, E. Nelson measured the physiological responses of male subjects to explicit sexual films, using the penis plethysmograph. (This is a device for measuring the changing volume of the penis from flaccid to erect.) Nine four-minute films were constructed from a large amount of commercial material, each film concentrating on one aspect of sexual activity, e.g. petting, intercourse male above female, cunnilingus, fellatio, *soixante-neuf*, orgies, intercourse *a tergo*, etc. Subjects were carefully chosen on the basis of personality inventories (E.P.I.) to represent the four groups of stable extraverts, stable introverts, unstable extraverts and unstable introverts; there were ten subjects in each group. Three films were shown to each person on three separate occasions, at least four days elapsing from occasion to occasion; there was a rest of four minutes between films on each occasion. Records were analysed for changes occurring

13

during each film, from film to film on any one occasion, and from one occasion to another.

This analysis showed that extraverts showed significantly more habituation (i.e. a lowering of penis volume) during the showing of each film, from film to film, and from occasion to occasion. This tendency was clearer for the stable extraverts and introverts, but it was also manifest for the unstable extraverts and introverts. Introverts showed no change in responsiveness from beginning to end, while extraverts showed a drop of 86 per cent of maximum erection to 66 per cent of maximum erection. Thus clearly habituation occurs more readily in extraverts, not only to simple sensory stimulation (as had been used in previous laboratory investigations) but also to visual sexual stimulation.

Prior to the experiments here published, there was only one study that attempted to look at these and similar predictions in an empirical manner (apart from the work of Schofield 1968 and Bynner 1969, which, although not making use of personality questionnaires, arrived at similar conclusions about the relationship between extraversion and explicit sexual conduct). The study in question was conducted by Giese and Schmidt (1968), who used a rather short scale for the measurement of E and administered questionnaires regarding their sexual conduct to over six thousand German students, both male and female; most of these were unmarried. Some of their relevant results are shown below (table 1.1a); only unmarried students are included in the tabulation, and groups are subdivided according to their extraversion scores into introverts (E_1), ambiverts (E_2) and extraverts (E_3). There were more men than women in this sample. It will be seen that extraverts masturbate less, pet to orgasm more, have coitus more frequently, have coitus earlier, adopt more different positions in coitus, indulge in longer precoital love-play, and practise fellatio and cunnilingus more frequently. It should be added that on some of these items differences are much greater for men than for women; this is expected on the grounds that in our society it is men who set the pace in sexual relationships, so that their personality is expressed more clearly in the procedure adopted. These results are in good agreement with our predictions.

Two studies reported by Zuckerman and others (1972) and Zuckerman (personal communication) did not use the E scale, but are relevant because the sensation-seeking scales used in these

Table 1.1a *Sexual activities of introverts* (E_1), *ambiverts* (E_2) *and extraverts* (E_3) (figures taken from Giese and Schmidt 1968)

	Males			Females		
	(percentages shown in italics)					
	E_1	E_2	E_3	E_1	E_2	E_3
1 Masturbation at present	*86*	*80*	*72*	*47*	*43*	*39*
2 Petting: at 17	*16*	*28*	*40*	*15*	*19*	*24*
Petting: at 19	*31*	*48*	*56*	*30*	*44*	*47*
Petting: at present age	*57*	*72*	*78*	*62*	*71*	*76*
3 Coitus: at 17	*5*	*13*	*21*	*4*	*4*	*8*
Coitus: at 19	*15*	*31*	*45*	*12*	*20*	*29*
Coitus: at present age	*47*	*70*	*77*	*42*	*57*	*71*
4 Median frequency of coitus per month (sexually active students only)	*3·0*	*3·7*	*5·5*	*3·1*	*4·5*	*7·5*
5 Number of coitus partners in last 1	*75*	*64*	*46*	*72*	*77*	*60*
12 months; unmarried students 2−3	*18*	*25*	*30*	*25*	*17*	*23*
only 4+	*7*	*12*	*25*	*4*	*6*	*17*
6 Long precoital sex play	*21*	*25*	*28*	*21*	*16*	*18*
7 Cunnilingus	*52*	*62*	*64*	*58*	*69*	*69*
8 Fellatio	*53*	*60*	*69*	*53*	*59*	*61*
9 More than three different coital positions	*10*	*16*	*26*	*12*	*18*	*13*
10 Experience of orgasm nearly always	—	—	—	*17*	*32*	*29*

studies correlate positively with E (and also with P), and thus make prediction possible (Zuckerman 1974). There are four such scales, concerned respectively with thrill and adventure-seeking, experience-seeking, disinhibition and boredom-susceptibility; these are summed to give a total score. Zuckerman constructed a sexual experience scale, listing types of sexual behaviour that the individual questioned either had or had not experienced (similar to our own scales given in chapters 2 and 3), going from kissing and breast-fondling to fellatio and cunnilingus. He also asked questions about the number of sexual partners each individual had had. The prediction would of course be that all the scales would correlate positively with the number of heterosexual activities endorsed, and the number of heterosexual partners. The scale involving heterosexual activities was administered to two separate populations, that regarding heterosexual partners only to one. The results are shown in table 1.1b; it will be seen that all the correlations are positive, both for males and for females. These results fit in well with those of Giese and Schmidt, and bear out prediction.

Neuroticism is conceived of as strong, labile emotionality, predisposing a person to develop neurotic symptoms in case of exces-

Table 1.1b *Correlations between sensation-seeking scales and sexual behaviour*

	Heterosexual activities 1		Heterosexual activities 2		No. heterosexual partners	
	M	F	M	F	M	F
General	0·51	0·15	0·39	0·29	0·40	0·27
Thrill and adventure-seeking	0·44	0·16	0·42	0·35	0·47	0·20
Experience-seeking	0·37	0·32	0·45	0·37	0·35	0·28
Disinhibition	0·33	0·43	0·39	0·33	0·42	0·29
Boredom susceptibility	0·36	0·29	0·23	0·20	0·25	0·20

sive stress. Traits correlating to define this 'type' are moodiness, sleeplessness, nervousness, inferiority feelings, irritability, etc. The physiological basis of this dimension of personality is believed to be the autonomic system, and in particular the visceral brain, which coordinates sympathetic and parasympathetic reactivity. High N scorers, in view of their strong, labile and lasting emotions of fear and anxiety to even mildly stressful situations (in which category we must include social contact generally, and perhaps sexual contact particularly), would perhaps be less likely to indulge in sexual contacts, to worry more about sex, to be disgusted by certain aspects of sex and to have fewer contacts with sexual partners; this would be particularly true of unmarried subjects, because of their well-known difficulties in social relations. In Miller's terms, sexual relations, to the neurotic, should present a conflict-laden area in which the conflict takes the approach–avoidance form; sexual desire makes the high N subject *approach*, while his fears and anxieties make him *avoid*. This ambivalence is of course well documented in the clinical literature, but our prediction would be that it could be found in normal (i.e. non-psychiatric) populations also. This prediction of conflict in the sexual field would be particularly acute in subjects combining high N and high E; high N would inflate the avoidance part of the equation, high E the approach part. Our work suggests that this is in fact so (Eysenck 1971c).

The only study of sexuality as related to neuroticism, prior to our own, is the work of Giese and Schmidt, already mentioned. Unfortunately they used a very short scale of N, which could not have been very reliable; it is perhaps for this reason that they found few significant correlation. High N scorers (male) were found to masturbate more frequently, have greater desire for coitus, and claim to have spontaneous erections more frequently than low N scorers. Females with high N scores had less frequent orgasm and stronger menstrual pains. As far as they go, these findings may lend some slight support to the deductions from theory outlined above, but clearly they do not help a great deal in understanding the relations involved.

Some work has been done on the relationship between orgasm capacity and psychiatric disorder, particularly neurotic disturbances, but this is contradictory on the whole. Terman (1951) found that, of a large sample of women, those lacking in orgasm capacity said, in reply to inventory questions, that they often felt miserable, experienced periods of loneliness, often felt grouchy, couldn't be optimistic when others around them were depressed; these are all N items, but so are others which did not discriminate. These items had also shown discrimination in a previous study (Terman 1938); others were significant only in the second, such as being burdened by a sense of remorse, often being just miserable, worrying too long over humiliating experiences, lacking in self-confidence and being affected by other people's praise and blame. There appears in these two studies a relationship between incapacity and N, but not a very strong one.

Thomason (1951) found similar differences between sexually well adjusted and poorly adjusted women, but of course used other criteria additional to orgasm capacity. Shope (1966) found a negative relationship in a very small sample of unmarried women; this inversion may have been due in part to the unmarried state of the girls in question. Fisher (1973), who gives a review of these studies, found some significant correlations between orgasmic incapacity and the Murray Anxiety Scale in one of his samples, but failed to do so in another; he also used some rather unusual and probably invalid techniques for the measurement of anxiety in other samples, without success. However, these samples were all quite small. Terman's conclusions are probably better based than those of the other authors mentioned, although even he used a rather poor measure of N.

Several authors have reported restricted orgasmic capacity in neurotic psychiatric patients (Landis and others 1940, Winokur and others 1958, Purtell and others 1951, and Coppen 1965). Cooper (1969) failed to find significant elevations in the N scores of women with orgasmic difficulties, but this of course is not a psychiatric diagnosis. Fisher (1973) concludes a review of these and other studies (mostly only marginally relevant) by saying that 'the existing data are not persuasive that general psychological maladjustment, as such, plays a major role in sexual responsiveness'. This leaves the probability that high neuroticism plays some part in orgasmic incapacity, even though perhaps not a major one.

✓ Whereas E and N are dimensions of personality that have been studied for many years (the first set of studies using this particular model of personality was presented by Eysenck 1947), and for which there is a good deal of theoretical and experimental background, the third dimension of personality here considered, psychoticism, has a much less opulent background. In conception it is not unlike neuroticism; just as N purports to be a personality variable stretching through the normal, non-psychiatric population, and measurable through questionnaires that do not involve actual psychiatric symptoms, so also psychoticism purports to be a personality variable stretching through the normal, non-psychiatric population, and the attempt has been made to measure it by means of questions that do not involve psychiatric symptoms but rather personality traits (Eysenck and Eysenck 1976). The assumptions underlying these scales and dimensions may be stated as follows.

1 Neurosis and psychosis are entirely different and separate disorders

2 Neurosis and psychosis are not qualitatively different from normal behaviour patterns, but are extremes along dimensions that run through the normal population

3 Diagnosed neurotics and psychotics may be used as criteria for measuring scales of N and P, in the sense that they ought to have high scores on scales for the measurement of N and P respectively

These points, and the evidence for them, are discussed elsewhere (Eysenck 1970a, Eysenck and Eysenck 1969, Eysenck and Eysenck 1975, 1976). For a consideration of psychoticism, it is this last reference that is of particular importance; it contains a survey of the relevant literature.

It is of particular interest in relation to P that genetically there appears to be a close link between psychosis and psychopathy (Eysenck 1975a); this would suggest that criminals as well as psychotic patients would show high P scores. This has in fact been found to be true (Eysenck and Eysenck 1970a, 1971a, 1971b) and reinforced our belief that the *P* scale measures something important, meaningful and genetically relevant.

It may be premature to attempt to describe the personality traits characteristic of the high *P* scorer, but in the absence of full knowledge on this point it may still be useful to quote the description given in the *Manual of the E.P.Q.* (*Eysenck Personality Questionnaire*) (Eysenck and Eysenck 1975) constructed for the measurement of the *P*, *E* and *N* variables.

[A high scorer may be described] as being solitary, not caring for people; he is often troublesome, not fitting in anywhere. He may be cruel and inhumane, lacking in feeling and empathy, and altogether insensitive. He is hostile to others, even his own kith and kin, and aggressive, even to loved ones. He has a liking for odd and unusual things, and a disregard for danger; he likes to make fools of other people, and to upset them. This is a description of adult high *P* scorers; as far as children are concerned, we obtain a fairly congruent picture of an odd, isolated, troublesome child; glacial and lacking in human feelings for his fellow-beings and for animals; aggressive and hostile, even to near-and-dear ones. Such children try to make up for lack of feeling by indulging in sensation-seeking 'arousal jags' without thinking of the dangers involved. Socialization is a concept which is relatively alien to both children and adults; empathy, feelings of guilt, sensitivity to other people are notions which are strange and unfamiliar to them. This description of course, refers in its entirety only to extreme samples; persons perhaps scoring relatively high, but nearer the middle range of scores, would of course be far more frequent than extremes, and would only show these behaviour patterns to a much less highly developed degree. Psychiatric terms which would seem to assimilate this kind of behaviour pattern are 'schizoid' and 'psychopathic'; 'behaviour disorders' is another term which springs to mind. Our concept of 'psychoticism' overlaps with all three of these diagnostic terms.

Predictions from this factor on to sexual behaviour are more difficult to make in view of the limited amount of knowledge we possess of its nature. The terms that spring to mind are 'impersonal sex' and 'aggressive sex', with their implications of lack of love and affection, the stress on physical relations purely and simply, and the failure to 'relate' in any sense to the sex object. It also

19

seems likely that high P scorers might behave in generally anti-social ways, and indulge in socially disapproved acts. These predictions are less explicit, and rather vague, as compared with those made in connection with E; the reason of course is simply that we know a good deal about E, but much less about P.

One important feature of P scores is that men tend to have much higher scores than women, and the general aggressiveness, lack of empathy and impersonal nature of the high P scorer is clearly allied to popular stereotypes of maleness.(2) It is also interesting that criminals score much more highly than non-criminals; there is a distinct tendency for criminals to be male. (The comparison between criminals and non-criminals is of course within the given sex; male criminals have higher P scores than male non-criminals, female criminals than female non-criminals.) If there is indeed a close and possibly causal link between maleness and high P scoring (perhaps through the mediation of androgens), then we would expect that the sexual attitudes and behaviours of high as opposed to low P scorers would be similar to those of males as opposed to females. This prediction is of course based on analogy, rather than on firm deduction, but may repay investigation.

In addition to these three major personality scales, there is a fourth scale which has been used in some but not all the studies to be described; this is the L (Lie) or dissimulation scale.

This scale, which was first incorporated in our series of questionnaires in the E.P.I. (Eysenck and Eysenck 1964), attempts to measure a tendency on the part of some subjects to 'fake good'; this tendency is particularly marked when the questionnaire is administered under conditions where such a tendency would seem appropriate (e.g. as part of an employment interview). A series of factorial and experimental studies has been carried out to investigate the nature of this scale in some detail (Eysenck and Eysenck 1970b, Michaelis and Eysenck 1971, Eysenck, Nias and Eysenck 1971). It is clear that the scale possesses a considerable degree of factorial unity, with individual items having high loadings on this factor and on no other; however, there are certain difficulties in regarding scores as nothing but indicators of dissimulation. The main difficulty seems to be that, in addition to measuring dissimulation, the L scale also measures some stable personality factor which may possibly denote some degree of orthodoxy or lawful rule-obeying behaviour (conformity to conventionality). The evidence is strong on both points.

The L scale does measure dissimulation; Michaelis and Eysenck (1971) have shown that it is possible to manipulate L scale scores by varying the experimental conditions from high to low motivation to dissimulate. However, if dissimulation were the only factor affecting the variance of this score, then the reliability of the score should be a function of the size of score; when scores are low, thus indicating that subjects are not dissimulating, then the scale should have low reliability. Empirically, this has not been found to be so; there is no lowering of reliability of the L scale under conditions of little dissimulation, and no increase in reliability under conditions of high dissimulation. Hence the scale must measure some stable personality function; unfortunately little is known about the precise nature of this function. (See Eysenck and Eysenck 1976.)

Michaelis and Eysenck have shown that the dissimulation-motivating conditions can be distinguished fairly adequately from the non-motivating conditions by noting the correlation between N and L. When conditions are such as to provide high degrees of motivation for dissimulation, the correlation between N and L is relatively high (approaching or even exceeding -0.5). When conditions are such as to provide little motivation for dissimulation, the correlation between N and L becomes quite small, or vanishes altogether. Thus, under conditions of little motivation to dissimulate, the L scale score may be used as a measure of whatever personality function is being measured by the scale; this would seem to constitute an important experimental problem. Under these conditions there is little point in trying to correct for dissimulation, and hence the scale should not be used for that purpose. Under conditions of high motivation to dissimulate, i.e. when the correlation between N and L is relatively high, the L scale may with advantage be used to screen out dissimulators, e.g. the highest 5 per cent of L scorers. No definite cut-off point is being suggested beyond which subjects should be eliminated, as this depends on the general level of scoring of the population, as well as its age; the L scale score decreases with age in children, and increases with age in adults.

In our investigation the L scale therefore fulfils a dual role. As a scale for the measurement of dissimulation it may be useful to discover whether in fact there has been any strong tendency in our population to dissimulate. As a personality scale for the measurement of some ill-defined dimension of conservative orthodoxy or social obedience (conformity; conventionality) we may be able

21

to link this with sexual behaviour patterns, predicting that high L scorers would prefer socially approved attitudes and behaviours.

We have now introduced the scales to be used to measure personality, and the theories to be tested; there remains one further point to be discussed before we describe the scales used for the measurement of sexual attitudes and behaviours, and go into details of the experimental procedures. We have criticised Kinsey and his followers in the opening paragraphs of this chapter for failure to use random samples; as will be seen presently, in our work too there is a marked departure from such random sampling. Does this mean that the criticisms that apply to Kinsey also apply to our own work? Such a conclusion would seem to be based on a confusion of the requirements of experimental designs subserving different purposes, and as this confusion is widespread it may be useful to discuss it in some detail. The discussion may be oriented by reference to a recent paper by Cochrane and Duffy (1974), specifically written to impress readers with the need for random samples, and criticising psychologists severely for their failure to use such samples.

Having reviewed samples of papers published in the *British Journal of Psychology* and the *British Journal of Social and Clinical Psychology*, and having found the sampling in most researches unacceptable, they write:

These findings obviously severely limit the generalizability of most of the results of our research endeavours. The most common procedure is for an author to assemble an aggregate of volunteers (to say 'sample' would be misleading) from a university. These may number less than 100 from a total student population of up to 20,000. It is impossible to generalize to the total student population of one college and, of course, nothing whatsoever can be said about the existence of any relationship found in the general population. Only 1–2 per cent of all studies reported in these two journals over the past four years based their findings on a true sample of the general adult population. [p. 120]

Even this, one might add, is an exaggeration; there never has been a 'true' sample of the general population, including mental defectives, schizophrenics, geriatric patients, alcoholics, colour-blind males, etc., in their correct proportions; the notion of a 'true' sample is a myth. Is it necessary or desirable?

The point here made is a very simple one. Cochrane and Duffy are basing their case on a quite erroneous conception of scientific method, using an inductive model that has been out of date for many, many years. In terms of this Baconian model, we discover facts from a sample, and then generalise these facts to a particular universe. But this is not the way modern science proceeds, and philosophers of science are quite explicit about this (Popper 1959, 1972). The purely inductive approach is philosophically invalid (even with a 'true' sample!) and scientifically meaningless. What happens instead is that we proceed by theory and falsification ('Conjectures and Refutations', in terms of Popper's famous book). We state a specific theory which has testable consequences; in so far as the consequences are in fact discovered when an empirical test is made, then in so far does our theory survive. Usually the theory will also predict the type of population to which it applies; the theory that resistance to the passage of an electric current grows as the conductor is heated clearly applies only to conductors (although it may also be found to apply to semi-conductors, etc.). Similarly in psychology; our theories are either general, i.e. are supposed to apply to all human beings (or to all mammals, or to all living organisms), or else they apply to extraverts, as opposed to introverts (Eysenck 1967), or to working-class children, as opposed to middle-class children (Jensen 1973). If a theory does not specify sub-groups to which it does not apply, then the assumption is that it applies universally. This assumption is of course subject to disproof, but it must govern the design of the experiments conducted to test the theory.

Putting the matter symbolically, we may say that the total population can be considered to be made up of (overlapping) sub-groups. Letting P stand for the whole population, we can write:

$$P = m, f; e, i; y, o; w, b; t, c; \text{etc.}$$

(in this expression m and f stand for male and female, e and i for extravert and introvert, y and o for young and old, w and m for working- and middle-class, w and b for white and black, and t and c for town and country dwellers). The hypothesis being tested states that $m=f$, $e=i$, $y=o$, $w=m$, $w=b$, $t=c$, etc.; consequently these distinctions are not relevant to our choice of subject. It may be of course that our hypothesis does include one of these terms; I have argued strongly that extraversion and introversion are relevant to many psychological experiments, and that we can formu-

23

late hypotheses that predict the way in which personality and experimental paradigm interact (Eysenck 1967). These predictions have often been verified, and in so far as such hypotheses exist, it becomes important to include reference to them in the selection and measurement of the experimental population. We may of course also be able to make predictions from some well considered theory about differences to be expected between young and old, male and female, white and black; if such hypotheses exist, then we must pay attention to them in our design. What is quite unscientific, however, is to demand random samples regardless of existing hypotheses; in this way no relevant hypotheses are being tested, and we are simply proceeding along a path of uncodified induction. That way lies chaos.

Let us consider a typical hypothesis in experimental psychology. To take one such at random, let us state that *reaction time increases linearly with increase in the number of bits of information in the stimulus.* This is a universal hypothesis; it does not specify that the prediction applies only to children, or to women, or to students, or to any particular group that can be induced to undergo the testing procedure and that understands and is willing to follow the instructions. It is not clear to me why, in testing it, we should go to the trouble of assembling a random sample of the population. A group of subjects assembled in the manner condemned by Cochrane and Duffy would do very well to test this prediction.

(In the same way can predictions made by astronomers about planetary orbits be tested in our planetary system, although this is a very poor sample of all possible planetary systems – on the basis of Cochrane and Duffy's argument astronomy could have very little reason for generalising findings from our system!) There may be personality and other differences between volunteers and non-volunteers, as Cochrane and Duffy argue, but these would be irrelevant to the prediction made by the theory, and consequently the theory can be tested equally well with volunteers as with conscripts.

Let us now turn to another type of research, involving the correlational method. It has been predicted that when social attitude items are intercorrelated and factor-analysed, then two major factors would emerge, which have been called conservatism–radicalism and toughmindedness–tendermindedness (Eysenck 1954). Such an hypothesis can be tested on any population within the Western world, being as universal (with that restriction) as the reaction time prediction. We have in fact tested it with as random a sample as the public opinion survey firms could manage to give us, and with many other more restricted samples, including student samples assembled in the manner criticised by Cochrane and Duffy. In all cases, the pattern of correlations behaved lawfully, and gave very similar solutions. We even tried to construct severely truncated samples, by using only Conservative, or only Labour, voters; even then the prediction was borne out. Solutions from different populations were mathematically transformable into identity by using Thompson's restriction of range formula, showing that only by choosing a population having zero range for one or other of the two variables could we fail to obtain the expected outcome. What would a random sample tell us that a non-random sample would not tell us just as well?

The only exception to this general rule would be a line of research that is of the least interest in science, namely the determination of population parameters (as in Kinsey's work). If the manufacturers of brassieres wish to know the average size of female breasts at a given age in this country, as well as the shape of the distribution, then of course they would be forced to use as random a sample as they could persuade to have their breasts measured. If we wish to know the average latency of reaction times to a given stimulus for the whole population, then of course we would have to test a 'random' sample. It is not clear to me why anyone should ever wish to do such a thing, but given the problem, then clearly this would be the solution. Needless to say, the resulting figure would have no scientific interest whatever.

Even problems of this kind can often be approached without the need of a 'random sample'. Let us take Milgram's (1974) work on obedience to authority as an example. When he demonstrated that a high proportion of Yale students were ready and willing to apparently torture and possibly kill a volunteer subject, it was argued that this might have been due to their status as students, and the special relation between students and instructor–experimenters, who gave the orders. Later work on non-student volunteers (who did not know what they were volunteering for, and who were paid for their trouble), and replications in many other countries, with many other types of sample, showed convincingly that this was not the correct explanation. Milgram's work generates a general hypothesis regarding obedience; this can be tested equally well with different types of samples. Differences between samples would be of considerable interest, and would require new hypotheses (or possibly they could be accounted for in terms of his own hypothesis, which could be used to generate predictions regarding different samples). But nowhere can it be said that a random sample would have added noticeably to the general interest or convincingness of his work. The precise mean value for the population, which could be obtained only from such a random sample, would be of precisely no interest at all.

Sometimes it is necessary to tailor an experiment to the specific nature of the sample, or even to individuals. If we wish to study the effect of stress on performance, we must make certain that our experimental procedure does indeed produce stress. The moving shape of a predatory bird produces stress in doves, but not in dinosaurs. Rapid presentation of serial rote-learning stimuli produces stress in high N subjects, but not in low N subjects. Having to listen to lectures on the inheritance of intelligence by A. R. Jensen without disruption and fisticuffs would, we may perhaps conjecture, produce stress in sociology students. Any experiment on stress would need to contain specific hypotheses of this kind; the use of a random sample of subjects would not guarantee equalisation of stress, and might in fact make it much more difficult to achieve this.

Cochrane and Duffy are worried about the applicability of statistical methods to non-random samples. The answer again lies in the hypothesis tested. If this hypothesis does not discriminate between different members of the total population, then all samples are random unless they are specifically selected by reference to the variables to be tested. If Milgram had selected only people known to be extremely obedient to authority, then obviously his results would be suspect. But short of this the hypothesis in most experiments mounted by psychologists contains the (usually silent) minor premise that for the purpose of this particular experiment all persons at risk of selection are equal – possibly the only occasion where extreme egalitarian demand is fully met! If this minor premise is justified, then clearly any selection of subjects is a random one, and the usual statistical methods are applicable. If the premise is not justified, then it is open to the critic to disprove it. In doing so *explicitly* the critic would add greatly to our knowledge of the natural phenomena in question; he would do so far more than if he simply argued for the desirability of random samples.

Cochrane and Duffy end by stating their distress at:

... the way in which the elementary rules of sampling are ignored, along with the known facts about biases being introduced by using college student volunteers as subjects. It is perhaps particularly unfortunate that virtually no one has the inclination, or the available resources, to test his hypothesis on the general population. Until we can do this routinely it appears that most of our research efforts into human behaviour will be essentially trivial. [p. 121]

The burden of the argument is that it is their criticisms that are essentially trivial, and that psychologists would be very ill-advised should they feel obliged to test random samples of the population whenever they wished to confirm or disprove specific theories. To use such samples routinely would imply a return to a long-abandoned scientific philosophy which has been given up quite universally by scientists and by philosophers of science. All the arguments in the Cochrane and Duffy article ultimately derive from this error.

It should not be thought that I have any wish to discourage the use of random samples in psychological research, or an extension of the usual research design from using sophomores to using other types of group. That would be to misunderstand my argument completely. There are many considerations that should be borne in mind in selecting a sample for one's research. To take but one instance, it would not be possible in the United States to use college students for an experiment of the Milgram type, simply because a large number of potential subjects would have heard all about the deception involved in the experiment, and would not be fooled. This would make a non-academic sample mandatory, and even there considerable caution would have to be observed. What we are opposing is a mindless rejection of non-random samples, either in planning one's own experiments or in evaluating other people's. The selection of a proper sample should derive from one's theoretical position, and not be imposed by irrelevant Baconian principles. In certain circumstances a random sample may be appropriate, in others not. These decisions cannot be anticipated by a fallacious appeal to imaginary 'scientific methods'; scientific research cannot be automated and made foolproof by laying down general rules of this kind.

We would conclude from this discussion that for our purposes random samples would not be needed; the hypotheses tested should be capable of being falsified in samples of students, variegated adults of all sorts or indeed any sample of volunteers selected without reference to their personality or their sexual behaviour. (If our population consisted entirely of extreme extraverts, or sexual perverts, then our predictions could not properly be tested, and we would have to conclude that the choice of subjects was unsuitable.)

It is desirable that our sample should not deviate too much from the normal distribution of scores on the *P, E, N* and *L* variables; as we shall see this deviation is in fact very small. Similarly, there is evidence that in sexual experience too at least some of our samples do not deviate from normalcy. This is all that is required for our purposes (McCloskey 1967).

The other problems considered in relation to Kinsey's work, i.e. conscious or unconscious falsification, do of course arise in relation to our own work also. They do not arise to the same extent because we have preserved strict anonymity, in contrast to the interviewing methods used by Kinsey. We shall present some arguments later on to show that subjects took the whole inquiry very seriously, and made every effort to answer truthfully and accurately; this does not guarantee truthful and accurate answers, but it does suggest a high degree of cooperation.

There is one further argument that derives from the internal structure of the results. It seems highly unlikely that the complex pattern of intercorrelations found, meaningful and replicable as it has turned out to be, could have been produced unless the great majority of the subjects had answered truthfully and conscientiously. But of course there is no final answer to the reader who chooses to doubt the accuracy of the answers to our questionnaires, and to the degree that this doubt may invalidate our conclusions there is no definitive reply. The reader may like to reconsider this point after reading the relevant comments in the following chapters.

1. For a survey of this work, and an extension to a French sample, see Simon (1972).

2. There are very many studies of sex differences in attitudes and behaviour; the major results have been well summarised by Kagan (1964, p. 143):

In sum, females are supposed to inhibit aggression and open displays of sexual urges, to be passive with men, to be nurturant to others, to cultivate attractiveness, and to maintain an effective, socially poised, and friendly posture with others. Males are urged to be aggressive in face of attack, independent in problem situations, sexually aggressive, in control of regressive urges, and suppressive of strong emotions, especially anxiety.

Fisher (1973), who also reviews some of the literature on 'being a woman', curiously enough attributes observed differences to cultural factors; his whole book does not contain any mention of genetic factors!

2

Sexual attitudes and behaviour in student populations

The first studies to be carried out in the attempt to determine the influence of personality on sexual behaviour and attitudes made use of an inventory specially constructed for the purpose, and covering a large number of separate issues relating to sex. In constructing this inventory we made use of existing questionnaires, particularly one constructed by Thorne (1966), and of discussions in the relevant psychological and psychiatric literature. Most of the major areas of sex are covered in this inventory, which is given below; also given in this table are the percentage 'Yes' answers of our male and female respondents. The second part of the inventory, dealing with actual behaviours, is given later in this chapter; here we are concerned more particularly with attitudes. Also administered to our subjects was another inventory, constructed to measure personality dimensions P (psychoticism), E (extraversion) and N (neuroticism). The inventory used was an earlier form of the E.P.Q. (Eysenck Personality Questionnaire) recently published (Eysenck and Eysenck 1975). Information about its construction and changes from earlier forms is given in detail elsewhere (Eysenck and Eysenck 1976).

The inventories described above were administered to 423 male and 379 female university students, aged from eighteen to twenty-two, all unmarried, under conditions of complete anonymity. The students came from several different universities, most were approached in groups and asked to volunteer for the purpose of contributing to a scientific study of sexual behaviour. There were few refusals; those who accepted were given copies of the questionnaire and asked not to give their names. Completed forms were either put into a large box, where they were obviously so mixed up with other questionnaires as to be untraceable to the person who had filled it, or else sent by post to the Institute in specially provided envelopes. Discussion with respondents indicated no worry about possible identification, and considerable interest in the project; in fact, many students who had not been approached wrote in or contacted the assistants who were distributing the questionnaires, indicating their regrets at having been left out, and their desire to participate. The rather lengthy questionnaires take a good deal of time to fill in; it seems unlikely that 'jokers' and others with intent to deceive would have gone to the trouble of spending so much time in order to fool the investigator. A few questionnaires had to be eliminated because questions had been left out by the subject, but these were far fewer in proportion than is usual in our experience. Many subjects added long comments to some of the questions, or wrote lengthy additions at the end, often on separately provided sheets of paper. There was no evidence of any 'response set', i.e. wholesale endorsement of Yes or No answers, or regular patterns of answering; these were carefully looked for by eye, and also by computer. The general impression (which must of course be subjective in the circumstances) was that the population sampled was unusually responsible and careful in the way they answered questions, and sincerely desired to make quite clear their actual attitudes and behaviours. Internal evidence to support this view will be given later on.

Ninety-six variables were taken from the inventory and intercorrelated separately by product–moment correlation for males and females; the items included were questions 1–94, age, and question 98 dichotomised as to whether respondent had or had not had intercourse. The resulting matrices were factor-analysed by principal components procedures; over thirty latent roots exceeded unity, and further analysis was restricted to the first fifteen factors. It will be seen that even this may be too many, and in fact only a dozen or so factors are meaningful. Factors so extracted were rotated by Promax (Hendrickson and White 1964) into oblique structure; these primary factors will be discussed first. Later sections will deal with higher-order factors. Indices of factor comparison (Eysenck and Eysenck 1969) were run between the fifteen male and the fifteen female factors extracted, and optimum matches were found reasonably easily for thirteen factors. One female factor had two roughly equally probable

INVENTORY OF ATTITUDES TO SEX

This questionnaire is anonymous, to encourage truthful answers

Read each statement carefully, then underline the 'yes' or the 'no' answer, depending on your views. If you just cannot decide, underline the '?' reply. Please answer *every* question. There are no right or wrong answers. Don't think too long over each question; try to give an immediate answer which represents your *feelings* on each issue. Some questions are similar to others; there are good reasons for getting at the same attitude in slightly different ways.

		Percentage 'YES' answers	
		Male	Female
1	The opposite sex will respect you more if you are not too familiar with them	38	59
2	Sex without love ('impersonal sex') is highly unsatisfactory	49	80
3	Conditions have to be just right to get me excited sexually	21	43
4	All in all I am satisfied with my sex life	40	60
5	Virginity is a girl's most valuable possession	16	24
6	I think only rarely about sex	4	13
7	Sometimes it has been a problem to control my sex feelings	46	44
8	Masturbation is unhealthy	7	21
9	If I loved a person I could do anything with them	55	46
10	I get pleasant feelings from touching my sexual parts	61	37
11	I have been deprived sexually	25	8
		Percentage 'YES' answers	
		Male	Female
12	It is disgusting to see animals having sex relations in the street	5	6
13	I do not need to respect a woman, or love her, in order to enjoy petting and/or intercourse with her	43	12
14	It is all right for children to see their parents naked	64	74
15	I am sexually rather unattractive	10	5
16	Frankly, I prefer people of my own sex	3	2
17	Sex contacts have never been a problem to me	35	41
18	It is disturbing to see necking in public	12	23
19	Sexual feelings are sometimes unpleasant to me	11	16
20	Something is lacking in my sex life	50	26
21	My sex behaviour has never caused me any trouble	43	36
22	My love life has been disappointing	39	23

23	I never had many dates	36	26
24	I consciously try to keep sex thoughts out of my mind	2	7
25	I have felt guilty about sex experiences	29	41
26	It wouldn't bother me if the person I married were not a virgin	68	73
27	I had some bad sex experiences when I was young	15	13
28	Perverted thoughts have sometimes bothered me	28	18
29	At times I have been afraid of myself for what I might do sexually	19	26
30	I have had conflicts about my sex feelings towards a person of my own sex	16	9
31	I have many friends of the opposite sex	71	80
32	I have strong sex feelings but when I get a chance I can't seem to express myself	23	12
33	It doesn't take much to get me excited sexually	56	31
34	My parents' influence has inhibited me sexually	30	25
35	Thoughts about sex disturb me more than they should	12	7
36	People of my own sex frequently attract me	4	4
37	There are some things I wouldn't want to do with anyone	53	47
38	Children should be taught about sex	94	97
39	I could get sexually excited at any time of the day or night	88	69
40	I understand homosexuals	44	35
41	I think about sex almost every day	84	52
42	One should not experiment with sex before marriage	7	21
43	I get sexually excited very easily	60	27
44	The thought of a sex orgy is disgusting to me	18	65
45	It is better not to have sex relations until you are married	6	31
46	I find the thought of a coloured sex partner particularly exciting	24	3
47	I like to look at sexy pictures	61	8
48	My conscience bothers me too much	18	26
49	My religious beliefs are against sex	7	13
50	Sometimes sexual feelings overpower me	32	27
51	I feel nervous with the opposite sex	25	15
52	Sex thoughts drive me almost crazy	6	2
53	When I get excited I can think of nothing else but satisfaction	24	15
54	I feel at ease with people of the opposite sex	66	80
55	I don't like to be kissed	2	3
56	It's hard to talk with people of the opposite sex	12	6
57	I didn't learn the facts of life until I was quite old	26	23

INVENTORY OF ATTITUDES TO SEX—*cont.*

	Percentage 'YES' answers	
	Male	Female
58 I feel more comfortable when I am with my own sex	24	16
59 I enjoy petting	92	78
60 I worry a lot about sex	22	13
61 The Pill should be universally available	84	65
62 Seeing a person nude doesn't interest me	11	43
63 Sometimes thinking about sex makes me very nervous	16	20
64 Women who get raped are often partly responsible themselves	57	53
65 Perverted thoughts have sometimes bothered me	26	18
66 I am embarrassed to talk about sex	9	8
67 Young people should learn about sex through their own experience	34	23
68 Sometimes the woman should be sexually aggressive	88	64
69 Sex jokes disgust me	4	22
70 I believe in taking my pleasures where I find them	44	7
71 A person should learn about sex gradually by experimenting with it	52	42

	Percentage 'YES' answers	
	Male	Female
72 Young people should be allowed out at night without being too closely checked	68	54
73 Did you ever feel like humiliating your sex partner?	20	12
74 I would particularly protect my children from contacts with sex	5	9
75 Self-relief is not dangerous so long as it is done in a healthy way	74	56
76 I get very excited when touching a woman's breasts	57	45
77 I have been involved with more than one sex affair at the same time	32	14
78 Homosexuality is normal for some people	74	70
79 It is all right to seduce a person who is old enough to know what he or she is doing	73	35
80 Do you ever feel hostile to your sex partner?	37	40
81 I like to look at pictures of nudes	63	10
82 Buttocks excite me	42	8
83 If you had the chance to see people making love, without being seen, would you take it?	41	12

No.	Statement		
84	Pornographic writings should be freely allowed to be published	59	32
85	Prostitution should be legally permitted	62	32
86	Decisions about abortion should be the concern of no one but the woman concerned	52	47
87	There are too many immoral plays on TV	6	13
88	The dual standard of morality is natural, and should be continued	32	26
89	We should do away with marriage entirely	9	2
90	Men marry to have intercourse; women have intercourse for the sake of marriage	7	3
91	There should be no censorship, on sexual grounds, of plays and films	63	39

Please underline the correct answer

92 If you were invited to see a 'blue' film, would you: — 80 — 37
  (a) Accept   (b) Refuse

93 If you were offered a highly pornographic book, would you: — 75 — 40
  (a) Accept it   (b) Reject it

61   4

94 If you were invited to take part in an orgy, would you:
  (a) Take part   (b) Refuse

95 Given availability of a partner, would you prefer to have intercourse:
  (a) Never
  (b) Once a month
  (c) Once a week
  (d) Twice a week
  (e) 3–5 times a week
  (f) Every day
  (g) More than once a day

96 Have you ever suffered from impotence:
  (a) Never
  (b) Once or twice
  (c) Several times
  (d) Often
  (e) More often than not
  (f) Always

97 Have you ever suffered from *ejaculatio praecox* (premature ejaculation)?
  (a) Very often
  (b) Often
  (c) Middling
  (d) Not very often
  (e) Hardly ever
  (f) Never

98 At what age did you have your first intercourse?

male matches, and one had none. Indices of factor comparison will be given in relation to each pair of factors presented. For each factor, items and loadings will be given in such a way that all loadings exceeding the arbitrary figure of 0·3 for either men or women are quoted (when indices of factor similarity are low, this rule has not always been followed in order to avoid swamping the tables with masses of irrelevant figures). The factors have been given names which are of course rather arbitrary; however, they help to identify factors and may serve a useful purpose in making possible verbal reference. Alternative labels might be preferred by many readers, but the actual names used are not of course of any great importance.

Factor 1. Sexual satisfaction

The index of factor similarity of the very clearly marked factor of sexual satisfaction is 0·97; in other words, men and women agree almost perfectly in the structure of this factor. Table 2.1 gives the numbers of the questions involved and the loadings for both men and women. The highest loadings are for questions indicating 'I am satisfied with my sex life', 'I have not been deprived sexually', 'Nothing is lacking in my sex life', 'My love life has not been disappointing', and 'I don't worry about sex'. There is only one reversal of sign between the sexes: men who are satisfied sexually agree that we should do away with marriage; women don't.

Table 2.1 *Loadings – sexual satisfaction*

Question	Males	Females
4	0·91	0·82
11	− 0·60	− 0·58
17	0·41	0·30
20	− 0·85	− 0·88
22	− 0·68	− 0·59
32	− 0·39	− 0·32
35	− 0·33	− 0·23
60	− 0·43	− 0·23
89	0·18	− 0·36

Factor 2. Sexual excitement

The index of factor similarity for sexual excitement is 0·94; here too there is great similarity in factor structure between the sexes. Table 2.2 gives all the details regarding the loadings for this factor.

The highest loadings are for items indicating 'It doesn't take much to get me excited sexually', 'I get excited sexually very easily', 'When I get excited I can think of nothing else but satisfaction', 'I get very excited when touching a woman's breasts', and 'Sometimes sexual feelings overpower me'. For such people, 'conditions don't have to be just right to get me excited sexually', and they don't think 'only rarely about sex'. It is interesting that the item 'I find the thought of a coloured sex partner particularly exciting' has a high loading only for women; for men this is quite negligible.

Table 2.2   *Loadings – sexual excitement*

Question	Males	Females
3	−0·31	−0·53
6	−0·43	−0·14
7	0·28	0·30
33	0·77	0·86
39	0·36	0·50
41	0·38	0·29
43	0·81	0·86
46	0·01	0·34
50	0·36	0·30
52	0·32	0·23
53	0·43	0·28
76	0·39	0·39

Factor 3. Sexual nervousness

Sexual nervousness too is clearly marked, with an index of factor similarity of 0·92. Table 2.3 gives the details concerning the factor. High-loading items are 'I don't have many friends of the opposite sex', 'I feel nervous with the opposite sex', 'I don't feel at ease with people of the opposite sex', 'I feel more comfortable when I am with my own sex'. There is no reason to assume any tinge of homosexuality in this factor; we will encounter a proper homosexuality factor later on.

37

Table 2.3 *Loadings – sexual nervousness*

Question	Males	Females
16	0·06	0·32
31	−0·49	−0·66
51	0·76	0·75
54	−0·88	−0·89
56	0·77	0·81
58	0·58	0·77
66	0·22	0·36

Factor 4. Sexual curiosity

The index of factor similarity for sexual curiosity is 0·90. The factor itself is very clear (table 2.4); high-loading items are 'I like to look at sexy pictures', 'Sex jokes don't disgust me', 'I like to look at pictures of nudes', 'I would take a chance of seeing people make love', 'I would agree to see a "blue" film', 'I would read a highly pornographic book'. These questions are all concerned with a liking for pornography and voyeurism and a desire to have vicarious sex experiences.

Table 2.4 *Loadings – sexual curiosity*

Question	Males	Females
10	0·34	0·37
47	0·78	0·77
62	−0·40	−0·45
69	−0·35	−0·07
81	0·84	0·77
82	0·41	0·27
83	0·34	0·49
92	0·32	0·54
93	0·27	0·54

Factor 5. Premarital sex(1)

The index of factor similarity for premarital sex is 0·79, indicative of some diversion in factor loadings between the sexes. The items which load highly for both groups are 'Virginity is a girl's most valuable possession', 'It would bother me if the person I married were not a virgin', 'One should not experiment with sex before marriage', 'It is better not to have sex relations until you are married', 'I have not had intercourse'. Other items, loading not so highly, are 'The Pill should not be universally available', 'It is not all right to seduce a person who is old enough to know what they are doing', 'Women should not be sexually aggressive'. Details about this factor are given in table 2.5. Growing older is associated with a shedding of these beliefs for women, but not for men.

Table 2.5 *Loadings – premarital sex*

Question	Males	Females
Age	0·03	0·45
5	0·57	0·70
23	−0·04	0·30
26	−0·72	−0·75
42	0·54	0·80
45	0·71	0·86
61	−0·34	−0·27
65	0·32	−0·02
68	−0·07	−0·40
79	−0·26	−0·44
90	0·12	0·34
98	0·42	0·81

Factor 6. Repression

The index of factor similarity for repression is 0·75; this is not very high and suggests that somewhat different items make up this factor for males and females. It can, therefore, not be expected to be as clearly interpretable as previous factors. High-loading items are 'Children should not be taught about sex', 'I would particularly protect my children from contact with sex', 'I think only rarely about sex', 'Masturbation is unhealthy', 'I don't think about sex almost every day', 'My religious beliefs are against sex', 'Self-relief is dangerous, even when done in a healthy way', 'Men marry to have intercourse, women have intercourse for the sake of marriage', 'I have strong sex feelings but when I get a chance I can't seem to express myself'. This factor has an almost Victorian flavour; it seems to be more prevalent with the younger members of our sample, although this is more true of men than of women. Details are given in table 2.6.

Table 2.6 *Loadings – repression*

Question	Males	Females
Age	−0·31	−0·13
6	0·30	0·51
8	0·37	0·28
32	0·33	0·10
38	−0·61	−0·59
41	−0·26	−0·32
42	0·35	0·11
49	0·00	0·60
74	0·16	0·66
75	−0·52	−0·32
90	0·38	0·13

Factor 7. Prudishness

The index of factor similarity for prudishness is 0·72; what was said about the previous factor is obviously equally relevant here. High-loading items are 'I don't like to be kissed', 'I don't enjoy petting', 'The thought of a sex orgy is disgusting to me', 'Sex jokes disgust me', 'It is disturbing to see necking in public', 'Sexual feelings are sometimes unpleasant to me', 'I consciously try to keep sex thoughts out of my mind', 'I had some bad sex experiences when I was young'; the remaining three items seem to load only for men, and refer to a preference for homosexual over heterosexual company. Table 2.7 lists the relevant items and loadings.

Table 2.7 *Loadings – prudishness*

Question	Males	Females
Age	−0·06	0·32
16	−0·56	−0·30
18	−0·24	−0·74
19	−0·22	−0·42
24	−0·08	−0·39
27	0·01	−0·33
30	0·40	−0·03
36	−0·64	−0·05
44	−0·04	−0·32
55	−0·75	−0·45
59	0·74	0·14
69	−0·23	−0·53

Factor 8. Sexual experimentation

Sexual experimentation has an index of factor similarity of 0·68, but the meaning is reasonably clear-cut as only three items have loadings on it. These are shown in table 2.8; they are 'Young people should learn about sex through their own experience', 'A person should learn about sex gradually by experimenting with it' and 'Young people should be allowed out at night without being too closely checked'.

Table 2.8 *Loadings – sexual experimentation*

Question	Males	Females
67	0·77	0·76
71	0·69	0·75
72	0·15	0·37

Factor 9. Homosexuality

Homosexuality has an index of factor similarity of only 0·60, but again the meaning is unmistakable. Items with high and congruent loadings are 'Homosexuality is normal for some people', 'I understand homosexuals', 'People of my own sex frequently attract me', 'I have had conflicts about my sex feelings towards a person of my own sex', 'I am embarrassed to talk about sex'. Items are listed in table 2.9.

Table 2.9 *Loadings – homosexuality*

Question	Males	Females
27	0·00	0·30
30	0·54	0·27
35	−0·07	−0·42
36	0·36	0·00
40	0·54	0·73
57	0·09	−0·33
61	−0·32	−0·12
66	0·39	0·28
78	0·64	0·76

Factor 10. Censorship

Censorship has an index of factor similarity of 0.52, but is again not difficult to interpret. Items with high and congruent loadings are 'There should be censorship on sexual grounds of plays and films', 'There are too many immoral plays on T.V.', 'Prostitution should not be legally permitted', 'Pornographic writings should not be freely allowed to be published', 'Young people should not be allowed out at night without close supervision', 'The Pill should not be universally available', 'It is disgusting to see animals having sex relations in the street'. Details about loadings are given in table 2.10.

Table 2.10 *Loadings − censorship*

Question	Males	Females
12	0·61	0·19
14	−0·35	0·10
61	−0·18	−0·45
72	−0·35	−0·29
74	0·54	0·12
84	−0·47	−0·65
85	−0·33	−0·41
86	0·12	−0·37
87	0·54	0·45
91	−0·50	−0·65

Factor 11. Promiscuity

The index of factor similarity for promiscuity is 0·50; nevertheless, interpretation is not too difficult. Items with high and congruent loadings are 'Sex without love ("impersonal sex") is not highly unsatisfactory', 'I do not need to respect a woman (man), or love her/him, in order to enjoy petting and/or intercourse with her/him', 'The thought of a sex orgy is not disgusting to me', 'I believe in taking my pleasures where I find them', 'I have been involved in more than one sex affair at the same time', 'I would see a "blue" film, read a pornographic book, or take part in a sex orgy'. Details regarding this factor are shown in table 2.11.

Table 2.11 *Loadings – promiscuity*

Question	Males	Females
Age	0·38	0·06
2	−0·24	−0·56
13	0·33	0·50
44	−0·76	−0·48
70	0·23	0·50
77	0·10	0·51
92	0·48	0·09
93	0·44	0·06
94	0·70	0·37

Factor 12. Sexual hostility

Sexual hostility has an index of factor similarity of only 0·48, and
its interpretation is not very certain. Details about loadings are given
in table 2.12. Items with high and reasonably congruent loadings
are 'I have felt like humiliating my sex partner', 'I have felt hostile
to my sex partner'; these are the only items that are both high
and congruent. Two further items, with much lower loadings, are 'I
have been involved in more than one sex affair at the same time', and
'Sexual feelings are sometimes unpleasant to me'.

Table 2.12 *Loadings – sexual hostility*

Question	Males	Females
7	0·00	0·32
19	0·24	0·33
21	−0·06	−0·47
25	0·11	0·35
60	0·04	0·45
63	−0·05	0·32
73	0·69	0·62
77	0·36	0·20
80	0·74	0·66
83	−0·02	0·38

Factor 13. Guilt

Guilt has an index of factor similarity of 0·82, but nevertheless

43

produces some problems in interpretation. These are due to the fact that one item was duplicated (28 and 65) in an attempt to check on the care with which the inventory was filled in; the very high correlation between these two identical items (0·78 and 0·82, respectively, for males and females) suggests reasonable reliability, but does of course produce spuriously high loadings for the two replications of these items. For the purpose of interpretation, these very high values should therefore be disregarded. High and congruent loadings are then found on the following items: 'I have felt guilty about sex experiences', 'At times I have been afraid of myself for what I might do sexually', 'My conscience bothers me too much', 'Sometimes sexual feelings overpower me', 'Sex thoughts drive me almost crazy', 'I worry a lot about sex', 'Sometimes thinking about sex makes me very nervous', 'Perverted thoughts have sometimes bothered me', 'Sometimes it has been a problem to control my sex feelings'. The general picture is clearly one of guilt-ridden neurotic reactions to sexual thoughts and experiences; details regarding loadings are given in table 2.13.

Table 2.13   *Loadings – guilt*

Question	Males	Females
7	0·49	0·19
19	0·31	0·04
25	0·49	0·31
28	0·70	0·90
29	0·55	0·23
30	0·10	0·64
34	0·35	0·02
35	0·37	0·15
36	0·06	0·30
48	0·45	0·23
50	0·32	0·05
52	0·05	0·32
60	0·41	0·07
63	0·41	0·14
65	0·67	0·92
82	0·32	0·13

Other factors

These thirteen factors exhaust the clearly replicated and interpretable factors; the remainder are difficult to interpret and do not

have obvious duplicates when male and female results are compared. One female factor has indices of factor comparison of 0·71
and 0·69 with two male factors; we shall call these two male factors
14 and 16. One of these factors may be called *inhibition* (factor 14);
items having high and congruent loadings are 'My parents' influence
has inhibited me sexually' (0·25; 0·40); 'I didn't learn the facts of
life until I was quite old' (0·33; 0·34), 'My sex behaviour has caused
me some trouble' (0·44; 0·18), 'Conditions have to be just right to
get me excited sexually' (0·35; 0·14), 'Sex contacts have been a
problem to me' (0·07; 0·38), 'Virginity is a girl's most valuable
possession' (0·32; 0·14), 'Self-relief is not dangerous so long as it
is done in a healthy way' (0·34; 0·03). Factor 16 is essentially a
doublet, consisting of items 9 and 37; these are worded almost
identically, with the exception that one is worded positively, the
other negatively. This factor is therefore an artefact of no interest.
Factor 15 exists only for the females, having no match among the
males; it might be called a *dual standard* factor, as item 88 has the
only high loading (0·74). Other items loading on this factor are
'The opposite sex will respect you more if you are not too familiar
with them' (0·39), 'There are things I wouldn't do with anyone'
(0·37), 'I have strong sex feelings but when I get the chance I
can't express them' (0·31). This factor is of marginal meaning and
interest.

The relations obtaining between these sex attitude factors on
the one hand and P, E and N on the other were investigated along
two lines. In the first place, a method was used of reflecting the
personality variables into the factor space, thus giving the estimated
factor loadings for the three personality variables on the fourteen
sex factors outlined above. Computations for the extension analysis
utilised a FORTRAN programme FAX.(2) The matrix of loadings for
the extension variables on the factors is computed as the triple-
product $R_{et} R_{tt}^{-1} P_{tf}$, where R_{et} is the matrix of correlations between
the extension variables and the variables or tests in the factor
analysis, R_{tt} is the matrix of the correlations among the variables
or tests in the factor analysis and P_{tf} is the matrix of primary factor
loadings for the variables or tests in the factor analysis. (This analysis
exploits the fact that the factor analysis has been carried out 'with
unities in the diagonal' and thus bypasses adjustment owing to communalities.)

In addition, a detailed analysis was made of the differences between high, medium and low scorers on *P*, *E* and *N* for each item loading above 0·3 on each of the factors. The final results of these analyses are incorporated on table 2.14, which shows the obtained relations by direction (+ or −) and by strength (number of + and − signs). A '0' means that there is no relation either way, single + or − symbols indicate a weak relation and two or three + or − signs indicate a moderate or strong relation. It will be seen that persons scoring high or low on any of the personality factors differ from each other and that the three personality traits have quite different patterns of sexual attitudes. On the whole, these patterns seem to bear out expectations quite well. A second method of analysing personality–attitude relations will be discussed after considering the superfactors arising from the correlations between the primary factors.

Table 2.14 *Relations between personality types P, E and N and sexual attitude factors**

	Factor	*P*	*E*	*N*
1	Satisfaction	−	+	− − −
2	Excitement	+	+	+ +
3	Nervousness	0	− − −	+ +
4	Curiosity	+ +	0	+
5	Premarital sex	+ +	+	0
6	Repression	−	0	0
7	Prudishness	+	− −	+
8	Experimentation	+	+	0
9	Homosexuality	+	0	+
10	Censorship	−	−	0
11	Promiscuity	+ + +	+ +	0
12	Hostility	+ + +	0	+ + +
13	Guilt	0	0	+ + +
14	Inhibition	+	0	+ + +

*+ and − signs indicate positive or negative relations; 0 indicates absence of any relation

Oblique factor analysis, using Promax methods of rotation, results in factors that are themselves correlated and thus enables the inter-correlations between factors to be in turn factor-analysed. A few examples may make the position clearer. In women, the premarital sex factor is correlated 0·37 with excitement, −0·38 with nervousness, −0·40 with prudishness and −0·32 with inhibition. In men, satisfaction is correlated −0·41 with nervousness and −0·26 with guilt, premarital sex −0·30 with inhibition, repression 0·26 with inhibition. Five second-order factors were extracted for the men, four for the women; these resemble in many ways the primary factors from whose intercorrelations they are inferred. For both sexes, the first factor is one of *satisfaction*, combining items from primary factors 1 and 3 reversed. When the three personality factors are reflected into this new sex factor, N has the highest loadings (-0.48 and -0.45 for men and women, respectively), with E also having respectable loadings (0.38 and 0.35); P has slight loadings of -0.07 and -0.19. This is not unexpected, as high P scorers also score low on nervousness and satisfaction; thus they score in opposite directions, on the two primary factors that go to make up this second-order factor. The index of factor similarity for the two sexes is 0.88.

Table 2.15 presents correlations among primary factors for the male sample, and table 2.16 the same data for the female sample. The factors are presented in order of extraction, but are identified by the labelling used in the body of the paper. Factors preceded by a minus sign have been multiplied by -1.

Male factor 4 and female factor 4 have an index of factor similarity of 0.87; this factor represents a combination of excitement and guilt. When the three personality factors are reflected into this new factor, P (0.22 and 0.21) and N (0.20 and 0.49) have positive loadings, E (-0.12 and -0.15) low negative ones. Male factor 3 and female factor 2 have an index of factor similarity of 0.80; this factor presents a combination of curiosity and promiscuity. Loadings of the three personality factors are P (0.15 and 0.46), N (0.17 and 0.23) and E (0.05 and 0.04). Extraversion is thus not related to this factor, but both P and N are.

The last female factor finds no ready match among the male factors; it resembles primary factor 6 (repression). Correlations with personality factors are 0.45 with N and -0.35 with E; with P the correlation is 0.19. Male factors 2 and 5 are not clearly enough defined to make interpretation meaningful, and no discussion will therefore be given on them here. It is not unusual to find that primary and third-order factors are more meaningful than second-order factors (Eysenck and Eysenck 1969), although why this should be is not clear. In any case, the intercorrelations among the second-order factors have again been factor-analysed, and for both men and women the analysis resulted in two clear-cut factors. These are almost identical for the two sexes, indices of factor

47

Table 2.15 Correlations among primary factors for male sample*

	1	11	13	2	10	4	12	16	3	7	9	5	8	6	14
1	1·00														
(−) 11	−0·01	1·00													
(−) 13	0·26	−0·09	1·00												
2	−0·07	−0·06	−0·08	1·00											
10	−0·10	0·15	−0·20	−0·00	1·00										
4	−0·08	−0·09	−0·06	0·14	−0·22	1·00									
12	0·12	0·06	0·03	0·15	−0·11	0·12	1·00								
16	0·03	−0·05	−0·07	0·18	−0·06	0·20	0·09	1·00							
3	−0·41	0·01	−0·22	0·01	0·14	0·09	−0·21	0·05	1·00						
7	0·23	−0·05	0·28	0·06	−0·06	0·03	0·03	−0·01	−0·22	1·00					
9	−0·04	0·08	−0·06	0·17	0·06	0·06	0·06	0·19	0·04	0·07	1·00				
5	−0·06	0·16	0·01	−0·09	0·18	−0·07	0·01	−0·28	0·07	0·00	0·03	1·00			
(−) 8	0·13	0·10	0·04	−0·08	0·14	−0·08	−0·22	−0·07	−0·00	0·09	−0·17	−0·04	1·00		
6	−0·12	0·03	−0·25	0·06	0·17	−0·11	−0·16	0·19	0·12	−0·22	0·01	−0·13	0·09	1·00	
14	0·08	0·18	0·04	−0·13	−0·05	−0·05	0·13	−0·41	−0·04	−0·02	−0·05	0·30	−0·08	−0·26	1·00

* Factors preceded by a minus sign have been multiplied by − 1 in order to give the direction of the factor as presented in the body of the paper

Table 2.16 Correlations among primary factors for female sample*

	5	3	2	13	4	7	11	10	1	14	8	15	6	9	12
5	1·00														
3	0·38	1·00													
2	−0·37	−0·24	1·00												
(−) 13	−0·03	−0·08	−0·22	1·00											
(−) 4	0·29	−0·07	−0·22	0·12	1·00										
7	−0·40	−0·31	0·09	0·17	−0·07	1·00									
11	−0·03	0·11	−0·07	0·04	−0·01	0·00	1·00								
(−) 10	−0·07	0·08	0·05	−0·21	−0·10	−0·02	−0·07	1·00							
1	−0·19	−0·28	0·07	0·29	0·05	0·25	0·05	−0·24	1·00						
14	−0·32	−0·19	0·17	−0·04	−0·11	0·30	−0·17	0·11	0·08	1·00					
8	−0·05	0·14	−0·12	0·16	−0·21	0·12	−0·06	0·13	0·03	0·03	1·00				
(−) 15	−0·18	−0·29	0·13	−0·02	0·13	0·12	0·05	−0·04	0·05	0·04	−0·32	1·00			
(−) 6	−0·25	−0·11	0·09	0·14	−0·11	0·18	0·17	−0·17	−0·17	−0·13	−0·11	0·32	1·00		
9	−0·20	−0·24	−0·03	0·13	0·08	0·17	0·22	−0·22	0·20	−0·12	−0·22	0·42	0·44	1·00	
12	−0·06	−0·06	0·20	−0·39	0·01	−0·06	−0·16	0·20	−0·20	0·14	−0·23	0·12	−0·06	−0·07	1·00

* Factors preceded by a minus sign have been multiplied by − 1 in order to give the direction of the factor as presented in the body of the paper

similarity being 0·95 and 0·93, respectively. We would expect these factors to be reasonably meaningful, and this expectation is not disappointed. Factor 1 combines all the aspects of pathology and deprivation that have found expression in the various primary factors listed; this factor may be named *sexual pathology*.(3) The second factor combines all the aspects of permissiveness and active sexuality that have been found in various other primary factors; this factor may be called *sexual libido*. These two factors are uncorrelated for both males and females.

√   The three personality factors were reflected into the sex questionnaire item space, and the results bear out what one would have expected from the detailed consideration of the various items reported in previous sections. Sexual pathology is correlated primarily with N, correlations being 0·40 for women and 0·47 for men. Correlations with P are also positive, but too low to be of much interest; they are 0·08 for women and 0·12 for men. Correlations with E are negative, as expected, and not very large; values are −0·23 for women and −0·27 for men. Thus dysthymics (high N, low E) would be most likely subjects for sexual pathology. Sexual libido is positively correlated with P, the correlations being as high as 0·40 for women and dropping to 0·19 for men; this difference may be related to the facts that men tend to score much higher on P than women and that strong sexual desires traditionally characterise men rather than women. N is also correlated with libido, but the correlation is only 0·29 for women and 0·06 for men; the latter correlation is clearly insignificant. E also shows only slight correlations with libido, 0·13 for women and 0·15 for men.

The data here given seem to establish that different personality types differ profoundly in their attitudes to sexual issues, as well as in their sexual behaviours. Such differences can be observed for most of the fifteen or so factors into which sexual attitudes were analysed. It is interesting that these factors appeared so clearly, and in so similar form, in both the male and the female samples, and that the personality differences in one sample tended to replicate those in the other. Of particular interest are perhaps the two main higher-order factors, pathology and libido; these make intuitive sense, as well as emerging so clearly from the analysis: and the relations with personality too are very much in line with expectation. It will of course be realised that our data apply only to a rather narrow sample of unmarried young undergraduates, and cannot be extended much beyond these limitations; later work with older and particularly with married groups has led to a modification of some of the conclusions that at present appear indicated. Nevertheless, as a pioneering study into these difficult and complex issues our results may certainly be regarded as suggestive; only replication with other samples will show how restrictive the limitations of the sample may have been. In spite of these limitations, there are certain reassuring trends in our data that fit in well with psychiatric experience; thus the combination in high N scorers of sexual pathology and strong sexual libido may be responsible for sexual conflict so often observed in neurotic patients.

Relating personality to sexual attitudes through factors is one way of describing the relationships obtaining; a more direct way is by way of subdividing the total sample into high, medium and low scorers on each of the three personality variables, and then calculating the percentage 'Yes' answers given to each question by members of these various groups. Tables 2.17, 2.18 and 2.19 give this information; also given there are correlations between items and personality scale score (r_p). The results are of course similar in essence to those contained in table 2·14, but may nevertheless repay some detailed description.

The first personality factor to be discussed is P. This presents an interesting combination of promiscuity, premarital sex and curiosity with hostility and lack of satisfaction; the picture is of a 'lady-killer' who has little love or kindness towards his victims, and who is on the whole dissatisfied with his sex life. Individual item correlations should be seen in the context of the pattern of factor loadings given in table 2.14. None of the loadings of P on these sex factors are very large (0·3, with premarital sex, is the highest, followed by 0·25 for promiscuity), but they form a meaningful pattern, and show congruence for the two sexes.

The highest loading individual items refer to lack of concern with virginity (items 5 and 26), liking for impersonal sex (2 and 13), premarital sex (42 and 45), libertinism (44 and 79), liking for pornography (47, 81 and 84), liking for prostitution instead of marriage (85, 89), dislike of sexual censorship (91, 92, 93, and 94), promiscuity (77), voyeurism (83) and strong sexual excitement (52, 3, 6, 7, 33, 37, 41, 46, 53, 82). These items indicate an intense preoccupation with sex in its biological aspect; other items indicate the morbid and indeed pathological aspect of the high P scorer's

51

Table 2.17 Percentage of 'yes' answers for **P+**, **P=** and **P−** subjects for 94 items of inventory; also correlations between P and each item

Item	P_M +	P_M =	P_M −	r_D	P_F +	P_F =	P_F −	r_D
1	35	36	42	−0·06	44	61	67	−0·17
2	27	47	58	−0·17	64	85	85	−0·26
3	21	15	25	−0·05	37	44	45	−0·14
4	29	38	48	−0·13	53	58	65	−0·10
5	11	18	18	−0·10	6	25	33	−0·30
6	1	7	5	−0·06	3	15	16	−0·15
7	51	49	43	0·09	49	48	36	+0·13
8	5	6	9	−0·04	15	23	23	−0·11
9	59	53	53	0·08	55	48	39	+0·09
10	65	59	59	0·05	43	41	31	+0·07
11	32	19	26	0·09	16	6	5	+0·22
12	5	6	5	0·00	7	6	4	−0·01
13	47	49	35	0·12	24	8	8	+0·22
14	66	60	65	0·04	75	77	71	+0·04
15	14	6	11	0·06	3	6	5	−0·06
16	6	1	3	0·10	5	2	1	+0·08
17	29	36	39	−0·08	41	39	43	−0·00
18	13	14	11	0·01	21	18	29	−0·06
19	12	14	8	0·06	16	18	15	−0·01
20	55	51	45	0·07	28	27	23	+0·04
21	38	43	46	−0·08	40	32	37	+0·01
22	45	39	34	0·10	35	27	18	+0·07
23	32	36	38	−0·01	25	29	23	+0·03
24	2	2	2	−0·02	7	4	11	−0·03
25	30	28	29	−0·02	40	43	40	−0·00
26	73	69	63	0·10	92	70	64	+0·23
27	20	14	13	0·10	22	9	11	+0·14
28	36	25	25	0·11	26	14	16	+0·11
29	22	17	19	0·01	33	27	21	+0·13
30	17	15	15	0·02	18	6	7	+0·15
31	67	68	76	−0·04	85	77	81	+0·03
32	24	23	22	0·02	15	15	7	+0·04
33	76	59	66	0·06	32	35	27	+0·10
34	33	32	26	0·07	31	25	20	+0·09
35	15	10	13	0·04	8	7	6	+0·10
36	5	2	3	0·12	3	6	4	+0·04
37	51	48	58	−0·12	48	49	46	−0·02
38	95	96	93	0·03	100	96	97	+0·09
39	90	86	89	−0·00	69	72	66	−0·01
40	52	38	43	0·07	48	31	31	+0·15
41	91	81	82	0·09	66	53	43	+0·19
42	7	6	9	−0·02	6	25	27	−0·23

43	68	51	61	0·04	30	30	21	+0·08
44	11	19	23	−0·17	43	73	69	−0·29
45	5	4	9	−0·08	13	37	35	−0·25
46	32	22	22	0·14	7	2	3	+0·08
47	61	62	60	0·02	15	8	5	+0·20
48	21	16	17	−0·01	24	27	27	−0·02
49	8	5	8	−0·03	11	15	12	−0·06
50	35	34	29	0·08	32	27	23	+0·07
51	27	20	27	−0·02	16	15	13	+0·05
52	13	4	5	0·21	5	0	1	+0·22
53	29	20	25	0·08	23	16	9	+0·18
54	61	72	65	−0·00	80	76	83	−0·07
55	5	1	1	0·10	5	2	3	+0·04
56	15	9	12	−0·01	7	6	5	+0·06
57	23	25	29	−0·05	22	21	27	−0·08
58	25	20	26	−0·01	14	14	18	−0·04
59	93	90	94	−0·03	86	78	74	+0·10
60	30	17	21	0·05	16	13	11	+0·06
61	85	82	85	0·03	78	62	61	−0·14
62	7	10	15	−0·04	33	40	51	−0·12
63	24	13	13	0·08	20	22	19	−0·06
64	55	61	55	0·03	56	58	45	−0·03
65	32	26	23	0·09	28	15	15	+0·13
66	9	7	10	−0·03	8	4	13	−0·04
67	37	34	31	0·07	29	25	18	+0·16
68	91	87	88	0·01	79	65	55	+0·19

69	8	3	3	0·08	20	20	24	−0·08
70	62	42	34	0·25	10	8	5	+0·09
71	56	55	46	0·11	44	42	42	+0·09
72	75	68	64	0·10	55	57	50	+0·04
73	30	23	12	0·21	23	14	3	+0·18
74	5	6	5	−0·06	6	11	9	−0·06
75	79	67	75	0·01	59	59	51	+0·06
76	58	52	61	−0·06	45	51	39	+0·03
77	39	38	22	0·16	23	11	11	+0·17
78	72	78	73	−0·02	74	70	68	+0·08
79	82	75	65	0·18	53	34	26	+0·32
80	43	45	27	0·20	60	42	27	+0·23
81	62	63	63	0·02	21	8	5	+0·27
82	39	45	41	0·01	11	8	7	+0·13
83	49	36	40	0·12	16	13	9	+0·12
84	69	58	53	0·18	41	30	28	+0·15
85	58	64	64	−0·01	47	36	31	+0·24
86	59	53	46	0·12	55	43	47	+0·07
87	5	4	9	−0·02	3	14	17	−0·14
88	33	33	31	−0·01	31	27	22	+0·00
89	19	7	5	0·23	3	2	1	+0·12
90	9	5	6	0·11	1	5	3	−0·06
91	72	62	57	0·16	57	35	33	+0·22
92	87	82	73	0·20	52	33	31	+0·20
93	82	75	73	0·09	57	37	33	+0·25
94	74	64	51	0·21	7	3	3	+0·18

Table 2.18 Percentage of 'yes' answers for E+, E= and E− subjects for 94 items of inventory; also correlations between E and each item

Item	E_M +	E_M =	E_M −	r	E_F +	E_F =	E_F −	r
1	31	38	45	−0·12	50	63	64	−0·15
2	42	54	49	−0·08	77	86	78	−0·09
3	17	23	22	−0·05	40	50	39	−0·07
4	42	42	37	−0·09	58	66	54	0·03
5	14	13	20	−0·04	21	23	27	−0·08
6	3	3	6	−0·03	8	14	16	−0·06
7	45	49	42	0·03	54	44	33	0·18
8	6	7	8	−0·04	23	20	21	−0·01
9	63	55	46	0·13	56	45	38	0·15
10	58	60	64	−0·06	36	42	34	0·02
11	16	24	34	−0·18	8	4	12	−0·13
12	5	7	4	−0·00	5	4	8	−0·09
13	51	40	39	0·09	14	11	11	0·04
14	67	62	63	0·05	75	74	74	−0·01
15	7	6	17	−0·17	4	5	6	−0·18
16	2	1	6	−0·07	1	2	4	−0·09
17	42	35	30	0·07	50	43	31	0·14
18	14	12	12	0·00	20	20	30	−0·12
19	7	9	16	−0·17	14	15	19	−0·11
20	40	47	62	−0·19	23	28	26	−0·05
21	48	40	42	0·00	31	40	37	−0·03
22	33	36	47	−0·11	17	20	32	−0·17
23	23	33	49	−0·27	12	18	46	−0·36
24	2	1	3	−0·01	4	10	7	−0·06
25	25	33	27	0·00	48	35	42	−0·00
26	77	65	62	0·06	80	71	68	0·16
27	14	15	15	0·00	12	11	14	0·00
28	22	28	33	−0·08	14	15	24	−0·15
29	17	19	22	−0·05	30	28	20	−0·08
30	15	15	18	−0·03	11	5	12	−0·04
31	84	76	54	0·29	93	86	62	0·40
32	13	23	31	−0·18	12	11	14	−0·05
33	71	64	65	0·05	37	32	25	0·12
34	23	28	37	−0·09	22	23	29	−0·07
35	3	13	19	−0·19	6	5	10	−0·12
36	2	2	7	−0·12	3	7	3	−0·02
37	50	52	56	−0·07	43	54	45	−0·07
38	93	96	94	−0·03	98	95	98	0·01
39	90	85	89	0·02	76	67	64	0·12
40	42	46	43	−0·05	37	38	29	0·08
41	87	82	83	0·01	58	53	45	0·16
42	6	8	8	−0·09	15	22	27	−0·13

#	2	4	7		15	20	30	
43	57	60	63	-0.03	32	28	20	0.18
44	11	20	23	-0.19	53	70	70	-0.19
45	3	4	11	-0.14	21	35	35	-0.14
46	28	26	20	0.13	5	2	4	0.03
47	56	63	62	0.00	8	7	10	-0.04
48	11	20	21	-0.11	29	25	26	0.00
49	7	7	7	0.02	10	16	13	-0.03
50	32	38	25	0.08	32	28	20	0.11
51	10	22	41	-0.29	9	10	25	-0.27
52	6	4	8	-0.07	1	2	2	-0.07
53	20	31	20	0.03	12	14	18	-0.03
54	83	70	47	0.28	87	86	66	0.27
55	0	1	5	-0.15	3	2	4	-0.10
56	2	8	25	-0.34	1	4	12	-0.26
57	15	27	35	-0.17	17	20	33	-0.13
58	17	23	30	-0.11	8	14	24	-0.24
59	96	96	86	0.11	86	80	70	0.21
60	14	21	30	-0.15	15	9	16	-0.05
61	91	79	84	0.01	69	64	62	0.05
62	10	12	12	0.01	39	44	45	-0.03
63	8	19	19	-0.14	15	21	25	-0.09
64	62	58	53	0.07	64	46	48	0.14
65	22	28	29	-0.03	13	15	26	-0.15
66	6	7	13	-0.15	3	5	16	-0.23
67	37	33	31	0.06	26	27	15	0.08
68	91	93	81	0.13	71	62	60	0.10
69	2	4	7	-0.15	13	5	3	-0.20
70	52	44	37	0.14	47	45	35	0.06
71	54	54	47	0.02	57	57	47	0.08
72	70	68	66	0.05	14	12	10	0.08
73	23	21	17	0.04	9	9	10	-0.02
74	6	4	6	-0.00	60	58	49	-0.09
75	70	74	77	-0.05	51	44	40	0.11
76	55	58	58	-0.04	19	11	12	0.07
77	48	30	19	0.22	72	71	67	0.09
78	71	76	75	-0.04	41	34	30	0.02
79	76	71	72	0.03	50	35	35	0.14
80	34	37	40	-0.04	10	10	9	0.04
81	58	65	65	-0.03	12	8	6	0.00
82	40	42	43	-0.01	11	14	10	0.12
83	42	33	49	-0.04	33	34	29	-0.02
84	66	58	52	0.11	38	31	29	0.07
85	68	66	54	0.12	51	50	40	0.09
86	59	49	48	0.05	14	11	14	0.09
87	3	6	9	-0.09	25	32	20	-0.07
88	34	30	32	0.01	4	1	2	0.04
89	10	10	8	0.07	6	3	2	0.04
90	5	6	9	-0.02	44	38	36	0.01
91	73	59	58	0.08	41	32	38	0.10
92	88	79	73	0.14	41	41	38	0.06
93	82	78	68	0.15	6	3	2	0.06
94	75	63	47	0.21	6	3	2	0.09

attitude. He considers himself deprived sexually (11) and dissatisfied with his sex life (4, 22), in spite of the fact that he has had more sexual experience than the low P scorer; he feels hostility to his sex partner (73, 80), is troubled by perverted thoughts (28, 29) and has homosexual leanings (16, 30, 36, 40). Taking one's pleasures where one finds them (70) has clearly not brought him much happiness; the libertinism is marred by a pathological streak which may justify the clinical connotations of the 'P' label.

✓ The high E scorer is also characterised by the promiscuity factor, but in him it is allied most prominently with lack of nervousness and with satisfaction. The highest loadings are with lack of nervousness (0·35) and with promiscuity (0·27); here apparently we have a happy philanderer, who derives satisfaction from his sexual behaviour. The individual items having the highest loadings emphasise the extravert's social facility with the opposite sex (23, 31, 56, 51, 54, 58, 66, 17), his like for sexual activity (59, 69, 9, 18, 19, 32, 41, 55), his contentment with his sexual life (11, 15, 20, 22) and his lack of worry about it (60, 63). He too is easily excited sexually, (7, 33, 39, 43, 46) and endorses premarital sex (26, 42, 45); he too is promiscuous (77, 44), but he lacks the pathological element of the high P scorer (28, 35), and his liking for pornography is very slight (84, 85, 91, 92, 93, 94). Homosexuality (36) is no problem to him, and offers no attraction.

✓ High N scorers show a different combination of excitement and approval for premarital sex with the other factors; they are characterised by low satisfaction and high guilt feelings. Loadings are highest on guilt (0·30) and lack of satisfaction (0·25); excitement loads more highly for the men (0·20). Individual items emphasise the same features; particularly prominent are the lack of satisfaction derived from sex (4, 20, 22), the guilt feelings associated with a strong conscience (48, 25), the worry about sexual activities (60, 63), the problem of controlling sex thoughts (35, 7, 28, 29) and the fears and difficulties with contacts with the opposite sex (56, 17, 54, 56, 31). Blame is attached to the inhibiting influence of the parents (34), religion (49) and 'bad experiences' (27). Sexual behaviour is seen as both troublesome (21, 19, 66) and disgusting (11), and the high N scorer stresses his inability to contact members of the other sex (15, 23); in spite of all this he has strong sexual drives (33, 41, 43, 50, 52) which he finds it difficult to control (32, 53). Homosexuality is a problem (16, 36, 40). There is some evidence

56

Table 2.19 *Percentage of 'yes' answers for N+, N= and N− subjects for 94 items of inventory; also correlations between N and each item*

	+	N_M	−	r_N	+	N_F	−	r_N		+	N_M	−	r_N	+	N_F	−	r_N
1	43	36	36	0.10	60	61	55	0.03	25	38	32	17	0.20	55	39	30	0.23
2	50	50	46	0.07	79	82	79	−0.05	26	59	66	77	−0.11	79	73	67	0.11
3	28	19	16	0.11	47	44	39	0.06	27	22	11	11	0.16	19	10	10	0.11
4	25	41	53	−0.27	49	53	77	−0.30	28	40	29	15	0.25	29	15	10	0.21
5	17	19	13	0.01	20	28	22	0.05	29	29	20	9	0.24	35	27	16	0.23
6	3	4	6	−0.12	6	15	15	−0.17	30	23	14	10	0.17	14	7	7	0.09
7	57	47	34	0.25	53	37	42	0.12	31	64	73	76	−0.12	79	77	85	−0.05
8	8	7	5	0.05	25	20	20	−0.02	32	35	22	11	0.26	23	7	6	0.19
9	59	58	48	0.07	48	44	47	0.02	33	73	64	62	0.14	38	27	29	0.03
10	64	61	57	0.09	42	39	31	0.14	34	39	33	18	0.18	39	22	14	0.27
11	37	22	16	0.25	13	9	2	0.20	35	24	11	2	0.33	12	7	2	0.18
12	5	6	5	0.04	8	7	2	0.09	36	6	2	2	0.14	6	4	3	0.05
13	45	44	41	0.02	11	13	11	0.00	37	55	49	54	0.04	49	48	45	0.02
14	64	61	66	−0.07	71	73	79	−0.05	38	95	95	94	0.01	97	96	98	0.02
15	18	5	7	0.15	8	4	3	0.10	39	91	88	85	0.08	60	71	75	−0.15
16	6	2	1	0.11	4	2	1	0.05	40	48	41	41	0.11	41	35	29	0.08
17	28	36	42	−0.16	25	45	52	−0.24	41	90	85	77	0.18	56	50	49	0.05
18	14	16	7	0.08	25	26	18	−0.07	42	7	9	6	0.01	15	27	21	−0.07
19	14	10	8	0.11	24	15	10	0.15	43	65	61	54	0.15	34	23	24	0.05
20	70	47	34	0.31	35	29	13	0.24	44	19	21	15	0.05	72	61	63	0.04
21	39	41	49	−0.08	30	36	41	−0.13	45	8	7	4	0.07	28	34	29	−0.03
22	53	37	26	0.29	34	26	10	0.28	46	27	21	24	0.04	4	2	4	0.01
23	42	36	30	0.12	27	28	22	0.04	47	65	64	54	0.08	13	7	5	0.13
24	4	1	1	0.09	9	7	6	0.04	48	30	17	7	0.27	48	21	12	0.33

Table 2.19—cont.

	+	N_M	−	r_N	+	N_F	−	r_N
49	9	9	3	0·14	16	13	10	0·03
50	42	30	26	0·18	34	25	22	0·14
51	41	16	17	0·30	23	15	6	0·21
52	14	2	2	0·27	3	1	0	0·08
53	33	24	16	0·16	23	15	7	0·19
54	53	68	77	−0·21	72	80	87	−0·14
55	4	1	0	0·18	4	3	2	0·04
56	20	7	9	0·22	8	6	3	0·11
57	35	23	20	0·15	34	23	13	0·15
58	32	22	17	0·23	22	15	10	0·11
59	88	95	94	−0·07	78	77	80	0·02
60	44	16	7	0·42	28	11	2	0·32
61	81	84	87	−0·07	66	66	63	0·09
62	9	13	13	−0·08	44	43	41	−0·06
63	30	11	6	0·34	39	15	9	0·33
64	60	59	52	0·06	53	53	52	−0·02
65	36	27	17	0·19	29	16	10	0·20
66	16	4	6	0·18	10	9	5	0·05
67	30	39	32	0·01	30	20	20	0·06
68	85	90	91	−0·10	72	60	63	0·05
69	6	4	3	0·08	27	19	20	0·04
70	47	42	43	0·05	8	7	7	−0·05
71	53	53	49	0·02	45	42	40	0·03
72	74	63	67	0·03	60	49	53	0·05
73	25	21	15	0·18	16	15	5	0·12
74	4	7	4	0·09	9	9	10	−0·03
75	77	71	73	0·06	57	55	55	0·02
76	54	63	55	0·05	52	44	40	0·05
77	35	33	29	0·02	14	16	12	0·02
78	75	72	76	−0·01	72	72	67	0·05
79	71	71	76	−0·06	41	36	28	0·12
80	50	36	26	0·21	53	39	29	0·18
81	65	67	57	0·10	12	9	8	0·05
82	47	46	33	0·16	11	7	8	0·09
83	59	41	33	0·14	16	9	11	0·07
84	60	56	60	0·01	36	31	29	0·06
85	63	61	63	−0·01	41	28	29	0·12
86	53	49	52	0·02	58	46	39	0·10
87	11	4	3	0·11	28	16	13	−0·06
88	33	32	30	0·02	28	24	26	−0·04
89	9	8	10	0·05	2	2	2	0·01
90	10	4	5	0·09	3	5	2	0·01
91	68	62	59	0·05	45	37	36	0·08
92	83	79	77	0·09	41	36	33	0·02
93	77	76	75	0·00	49	38	34	0·10
94	61	59	64	0·05	3	4	4	0·10

of liking for pornography (83, 85, 93, 94), but much less so than in the high P scorer; it almost seems a substitute for the unattainable sexual contacts with real life partners. Lastly, there is a tendency to be hostile to the sex partner (80, 73), but again in the context suggests a different interpretation to the hostility of the high P scorer; here the hostility may spring from the failure to acquire a sex partner in the first place!

Taking an overall view, one might say that, as expected, high P and N scorers show a distinctly pathological pattern of sexual reactions. Both are characterised by strong sexual drives (the former less so than the latter), but whereas the high P scorer 'acts out' his libidinous, promiscuous and perverse desires, the high N scorer does not; instead he is beset by a whole set of inhibitions, worries and guilt feelings which effectively prevent him from consummating his desires. Yet both groups are dissatisfied with their patterns of sexual performance, although presumably for different reasons; this dissatisfaction constitutes the strongest evidence for the hypothesis that both are to some degree 'pathological'. (It would clearly not be adequate to justify this term on the grounds of either statistical infrequency of occurrence, or of moral and ethical undesirability of the conduct in question; it is because both groups are so dissatisfied with their behaviour that one may justly infer that it is not appropriate.) Both groups are similar in that they view their sex partners with some hostility, like pornography, and have homosexual leanings; yet as already pointed out, the different setting in which these items occur suggests different interpretations of the motivation involved, at least for the first two points.

As regards the E factor, the evidence would seem to suggest that here we have non-pathological ways of sexual adjustment, the extraverted and the introverted, which are opposed in a very meaningful manner. The extravert endorses the 'permissive', promiscuous approach to sex, with frequent change of sex partner and much 'healthy appetite' for frequent sexual contacts. The introvert endorses the orthodox Christian approach with fidelity, stress on virginity and less purely biological factors as the prime contents. Taken to their extremes, these approaches become the 'libertine' and the 'puritan' respectively, but if not taken to excess they are probably both viable modes of adjustment. The extravert seems more satisfied with his way of life, and is of course better able to contact members of the opposite sex, but this may be an artefact of the particular sample taken; at twenty, unmarried youngsters quite naturally have some difficulties in living up to introverted ideals. At forty, the happily married introvert may show better adjustment than the extravert suffering from the 'seven-year itch'. This is of course merely speculation, but it may serve to emphasise the restrictions imposed on interpretation by the specific nature of the sample studied.

The data presented in tables 2.17, 2.18 and 2.19 enable us to say something about the consistency of the personality–attitude relations between sexes, and also about the similarity or dissimilarity of attitudes held by different personality types. Given in these tables are six columns (r_P, r_E and r_N, each replicated for males and females) which report the correlations of each of the ninety-four items with P, E and N. These six columns were themselves correlated, in the hope that the results would throw some light on the two problems mentioned above. First consider the male–female correlations within the personality type, i.e. P_M v. P_F=0·69; E_M v. E_F=0·80; N_M v. N_F=0·77. These demonstrate that personality scale–attitude item correlations that are high for one sex are also high for the other; there is clearly a considerable amount of consistency here, particularly for the E scale, slightly less so for the N scale, and least of all for the P scale. This is not unexpected, as the P scale is the least reliable and has had much less experimental work associated with it than the other two scales. When we turn from these intra-scale correlations to inter-scale correlations, we find results which may be set out in the form of table 2.20.

Table 2.20 *Correlations between columns of tables 2.17, 2.18 and 2.19*

	$P \times E$	$P \times N$	$E \times N$
Male v. male	0·28	0·23	−0·61
Female v. female	0·39	0·38	−0·25
Male v. female	0·22	0·33	−0·39
Female v. male	0·32	0·14	−0·44

Clearly, the sexual attitudes of high P scorers are a little like those of high E scorers, and also a little like those of high N scorers; the degree of similarity does not amount to more than about 8 per cent or 9 per cent of the variance. High E scorers are somewhat more markedly unlike high N scorers; the degree of dissimilarity amounts to something like 17 per cent of the variance. The within-sex comparisons are no different on the whole from the between-sex comparisons, and all are in good agreement with each other. The between-scale correlations are clearly lower than the within-scale correlations, demonstrating that our results are consistent across sex. On the whole these figures are very encouraging; they suggest that different personality types do indeed have different attitudes towards sex, regardless of the sex of the respondent.

Having thus briefly discussed the sexual attitudes associated with P, E and N, it may be worthwhile to devote a few sentences to a discussion of the observed differences between male and female attitudes. The items showing the greatest differences are given in table 2.21 (Eysenck 1971b).

Overwhelmingly outstanding among items giving marked differences between the sexes are items relating to pornography (47, 81, 84, 91, 92, 93), orgies (44, 94), voyeurism (83, 62) and prostitution (85), closely followed by impersonal sex (2, 13). Sexual excitement is close behind (33, 41, 43, 46, 82, 3, 39); in all those of course males have higher rates of endorsement than females. Premarital sex is also favoured more by the males (45, 70, 79, 42), as is promiscuity (77). But contentment in their sex life is more marked among women (4, 20, 11, 22), perhaps unexpectedly. Masturbation is more a male pastime (10, 8), and men are also less prudish in general (18, 68, 69, 59) and feel less guilt (25).

Most of these differences are not unexpected, although one should not over-interpret them; some of the replies may represent little but widely held views unthinkingly endorsed. The only unexpected feature of the study is the apparent satisfaction of the women with their sex lives; it used to be thought that the 'permissive' society favoured men, as did the Victorian era. Possibly the clue lies in the greater sex drive apparent in the men, and the difficulties that this strong drive must give rise to when confronted with the stark reality that over half the women in our samples were still virgins and apparently intent on holding on to this status. In this sellers' market, women clearly have the upper hand, and may enjoy this status; again the nature of our sample may be responsible for a finding that is not likely to be duplicated for older men and women. There is an interesting finding in Schofield's book (1968), in

Table 2.21 *Percentage differences in endorsements of twenty-seven items on the sex inventory between men and women*

	M–F differences
If you were invited to take part in an orgy, would you: (a) accept it? (b) refuse?	57
I like to look at pictures of nudes	53
I like to look at sexy pictures	53
The thought of a sex orgy is disgusting to me	–47
If you were invited to see a 'blue' film, would you: (a) accept? (b) refuse?	43
It is all right to seduce a person who is old enough to know what they are doing	38
I believe in taking my pleasures where I find them	37
If you were offered a highly pornographic book, would you: (a) accept it? (b) refuse it?	36
It doesn't take much to get me excited sexually	35
Buttocks excite me	34
I get excited sexually very easily	33
I think about sex almost every day	32
Seeing a person nude does not interest me	–32
Sex without love ('impersonal sex') is highly unsatisfactory	–31
I do not need to respect a woman, or love her, in order to enjoy petting and/or intercourse with her	31
Prostitution should be legally permitted	–30
If you had a chance to see people making love, without being seen, would you take it?	29
Pornographic writings should be freely allowed to be published	27
It is better not to have sexual relations until you are married	–25
Sometimes the woman should be sexually aggressive	24
I get pleasant feelings from touching my sexual parts	24
Something is lacking in my sex life	24
There should be no censorship, on sexual grounds, of plays and films	34
Conditions have to be just right to get me excited sexually	–22
I find the thought of a coloured sex partner particularly exciting	21
The opposite sex will respect you more if you are not too familiar with them	–21
All in all I am satisfied with my sex life	–20

which he showed that female adolescents who had had intercourse were not very attractive on the whole, while male adolescents who had had intercourse were; the explanation presumably is again in terms of the sellers' market – men must be attractive to get a girl, but a girl who is attractive does not need to trade her virginity for male attention. Specific research devoted to a clarification of these relations might be of considerable interest. Figure 2.1 shows the distribution of scores on a scale made up of the most discriminating male–female items.

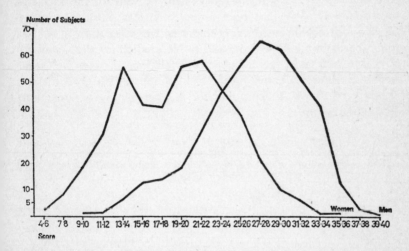

Figure 2.1 *Scores of men and women on masculinity–femininity in sex attitudes inventory*

It is of some interest to note that male–female differences on our sex attitude inventory are similar to the high *P* v. low *P* differences, as shown in table 2.17. In other words, the pattern of male v. female response differences is similar to that of high-*P* males v. low-*P* males, or of high-*P* females v. low-*P* females. This is not unexpected; in our previous work with *P* we have noted that males have much higher *P* scores than females, and that criminals (who are of course predominantly male in society) have higher *P* scores than do non-criminals. This suggestion deserves investigation and the following calculations have been carried out accordingly.

For the purpose of analysis, the percentage of 'Yes' answers on

63

each question was established for men and women separately, and that for women subtracted from that for men; this difference score will be called the *M–F* score. Next, product–moment correlations were established, separately for the two sexes, between each personality dimension (*P*, *E* and *N*) and between each of the ninety-four items in the inventory. There are thus six sets of correlations: three dimensions, two sexes. These six sets of correlations were in turn correlated with the *M–F* score, our expectation being that *M–F* score would correlate positively and highly with the *P* factor correlations, for both men and women. In view of the fact that masculinity–feminity has been observed to load positively on extraversion it also seemed likely that positive correlations would be found between the *M–F* score and *E*. No predictions were made for *N*. Table 2.22 gives the actual intercorrelations between our seven variables. Interest centres on the last column, which gives the correlations of the *M–F* score and the sex personality–sex inventory correlation scores.

Table 2.22 *Correlations between M–F score differences and sets of personality inventory score–sex inventory item correlations. Asterisked values significant at < 0·01, doubly asterisked values significant at < 0·001 levels of p*

			2	3	4	5	6	7
P	M	2	0·70**	0·31*	0·23	0·23	0·33*	0·54**
	F	2		0·34**	0·38**	0·14	0·38**	0·74**
E	M	3			0·81**	−0·56**	−0·34**	0·31*
	F	4				−0·45**	−0·24*	0·30*
N	M	5					0·77**	0·10
	F	6						0·21*
M–F		7						

As expected, the correlations of the *M–F* score are very high and positive with *P*, for both sexes. They are considerably lower, although still significant at the $p < 0·01$ level, for *E*. For *N*, the correlations are for all practical purposes negligible, although both are positive, and that for females is significant at the $p < 0·05$ level. It is clear that our hypothesis receives strong support from these data; male attitudes towards sex, as compared with females ones, are similar to those of high *P* scoring males (or females) as compared to low *P* scoring males (or females). These correlations, in fact, are to the same order as the correlations between males and females on the psychoticism scale.

One further item of interest may support our view. Eysenck (1971c) found that high *P* scorers, as compared with low *P* scorers, had indulged significantly more frequently in minor perversions (fellatio, cunnilingus, '69'). So had men as compared with women, when only respondents having had intercourse were included in the tabulation. However, taking part in an activity is not identical with enjoying it, and it seems likely on our hypothesis that of those who had actually indulged in these perversions, men would have enjoyed them more than women. Some evidence is furnished on this point in a study by Kolaszynska-Carr (unpublished) in which male and female subjects who had indulged in these activities (between 40 and 50 of each sex, depending on the activity in question) reported on their enjoyment of their experiences. Taking fellatio as typical of this category of conduct, 39 out of 41 male subjects reported enjoyment, but only 24 out of 42 females. Even for such items as manual genital manipulation, male by female, the percentages are quite different (94 and 64 per cent); for mutual manual genital manipulation they are 96 and 68 per cent. It would seem that for even slightly unusual practices women are much less likely to report enjoyment; no such sex differences were found for petting behaviour of a more innocent kind (fondling of the female breast, kissing of nipples, etc.). This whole area of enjoyment of sexual activity deserves to be studied in much greater detail.

It is of some interest to note that in some unpublished research imprisoned sex offenders scored very significantly higher on the *P* scale than did other prisoners (who in turn of course scored very significantly higher on the *P* scale than did matched non-prison controls). The mean *P* value for the sex offenders was 11·07, as compared with a prisoner mean of 6·25; $p < 0.01$. The offences in question included rape, indecent assault and buggery.

Sexuality thus seems to constitute a continuum that is largely colinear with *P* and with masculinity; it would seem important to investigate possible hormonal and other biochemical correlates of *P* in suitably chosen samples. But even without such obvious biological assays, it may be said that our data furnish important support for the view that the *P* scale appears to be closely related to the masculinity–feminity dimension.(4)

Two questions in the inventory are related to sexual reactions that might be considered medically pathological, although use of this term is of course somewhat arbitrary in this context. The questions relating to male subjects are numbers 95 and 96; they are concerned with impotence and *ejaculatio praecox* respectively. For the women, these two questions refer instead to frigidity (from (a)= never to (f)=always) and orgasm during intercourse (from (a) =very often to (f)=never). The actual wording of the possible answers ((a) to (f)) is identical to that of the male questions. The wording of the female questions is: 'Have you ever suffered from frigidity?' and 'Do you usually have orgasm during intercourse?' These questions are only meaningful for respondents who have in fact had intercourse, and were only answered by them; in consequence they could not be included in the factor analysis, and results are discussed separately in this section.

The distributions of replies, as expected, are very asymmetrical, and in order to make possible the use of *t* tests an attempt was made to divide the distribution at a point that would give as nearly as possible groups of equal size; this aim was not accomplished with any very great success, owing to the piling up of data in certain categories. Nevertheless, the results are suitable for statistical treatment. The male results will be discussed first, followed by the female results. In each case, the *P*, *E* and *N* scores of the groups that showed or did not show the pathological behaviour in question were calculated and compared, significance of differences being assessed by means of the *t* technique.

1 *Male impotence.* The great majority of men gave answer (a), i.e. 'never' to this question ($n=164$); consequently all other answers were grouped together to form the 'pathological' group ($n=120$). Mean scores on *P*, *E* and *N* are shown in table 2.23; it will be seen that impotent men are somewhat (non-significantly) higher on *P*, more introverted and significantly ($p < 0.05$) higher on *N*.

Table 2.23 *Mean* P, E *and* N *scores of students pathological and non-pathological with respect to four sexual disorders*

		P	E	N
1 Male Impotence	Non-pathological	4·37	13·09	10·58
	Pathological	4·82	12·65	11·84
2 *Ejaculatio praecox*	Non-pathological	4·62	13·04	10·54
	Pathological	4·48	12·70	11·70
3 Frigidity	Non-pathological	3·00	12·59	12·05
	Pathological	2·80	11·58	13·41
4 Orgasm	Non-pathological	3·06	11·87	12·29
	Pathological	2·77	11·84	13·75

2 *Ejaculatio praecox.* A majority of men gave answers (e) and (f), i.e. never or hardly ever ($n=152$); consequently all other answers were grouped together to form the 'pathological' group ($n=132$). Mean scores on P, E and N are shown in table 2.23; it will be seen that men suffering somewhat from *ejaculatio praecox* are slightly (non-significantly) lower on P, slightly more introverted and significantly higher on N.

3 *Female frigidity.* The great majority of women gave answer (b), i.e. once or twice; this was grouped with answers (c) to (f) to constitute the 'pathological' group, with those answering 'never' (a) constituting the non-pathological group. Mean scores on the personality dimensions are given in table 2.23; frigid women (using this term somewhat inaccurately for our 'pathological' group) are somewhat more introverted, but not significantly so, and score higher on N, but also not significantly so. Numbers are only 49 in the non-pathological group and 122 in the pathological group; had the numbers been as large as those in the male groups, these differences might have reached significance. Clearly repetition of the study with larger numbers is called for.

4 *Orgasm.* Many women gave answer (a), i.e. 'very often' or (b), i.e. 'often'; these were combined to form the non-pathological group ($n=83$). The other answers were combined to form the 'pathological' group ($n=86$). Neither P nor E seem to be related to orgasm frequency; N, however, differentiates the two groups at the 0·05 level of statistical significance: higher N scores go with lower orgasm frequency.

The results of this analysis are not unexpected; it is found that sexual pathology as defined here is associated with neuroticism (significantly in three cases out of four, and almost significantly in the fourth case). Introverts show slightly greater pathology, but these differences never reach significance. High P scorers do not differ significantly from low P scorers, and may in fact have slightly less pathology as regards these indices of behaviour.

It is doubtful if the behaviours called 'pathological' really deserve this name, in view of the frequency with which they occur in this normal group, and it seemed of some interest to study the personality correlates of the much smaller more extreme groups giving more definitely pathological reactions. Five males admitted to having suffered from impotence often, more often than not or always; they showed a markedly elevated P score of 7·00, which is significantly higher than average. The E score of this group fell to 11·9, and the N score rose to 12·8; these changes are in line with expectation, but not significant in view of the very small size of the sample. Six women admitted to frigidity often, more often than not or always. Their P scores went up to 4·58, and their N score reached the very high value of 17·83; the latter value is significant beyond the 1 per cent level, but the former is not significantly different from average.

The other extreme groups do not add anything of interest to the data already presented. It is interesting that, in spite of the small size of the sample of frigid women, the greater degree of pathology involved has now made the relation with N significant. We may conclude, therefore, that all four types of sexual pathology are related to N, but that P is involved significantly only with high frequency of impotence.

Discussion of the results will be confined to two main points:

1 the problems of sampling and
2 the problem of veridical report.

The correlations here established between sexual attitudes and personality variables are meaningful only in so far as they can be considered to transcend the particular sample on which they were established. Correlations are not as subject to sampling distortions as are population parameters such as means, but nevertheless some evidence is required to show that our sample is not so highly selected with respect to relevant variables as to make the conclusions of doubtful generality. Eysenck (1972) has shown that the sample is very similar to unselected population samples of similar age with respect to percentage of men and women with experience of coitus, and also with respect to the scores on P, E and N. In other words, our sample is representative of the population of unmarried adolescents of eighteen to twenty-two years of age with respect to the two main variables we are concerned with, i.e. sexual experience and personality; it seems unlikely that our data are entirely idiosyncratic and unrepresentative. No doubt some distortion of sampling has taken place through the act of volunteering and other associated factors, but these are probably not so serious as to invalidate the results.

As regards veridical reports, we have two lines of argument.

The first relates to internal evidence; thus, duplicated items gave very highly correlated results, which suggests that items were not filled in randomly or with intention to deceive. The large number of comments written on the questionnaire returned suggested that respondents took the task very seriously. Most important, meaningful factors are not likely to arise from an analysis of correlations between items that were not in fact completed with some degree of honesty. Furthermore, the higher correlations between sexual behaviour patterns and personality in males to be discussed presently are unlikely to have arisen from faked data.

More convincing perhaps are various bits of external evidence. If the relations established in this paper are real, then it should be possible to find evidence in the literature of factual consequences of these relations. Eysenck (1971a) has argued, for instance, that if extraverts are in fact more promiscuous, then V.D. patients and unmarried mothers should be particularly extraverted; Eysenck (1961) and Wells (1969) have found evidence in favour of these predictions. Sex differences in line with our results have been discovered in an experimental investigation by Sigurt and others (1970). Psychiatrists have repeatedly found a relation between neurosis and sexual pathology; our data are very much in line with these suggestions. Ultimately, of course, there can be no absolute proof for the veridical nature of the answers given, but such evidence as has been quoted makes it unlikely that the data seriously misrepresent the truth. After all, respondents were assured of anonymity and had no motivation to tell lies; furthermore, much concentrated work was required to fill in the various questionnaires properly and post them back to the author, and few people would be likely to undertake all this just in order to mislead.

It might also be pointed out that other writers, using different methods, have reported results that, where comparable, were similar to ours. Mention has been made of the work of Giese and Schmidt; we might also mention the interviewing studies of Schofield (1968), and of Bynner (1969). There is thus beginning to build up a set a of findings linking personality factors with sexual attitudes and behaviours that seems to hang together and be reproducible from study to study, even when different methods of information-gathering and different samples, of different nationality, are involved. Finally, it should be noted that these results are for the most part in excellent agreement with prediction from theory; respondents could hardly have known these theories, or filled in their inventories in such a way as to support prediction!

We must next turn to the results of our sexual behaviour questionnaire. This is reproduced in table 2.24.(5)

Table 2.24 *Sexual behaviour inventory*

Here are brief descriptions of sexual behaviour patterns which people indulge in. Indicate by putting a cross (X) in Column 1 *whether you have ever* indulged in this type of behaviour.

(Note: *Manual* = by hand/*Oral* = by mouth)   (column 1)
                                                                       Have done

1 One-minute continuous lip kissing	———
2 Manual manipulation of male genitals, over clothes, by female	———
3 Kissing nipples of female breasts	———
4 Oral manipulation of female genitals	———
5 Sexual intercourse, face to face	———
6 Manual manipulation of female breasts, over clothes	———
7 Oral manipulation of male genitals, by female	———
8 Manual manipulation of male genitals to ejaculation, by female	———
9 Manual manipulation of female breasts, under clothes	———
10 Manual manipulation of male genitals, under clothes, by female	———
11 Sexual intercourse, man behind woman	———
12 Manual manipulation of female genitals, over clothes	———
13 Manual manipulation of female genitals to massive secretions	———
14 Mutual oral manipulation of genitals to mutual orgasm	———
15 Manual manipulation of female genitals, under clothes	———
16 Mutual manual manipulation of genitals	———
17 Oral manipulation of male genitals to ejaculation, by female	———
18 Mutual manual manipulation of genitals to mutual orgasm	———
19 Mutual oral genital manipulation	———

Details of this study are given in Eysenck (1972), where a factor analysis of the intercorrelations between the individual items is reported. Factor 1 has high loadings on items relating to petting (kissing, manipulation of female breasts over or under clothes, kissing nipples of female breast). Factor 2 has high loadings on items related to intercourse and manual manipulation of sexual organs, such as would unavoidably be part of intercourse. Factor 3 has high loadings on items related to oral manipulation of partner's sexual organs (fellatio and cunnilingus). For the sake of convenience, we may perhaps speak of these factors in terms of petting, intercourse and perversion. Factor loadings, for males and females separately, are given in table 2.25.

70

Table 2.25 Correlations of nineteen sex behaviours with personality and age

Item	P M	P F	E M	E F	N M	N F	Age M	Age F	Factor loadings (M) 1	Factor loadings (M) 2	Factor loadings (M) 3	Factor loadings (F) 1	Factor loadings (F) 2	Factor loadings (F) 3	Percentage scores in terms of normal curve deviate M	Percentage scores in terms of normal curve deviate F
1	0·00	0·08	0·23	0·20	−0·08	0·08	−0·03	0·12	0·94	−0·19	0·03	0·59	0·02	−0·08	−1·60(19)	−1·41(19)
2	0·01	0·17	0·23	0·18	−0·14	0·04	−0·11	0·21	0·05	0·85	−0·08	0·08	0·85	−0·06	−0·54(13)	−0·37(11½)
3	−0·01	0·10	0·19	0·18	−0·15	−0·04	−0·10	0·18	0·41	0·48	0·02	0·84	0·11	−0·02	−0·86(16)	−0·47(14)
4	0·02	0·10	0·11	0·11	−0·03	−0·02	−0·20	0·20	0·07	0·08	0·71	0·44	−0·05	0·55	0·41(6)	0·26(7)
5	0·12	0·25	0·25	0·16	−0·07	0·04	−0·14	0·29	0·27	0·35	0·21	−0·02	0·48	0·37	−0·48(11)	0·14(8)
6	0·02	0·06	0·30	0·15	−0·13	0·04	−0·01	0·06	0·97	−0·09	0·02	1·05	−0·28	−0·01	−1·37(18)	−0·84(18)
7	0·14	0·14	0·12	0·12	−0·04	−0·02	0·17	0·28	−0·01	0·21	0·68	0·02	0·17	0·75	0·44(5)	0·44(6)
8	0·00	0·19	0·18	0·21	−0·20	0·07	0·11	0·28	−0·21	0·86	0·07	−0·04	0·88	0·01	−0·05(8)	−0·13(10)
9	0·04	0·08	0·32	0·13	−0·12	0·04	0·02	0·10	0·88	0·07	−0·00	0·99	−0·09	−0·03	−1·23(17)	−0·63(17)
10	0·05	0·16	0·18	0·22	−0·10	0·04	0·12	0·32	0·05	0·81	−0·02	0·15	0·88	−0·10	−0·48(11)	−0·49(15)
11	0·04	0·17	0·11	0·11	−0·04	−0·03	0·26	0·24	0·10	−0·02	0·64	0·01	0·11	0·65	0·82(4)	0·76(4)
12	0·08	0·08	0·29	0·17	−0·16	−0·00	0·09	0·11	0·41	0·47	−0·04	0·85	0·08	−0·05	−0·69(14)	−0·53(16)
13	0·09	0·13	0·18	0·14	−0·09	−0·02	0·12	0·14	0·01	0·72	−0·00	0·45	0·25	0·19	−0·32(9)	0·10(9)
14	0·08	0·08	0·14	0·07	−0·04	−0·04	0·10	0·15	−0·03	−0·10	0·76	−0·14	−0·10	0·77	1·44(1)	1·60(1)
15	0·03	0·12	0·25	0·15	−0·12	0·03	0·11	0·14	0·28	0·72	−0·12	0·76	0·24	−0·04	−0·79(15)	−0·44(13)
16	0·03	0·14	0·23	0·20	−0·08	0·01	0·15	0·31	0·04	0·82	−0·01	0·08	0·91	−0·06	−0·48(11)	−0·37(11½)
17	0·12	0·16	0·17	0·18	−0·01	−0·05	0·08	0·19	−0·07	0·06	0·74	−0·06	−0·07	0·87	0·91(3)	1·01(2)
18	0·03	0·04	0·16	0·18	−0·13	−0·01	0·16	0·12	−0·30	0·79	0·10	−0·25	0·77	0·11	0·21(7)	0·47(5)
19	0·06	0·12	0·13	0·10	−0·03	−0·02	0·15	0·21	0·03	−0·10	0·89	−0·01	−0·01	0·85	0·95(2)	0·82(3)

Significant at 5 per cent level: 0·10
Significant at 1 per cent level: 0·13

The first 8 columns in table 2.25 give the correlations, for males and females separately, of P, E, N and age with the nineteen items of the Sex Behaviour Questionnaire. Correlations of 0·10 are statistically significant at the 5 per cent level, correlations of 0·13 at the 1 per cent level; only two-tailed tests are used in this comparison. Before discussing the three personality variables, it may be worthwhile to look at age as a factor; this has not been partialled out as it does not correlate with P, E or N within the narrow range of ages here sampled. It does however correlate with sexual experience; as one might have expected, all the correlations (with two trivial exceptions) are positive, and the tendency is clearly for females to have rather higher values than males. The highest values, for both sexes, are with items loading on factors 2 and 3; correlations of age with factor 1 items are uniformly low, or even negative. Petting, in these groups, is probably so universal, even at seventeen to eighteen years, that there is little increase; it is the more serious items in factors 2 and 3 that show such an increase. Even so, the values are perhaps somewhat lower than one might have expected; age never seems to account for more than 10 per cent of the variance.

Correlations with P are almost uniformly positive; high P scorers have more experience in all forms of sexual conduct. Figures are pretty uniformly higher for females than for males; the most notable difference is in connection with item 5 (intercourse), where the correlations are 0·12 and 0·25. Correlations are highest, for both sexes, in connection with items loading on factors 2 and 3; they are insignificant for items loading factor 1. Hence P influences sexual conduct only when this is going beyond simple petting; in terms of our theory it seems possible that petting involves a less impersonal element of interaction, although this hypothesis may be quite beside the point. The variance contributed by this dimension of personality is not high, but it should be remembered that the distribution of P scores is rather J-shaped, with very few students having high scores; this would tend to lead to an underestimation of the importance of P.

Correlations with E, as predicted, are all positive, and, as also predicted, are higher for males than for females as far as the majority of items are concerned. Particularly large differences are observed in relation to items 5, 6, 9, 12, 14 and 15; slight inversions of the general rule occur with a few items. The 'perversion' factor items on the whole tend to have lower correlations with E, although

72

still positive; petting, intercourse and manual manipulation of partner's sexual parts tend to give higher correlations. It is not clear why this should be so; possibly the small number of subjects who indulged in 'perverted' practices of this kind is responsible for the observed facts.

Correlations with N, as predicted (although without much confidence) tend to be negative – uniformly so for the men, less so for the women. In addition, the correlations for the men tend to be bigger than those for the women. This again is understandable in terms of the more active role that the male traditionally assumes in this field; the high N male may have difficulties in initiating sexual meetings and practices, while the high N female may have less difficulties in simply responding. Indeed, she may have some difficulties in not responding – to react in a negative fashion may require anxiety-provoking self-assertion and independence! The general run of the correlations is not high; they tend to be intermediate between those for P and those for E, perhaps somewhat nearer the former than the latter.

The studies described so far have dealt only with students; would differently selected groups of the population show similar patterns of sexual attitudes, and similar correlations with personality? In another study (Eysenck 1973a) the same questionnaires were administered, with the exception of the sexual behaviour one but with the addition of a questionnaire on conservatism, to 241 male prisoners, all of whom were adult volunteers. The conclusion reached was that:

... this study has demonstrated that the patterning of sexual attitudes is very similar in prisoners to what had been found in younger samples of males of higher social class, education and intelligence. Furthermore, the relations observed between the clusters of sex attitudes and the personality factors measured were very similar in size and direction. This seems to justify the conclusion that the results obtained from unrepresentative samples (students, prisoners) may have greater generality than one might have thought; the fact that the results fit in well with the personality theory developed by the writer also supports this view. [p. 305]

Another study suggested the possibility that, in addition to P, E and N, there might be another personality variable that could exert an influence on attitudes towards sex. This suggestion arose

73

from a study reported by Eysenck and Eysenck (1971c). Our previous work had left somewhat open the question of the truthfulness of responding, and the study in question sought to answer this question by using a Lie scale, taken from E.P.I. (Eysenck and Eysenck 1964) and consisting of eighteen items. It was hypothesised that if sex attitude questions were answered truthfully, then they would have low loadings on the Lie scale; high loadings would suggest defensive or 'fake good' behaviour. A random sample of the available population, consisting of 228 male and 263 female subjects, filled in the questionnaire; these subjects had been assembled by a market research firm for other purposes and had filled in the questionnaire between other, commercial, duties. The population thus contrasted with that previously used, which was comprised of university students. Apart from the Lie scale the questionnaire contained 47 psychoticism items, similar in kind to those used on previous occasions, and 12 extraversion and 12 neuroticism items, taken from the E.P.I. Interest centred on the possibility of using sex attitude items as part of the Psychoticism scale, as in our previous study (Eysenck 1971c) correlations with psychoticism had been the outstanding characteristic of many sex-attitude items. Many of these items were too explicit to be used with a random audience, but the following eight items were used in the present investigation:

1 Do you think that sex without love is highly unsatisfactory?

2 Do you think people must necessarily be in love to enjoy love-making with each other?

3 Would it bother you if the person you married were not a virgin?

4 Do you think it is all right to seduce a person who is old enough to know what he is doing?

5 Would you object to pornographic writings being freely published?

6 Do you think that marriage is old-fashioned and should be done away with?

7 Do you disapprove of censorship of films and plays?

8 Do you think that 'wife swapping parties' are disgusting?

The last of these items had not been included in the original questionnaire; some of the others were slightly reworded, so that items 2, 3 and 5 now require an answer in the opposite direction

74

in order to give correlations with psychoticism having the same sign as before. Results of a factor analysis (principal components, followed by Promax rotation) disclosed four clear-cut factors, labelled psychoticism, extraversion, neuroticism and lie; the sex attitude items had sizeable loadings only on psychoticism and lie, and these loadings are given in table 2.26, together with the correlations of these items on the original study with psychoticism (no Lie scale had been used then, so that these correlations are not available).

Table 2.26 *Loadings on* P *and* L *of eight sex-attitude items*

Items	Original P correlations		P loadings new sample		L loadings new sample	
	Male	Female	Male	Female	Male	Female
1 (2)	−0·17	−0·26	−0·01	−0·28	0·49	0·53
2 (−13)	0·12	0·22	−0·07	−0·22	0·59	0·56
3 (−26)	0·10	0·23	−0·18	0·03	0·25	0·42
4 (79)	0·18	0·23	0·05	0·14	−0·45	−0·26
5 (−84)	0·18	0·15	−0·12	−0·14	0·45	0·48
6 (−89)	0·23	0·12	0·43	0·24	−0·18	−0·03
7 (91)	0·16	0·22	0·24	0·21	−0·38	−0·17
8 (−)			−0·27	−0·43	0·56	0·42

It will be seen that the sex attitude items have loadings on the psychoticism factor that are similar in size and identical in sign to the originally observed correlations between these items and psychoticism. The numbers of the items in the original scale are given in parenthesis, so that readers can check details in the original paper (Eysenck 1971a). The minus sign preceding numbers 13, 36 and 84 is intended to remind the reader that these were reversed in the rewording, so that the signs of the correlations are opposite for the two samples. Considering the difference between the two samples, the agreement between the two sets of correlations is reasonable.

The last two columns give the loadings of the eight items on the Lie scale; it will be seen that almost all the items have very high loadings on this scale and that these loadings are much higher than the loading on psychoticism. This suggests that dissimulation ('faking good') may have played a considerable part in the process of answering these questions. There are reasons to doubt this interpretation. Table 2.27 gives the intercorrelations between the factors:

it will be seen that these are quite independent, and in particular that Neuroticism and Lie scales are orthogonal.

Table 2.27 *Intercorrelations between personality factors* N, E, P *and* L, *for male and female subjects*

	NL	NP	NE	LP	LE	PE
Men	0·09	0·01	−0·08	−0·00	−0·09	0·02
Women	0·03	0·09	−0·12	0·14	−0·15	−0·05

This observation is relevant to the question of the interpretation of the Lie scale. Michaelis and Eysenck (1971) have shown that, as motivation to dissimulate increases in a population, lie scores go up, neuroticism scores go down and the correlation between the two becomes more negative. The failure of these scales to show such a high, negative, correlation suggests that dissimulation played little part in the answering behaviour of this group and that the correct interpretation may lie rather in the personality structure of high lie scorers when motivation to 'fake good' is low. We have surmised that such people are conformist, orthodox and conservative in their beliefs (Eysenck and Eysenck 1976, Wilson 1973), and there is evidence that the *L* scale does correlate with conservatism in the studies mentioned.

Some direct evidence in support of this view is available in the work of Joe (1976). He administered the Wilson Conservatism scale to 66 male and 64 female undergraduates, together with the Zuckerman Heterosexual Experience scale, finding negative correlations between conservatism and heterosexual experience ($r = -0·44$). 'These results suggest that low conservative subjects on the whole engaged in a greater number and range of sexual experiences than high conservative subjects. For both male and female, low conservative subjects have advanced to coital activities while high conservatives have advanced to only foreplay activities (e.g. manipulation of the genitals).' High conservatives also had fewer experiences of viewing 'X'-rated movies.

These results suggest that our findings, as reported in table 2.26, can best be explained not in terms of dissimulation, but rather in terms of the conventional, conformist, conservative nature of the high *L* scorer. Further data to support this interpretation will be given in the next chapter.

1. Strictly speaking, this should be 'Lack or absence of premarital sex'. For ease of understanding, the loadings have been multiplied by -1 for later analyses, so that this factor will be properly named as in the text.

2. The programme was written especially by Dr O. White, and is available from this Department.

3. It might also be named by its opposite aspect, 'sexual satisfaction'; we have used this second name in later chapters.

4. The relationship between the masculinity–femininity scale and the libido scale would find an easy explanation if it were true, as Money (1961a, 1961b), Foss (1951) and others suggest, that 'the clinical evidence ... supports the view that, in adulthood, androgen is the libido hormone for both men and women. The androgens of eroticism in normal, untreated women may be of adrenal origin or may derive metabolically from the closely related progestins' (Money 1965, p. 76). However, as Davidson (1972) has pointed out, 'the fact that testosterone in the doses administered in these studies causes clitoral hypertrophy vitiates the worth of this evidence ... Doses of androgen which produce clitoral hypertrophy would be clearly supraphysiological and indeed this change may be responsible for the reported increase in "libido".' (p. 96). He concludes that 'there is no adequate evidence that the effects of androgens on feminine sexual behaviour represent any important physiological function under normal circumstances.' (p. 96). The possibility that some such relation may nevertheless exist must remain open. The evidence is more decisive as far as the importance of androgens on aggressive behaviour is concerned (Conner 1972), but even here there are many complications in the way of arriving at any clear-cut statement of the position.

5. The inventory is based on the pioneering work of Brady and Levitt (1965) and Bentler (1968).

3

Sexual attitudes and behaviour in adult populations

Our first series of studies, using the ninety-eight-item questionnaire and a student population, was followed by another series, using a rather longer and more detailed questionnaire and a more mature population, many of them married or living together. It seemed likely that these changes in measuring tool and population would make for certain minor changes in the conclusions, but that on the whole similar findings would re-emerge. Such at least was our hope. None of the data collected has been published previously (unlike the data in the previous chapter) and consequently, a more detailed discussion will be given.

The sample for this investigation of the major factors in people's attitudes to sex consisted of 427 males and 436 females, ranging in age from eighteen to sixty, with an average of around thirty years. The questionnaires for men and women were almost identical, but occasionally questions had to be reworded to make them applicable to the other sex; e.g., a question put to the males, regarding whether they felt excited when feeling a woman's breasts, when put to the women asked whether they felt excited when men felt their breasts. The actual questionnaire used is given below (table 3.1). When there were differences between the questions asked of the men and women, the male form is given first, the female form second; in addition, the letters 'M' and 'F' respectively are attached to the number of the question. There were 158 questions for the males and the same number for the females. The percentage of 'Yes' answers for each question for the males and females respectively is given in each case after the actual question. These questions, when repeatedly referred to in the text, or in the tables giving the factors extracted from the factor analyses, have been paraphrased in order to save space; the numbers are given in each case so that reference is possible to the actual form of the question given in the questionnaire.

The sample of men and women is not representative of the population, but it does include reasonable numbers of different ages, as well as a reasonable selection of people of different social classes, income group and educational backgrounds. An effort was made to attract volunteers in many different ways, including circulating student groups, approaching individuals and groups (such as the Salvation Army) personally, advertising and generally making the existence of the inquiry known as widely as possible. The results clearly cannot be used to estimate population parameters, but this is not the aim of the study; we are concerned rather with the degree to which questions are correlated, the factors they give rise to and the degree to which these factors correlate with personality variables. Such data are much less vulnerable to faulty sampling, and in addition we have two safeguards against errors arising from this factor.

1 We can compare the factors and correlations obtained with those obtained from other samples selected on other principles; if the factors and correlations agree in broad outline, then clearly the different ways of obtaining the samples cannot have given rise to large errors, nor can the resulting factors be pure artefacts.

2 In the second place, we can look at the scores of our group in respect to the personality inventory used, and compare the results with population estimates obtained with these instruments. We shall see that, with respect to these personality variables, our sample is not dissimilar to that used for standardising the personality inventory used, and consequently does not differ too much in one very important respect from the general population. These considerations encourage us to believe that our results have wider applicability than just to the sample tested.

The number of items used in the questionnaire was too large to make possible a factor analysis on the University of London computer, and consequently a sub-set of 135 variables was chosen for analysis. The choice was based on such considerations as avoidance of items having endorsements in excess of 90 per cent or in default of 10 per cent, duplication of meaning and high loadings

Table 3.1 *Inventory of attitudes to sex, including percentage 'yes' answers of men and women*

AGE: _____   SEX: _____

MARRIED/SINGLE/SOME FORM OF PERMANENT OR SEMI-PERMANENT UNION
(underline correct response)

This questionnaire is anonymous, to encourage truthful answers.

Read each statement carefully, then underline or circle the 'yes' or the 'no' answer, depending on your views. If you cannot decide, underline the "?" reply. Please answer *every* question. There are no right or wrong answers. Don't think too long over each question; try to give an immediate answer which represents your *feeling* on each issue. Some questions are similar to others; there are good reasons for getting at the same attitude in slightly different ways.

					M	F
1	The opposite sex will respect you more if you are not too familiar with them	YES	?	NO	45	48
2	Sex without love ('impersonal sex') is highly unsatisfactory	AGREE	?	DISAGREE	43	60
3	Conditions have to be just right to get me excited sexually	YES	?	NO	15	42
4	All in all I am satisfied with my sex life	YES	?	NO	64	70
5	Virginity is a girl's most valuable possession	YES	?	NO	8	12
6	I think only rarely about sex	AGREE	?	DISAGREE	5	12
7	Sometimes it has been a problem to control my sex feelings	YES	?	NO	50	38
[8]	Masturbation is unhealthy	YES	?	NO	4	4
9	If I love a person I could do anything with them	YES	?	NO	69	61
10	I get pleasant feeling from touching my sexual parts	YES	?	NO	81	66
11	I have been deprived sexually	YES	?	NO	22	15
[12]	It is disgusting to see animals having sex relations in the street	YES	?	NO	5	6
13	(M) I do not need to respect a woman, or love her, in order to enjoy petting and/or intercourse with her	YES	?	NO	43	26
13	(F) I do not need to respect a man, or love him, in order to enjoy petting/or intercourse with him	YES	?	NO		
14	I am sexually rather unattractive	YES	?	NO	10	6
15	Frankly, I prefer people of my own sex	YES	?	NO	4	3

#	Statement				M	F
16	Sex contacts have never been a problem to me	TRUE	?	FALSE	32	49
17	It is disturbing to see necking in public	YES	?	NO	12	13
18	Sexual feelings are sometimes unpleasant to me	TRUE	?	FALSE	6	11
19	Something is lacking in my sex life	YES	?	NO	35	30
20	My sex behaviour has never caused me any trouble	TRUE	?	FALSE	54	57
21	My love life has been disappointing	YES	?	NO	24	20
22	I never had many dates	TRUE	?	FALSE	45	25
23	I consciously try to keep sex thoughts out of my mind	YES	?	NO	3	4
24	I have felt guilty about sex experiences	YES	?	NO	34	36
25	It wouldn't bother me if the person I married were not a virgin	TRUE	?	FALSE	78	83
26	At times I have been afraid of myself for what I might do sexually	YES	?	NO	16	17
[27]	I have had conflicts about my sex feelings towards a person of my own sex	YES	?	NO	20	14
[28]	I have many friends of the opposite sex	YES	?	NO	56	68
29	I have strong sex feelings but when I get a chance I can't seem to express myself	YES	?	NO	17	19
30	It doesn't take much to get me excited sexually	TRUE	?	FALSE	75	44
31	My parent's influence has inhibited me sexually	YES	?	NO	29	35
32	Thoughts about sex disturb me more than they should	TRUE	?	FALSE	9	5
[33]	People of my own sex frequently attract me	YES	?	NO	5	10
34	There are some things I wouldn't want to do with anyone	TRUE	?	FALSE	50	53
[35]	Children should be taught about sex	YES	?	NO	96	97
36	I understand homosexuals	YES	?	NO	57	53
37	I think about sex almost every day	YES	?	NO	87	61
38	One should not experiment with sex before marriage	AGREE	?	DISAGREE	7	8
39	I get excited sexually very easily	YES	?	NO	68	40
40	The thought of a sex orgy is disgusting to me	YES	?	NO	15	40
41	It is better not to have sex relations until you are married	TRUE	?	FALSE	10	12
42	I find the thought of a coloured sex partner particularly exciting	YES	?	NO	32	11
43	I like to look at sexy pictures	YES	?	NO	80	45
44	My conscience bothers me too much	YES	?	NO	13	20
[45]	My religious beliefs are against sex	YES	?	NO	1	4
46	Sometimes sexual feelings overpower me	YES	?	NO	25	27

81

Table 3.1—*cont.*

					M	F
47	I feel nervous with the opposite sex	YES	?	NO	20	11
48	Sex thoughts drive me almost crazy	YES	?	NO	7	3
49	When I get excited I can think of nothing else but satisfaction	YES	?	NO	24	31
50	I feel at ease with people of the opposite sex	YES	?	NO	76	83
51	I don't like to be kissed	TRUE	?	FALSE	3	5
52	It is hard to talk with people of the opposite sex	YES	?	NO	8	6
53	I didn't learn the facts of life until I was quite old	TRUE	?	FALSE	31	35
[54]	I feel more comfortable when I am with my own sex	YES	?	NO	14	10
55	I enjoy petting	YES	?	NO	95	88
56	I worry a lot about sex	YES	?	NO	13	12
57	The Pill should be universally available	YES	?	NO	85	81
58	Seeing a person nude doesn't interest me	TRUE	?	FALSE	6	28
59	Sometimes thinking about sex makes me very nervous	YES	?	NO	11	11
60	Perverted thoughts have sometimes bothered me	YES	?	NO	24	15
61	I am embarrassed to talk about sex	YES	?	NO	6	6
[62]	Young people should learn about sex through their own experience	YES	?	NO	39	31
63	Sometimes the woman should be sexually aggressive	YES	?	NO	95	88
64	Sex jokes disgust me	YES	?	NO	7	10
65	I believe in taking my pleasures where I find them	YES	?	NO	34	19
[66]	A person should learn about sex gradually by experimenting with it	YES	?	NO	58	59
67	Young people should be allowed out at night without being too closely checked	YES	?	NO	69	54
68	I have sometimes felt like humiliating my sex partner	YES	?	NO	22	16
69	I would particularly protect my children from contacts with sex	YES	?	NO	6	12
[70]	Self-relief is not dangerous as long as it is done in a healthy way	YES	?	NO	84	80
71	(M) I get very excited when touching a woman's breasts	YES	?	NO	74	
71	(F) I get very excited when men touch my breasts	YES	?	NO		60
72	I have been involved with more than one sex affair at the same time	YES	?	NO	42	33
73	Homosexuality is normal for some people	YES	?	NO	87	87
74	It is all right to seduce a person who is old enough to know what they are doing	YES	?	NO	67	58
75	I have sometimes felt hostile to my sex partner	YES	?	NO	54	59

					M	F
76	I like to look at pictures of nudes	YES	?	NO	84	44
77	If I had the chance to see people making love, without being seen, I would take it	YES	?	NO	67	37
78	Pornographic writings should be freely allowed to be published	YES	?	NO	74	55
79	Prostitution should be legally permitted	YES	?	NO	82	63
80	Decisions about abortion should be the concern of no one but the woman concerned	YES	?	NO	56	68
81	There are too many immoral plays on T.V.	YES	?	NO	9	11
82	The dual standard of morality, allowing men greater freedom, is natural, and should be continued	YES	?	NO	19	14
83	We should do away with marriage entirely	YES	?	NO	8	8
84	I had some bad sex experiences when I was young	YES	?	NO	13	20
85	There should be no censorship, on sexual grounds, of plays and films	AGREE	?	DISAGREE	73	53
86	Sex is far and away my greatest pleasure	YES	?	NO	35	26
87	Sexual permissiveness threatens to undermine the entire foundation of civilized society	YES	?	NO	9	14
88	Sex should be used for the purpose of reproduction, not for personal pleasure	TRUE	?	FALSE	0	1
89	Absolute faithfulness to one partner throughout life is nearly as silly as celibacy	YES	?	NO	41	28
[90]	I prefer to have intercourse under the bedcovers and with the light off	YES	?	NO	7	13
91	The present preoccupation with sex in our society has been largely created by films, newspapers, television and advertising	TRUE	?	FALSE	45	54
92	I would enjoy watching my usual partner having intercourse with someone else	YES	?	NO	18	6
93	Sex play among young children is quite harmless	YES	?	NO	78	74
[94]	Females do not have such strong sexual desire as males	TRUE	?	FALSE	17	22
95	I would vote for a law that permitted polygamy	YES	?	NO	31	11
96	Even though one is having regular intercourse, masturbation is good for a charge	YES	?	NO	55	39
97	I would prefer to have a new sex partner every night	YES	?	NO	7	2
[98]	I only get sexually aroused at night; never in the daytime	YES	?	NO	1	3
99	I prefer partners who are several years older than myself	YES	?	NO	6	25
100	My sexual fancies often involve flogging	YES	?	NO	9	6
101	I make lots of vocal noises during intercourse	YES	?	NO	26	53
102	Sex is more exciting with a stranger	YES	?	NO	21	7
103	I could never discuss sex with my parents	TRUE	?	FALSE	64	60
104	There are some things I only do to please my sex partner	TRUE	?	FALSE	45	47

Table 3.1—*cont.*

				M	F
105	I don't always know for sure when I have had an orgasm	TRUE ?	FALSE	3	23
106	To me the few things are more important than sex	TRUE ?	FALSE	44	26
[107]	I am very keen on babies	YES ?	NO	29	45
108	My sex partner satisfies all my physical needs completely	YES ?	NO	44	57
109	Sex is not all that important to me	TRUE ?	FALSE	11	19
110	Most men are sex-mad	TRUE ?	FALSE	12	16
111	Being good in bed is terribly important to my marriage partner	YES ?	NO	57	60
112	I enjoy very lengthy pre-coital love play	YES ?	NO	69	70
113	(M) I find it easy to tell my sex partner what I like or I don't like about her love-making	YES ?	NO ⎫	65	66
113	(F) I find it easy to tell my sex partner what I like, or don't like about his love-making	YES ?	NO ⎬		
114	I would like my sex partner to be more expert and experienced	YES ?	NO	39	29
[115]	To me, psychological factors in my sex partner are more important than physical ones	YES ?	NO	55	63
116	I sometimes feel like scratching and biting my partner during intercourse	YES ?	NO	53	67
117	No one has ever been able to satisfy me sexually	TRUE ?	FALSE	5	7
118	I feel sexually less competent than my friends	YES ?	NO	11	11
119	Group sex appeals to me	YES ?	NO	33	10
120	The thought of an illicit relationship excites me	YES ?	NO	52	32
121	I usually feel aggressive with my sexual partner	YES ?	NO	24	18
122	I believe my sexual activities are average	YES ?	NO	66	72
123	It disturbs me to look at sexy photographs	YES ?	NO	8	10
124	I am afraid of sexual relationships	YES ?	NO	6	7
125	(M) I often wish that women would be more forthcoming sexually	YES ?	NO ⎫	69	14
125	(F) I often wish that men would be less demanding sexually	YES ?	NO ⎬		
126	I can't stand people touching me	TRUE ?	FALSE	6	7
127	Physical sex is the most important part of marriage	YES ?	NO	21	20
128	I prefer my partner to dictate the rules of the sexual game	YES ?	NO	9	37
129	I find 'straight sex' unsatisfactory	TRUE ?	FALSE	19	21
[130]	I always make love in the nude	YES ?	NO	38	38
131	Physical attraction is extremely important to me	YES ?	NO	63	56
132	In a sexual union, tenderness is the most important quality	YES ?	NO	53	58

84

				M	F
133	(M) Female genitals are aesthetically unpleasing (F) Male genitals are aesthetically unpleasing	AGREE	?	DISAGREE	13	17
					41	41
134	I object to four-letter swear words being used in mixed company	YES	?	NO	37	63
135	The idea of 'wife swapping' is extremely distasteful to me	TRUE	?	FALSE	16	15
[136]	Romantic love is just puerile illusion	YES	?	NO	16	13
[137]	The need for birth control upsets my love-making because it makes everything so cold blooded and planned	YES	?	NO	83	58
[138]	I love physical contact with members of the opposite sex	YES	?	NO	3	5
139	(M) I cannot discuss sexual matters with my wife (or habitual sex partner) (F) I cannot discuss sexual matters with my husband (or habitual sex partner)	TRUE	?	FALSE	5	8
[140]	People who attend 'strip-tease' shows are sexually abnormal	YES	?	NO	90	81
141	The naked human body is a pleasing sight	YES	?	NO	41	55
[142]	I can take sex and I can leave it alone	TRUE	?	FALSE	26	44
[143]	I think taking the 'Pill' for any length of time is dangerous to a woman's health	YES	?	NO	36	32
144	(M) It would not disturb me overmuch if my sex partner had sexual relations with someone else, as long as she returned to me (F) It would not disturb me overmuch if my sex partner had sexual relations with someone else, as long as he returned to me	TRUE	?	FALSE	55	39
145	(M) Men are more selfish in their love-making than women (F) Women are more selfish in their love-making than men	YES	?	NO	15	30
146	Some forms of love-making are disgusting to me	YES	?	NO	29	43
147	It is right that man should be the dominant partner in a sex relationship	YES	?	NO	59	68
[148]	Women often use sex to gain all sorts of advantages	YES	?	NO	22	29
149	The reading of 'girlie' magazines suggests failure to achieve adult attitudes to sex	YES	?	NO	20	20
150	In matters of sex, women always seem to come off second-best	YES	?	NO		

Please underline the correct answer

		M	F
151	If you were invited to see a 'blue' film would you: (a) Accept (b) Refuse	85	72
152	If you were offered a highly pornographic book, would you: (a) Accept it (b) Reject it	86	72

Table 3.1—*cont.*

	M	F
153 If you were invited to take part in an orgy, would you:	48	17
(a) Take part (b) Refuse		
154 Ideally, would you prefer to have intercourse:	e	e
(a) Never (d) Twice a week		
(b) Once a month (e) 3-5 times a week		
(c) Once a week (f) Every day		
(g) More than once a day		
155a (M) Have you ever suffered from impotence:	b	b
(a) Never (d) Often		
(b) Once or twice (e) More often than not		
(c) Several times (f) Always		
155a (F) Have you ever suffered from frigidity:		
(a) Never (d) Often		
(b) Once or twice (e) More often than not		
(c) Several times (f) Always		
155b (M) Have you ever suffered from *ejaculatio praecox* (premature ejaculation)?	d	–
(a) Very often (d) Not very often		
(b) Often (e) Hardly ever		
(c) Middling (f) Never		
155b (F) Do you usually have orgasm during intercourse:	–	–
(a) Very often (d) Not very often		
(b) Often (e) Hardly ever		
(c) Middling (f) Never		
156 At what age did you have your first intercourse (if virgin, leave blank)	19·84	19·52
157 Rate the habitual strength of your sexual desire from 10 (absolutely overwhelming and all-embracing) to 1 (very weak and almost non-existent). Rating	7·33	6·82
158 Rate the strength of the influences that inhibit you sexually (moral, aesthetic, religious, etc.) from 10 (terribly strong, completely inhibiting) to 1 (very weak and almost non-existent). Rating	2·58	2·95

86

of the items on previous analyses. The items omitted from analysis are enclosed in square brackets in the questionnaire. Phi coefficients were used for intercorrelating the items. The use of this coefficient has been criticised in connection with factor analytic work because it is affected by the marginal proportions to such an extent that its maximum possible value is restricted where proportions vary from one another; this particular phenomenon has been thought to be responsible for the introduction of spurious 'difficulty' factors (Cattell 1952, Ferguson 1941, Wherry and Gaylord 1944). Tetrachoric coefficients and a corrected phi coefficient (phi/phi max.) have often been preferred. The whole problem has been examined empirically by Comrey and Levonian (1958); they state that 'it seems reasonable to conclude that the phi coefficient is the method of choice in point correlation work where factor analysis is to follow. This thesis is strengthened by the fact that the number of significant centroid factors obtained is at least as great with phi-over-phi-max and tetrachoric *r* as with phi. Hence, if spurious factors exist with factor analysis of phi coefficients, they may be no less evident with phi-over-phi-max or tetrachoric coefficients.' (p. 753). Phi coefficients resulted in analyses relatively free of excessively high communalities encountered when using the other two types of coefficients. It may be concluded that the use of phi coefficients in this study is not contra-indicated by the best available opinion.

The analyses were done by Promax rotation of principal components, using the method of Hendrickson and White (1964). Fifteen factors were orginally extracted, although eigenvalues in excess of unity were found for some forty factors. However, in this as in our previous studies, we found that only about a dozen factors could be interpreted with any confidence, so that the number extracted is if anything in excess of the number of 'true' and meaningful factors contained in the matrices. Factor comparison was made of the fifteen male and the fifteen female factors and those factors showing the largest comparison coefficients were then matched. The method of factor matching was that described in Eysenck and Eysenck (1969). The factors were interpreted and named in terms of the items having the highest loadings; table 3.2 presents the results. Given are the extraction numbers of the factors for males and females, the coefficient of factor comparison and the tentative name given that factor. It is of course realised that such names are inevitably subjective, but they have a useful function to perform in making reference to a given factor easier to follow. In any case, it is possible for the reader to check the adequacy of the naming procedure by looking at the detailed results for each factor given below.

Table 3.2 *Factor comparisons for males and females on sex questionnaire*

Male (Extraction factor number)	Female	Factor comparison coefficient	Name of factor
1	1	0·93	(1) Permissiveness
2	2	0·92	(2) Satisfaction
5	9	0·95	(3) Neurotic sex
6	5	0·97	(4) Impersonal sex
4	11	0·91	(5) Pornography
13	6	0·89	(6) Sexual shyness
7	13	0·76	(7) Prudishness
8	15	0·75	(8) Dominance–submission
15	14	0·71	(9) Sexual disgust
9	3	0·70	(10) Sexual excitement
3	7	0·66	(11) Physical sex
11	4	0·52	(12) Aggressive sex

We now proceed to give the actual items having loadings of 0·3 or above that go to make up each factor. Factor 1 is called 'Permissiveness', and the items seem to make this name quite appropriate. The index of factor comparison is 0·93, suggesting that both sexes are very closely in agreement on their interpretation of the items that go to make up this factor.

Factor 1: Permissiveness

Item	Loading	Item
Males		
5	−0·37	Virginity is a girl's most valuable possession
17	−0·45	Disturbing to see necking in public
25	0·37	Wouldn't bother if person married not virgin
38	−0·53	Shouldn't experiment with sex before marriage
40	−0·38	Thought of sex orgy disgusting
41	−0·62	Better not to have sex until married
57	0·61	'Pill' should be universally available
64	−0·42	Sex jokes disgust
67	0·54	Young people out at night not too closely checked
78	0·76	Pornographic writings should be freely published
79	0·44	Prostitution should be legally permitted
80	0·35	Abortion should be the concern of no one but the woman concerned

Item	Loading	Item
Males		
81	− 0·68	There are too many immoral plays on T.V.
85	0·72	There should be no censorship on sexual grounds in films and plays
87	− 0·70	Sexual permissiveness threatens to undermine civilisation
93	0·34	Sex play among children is harmless
134	− 0·49	Object to four-letter words in mixed company
157	− 0·38	Age at first intercourse low
Females		
1	− 0·46	Opposite sex will respect more if not too familiar
5	− 0·52	Virginity valuable possession
17	− 0·51	Disturbing to see necking in public
25	0·40	Wouldn't bother me if person I married was not a virgin
38	− 0·68	Should not experiment with sex before marriage
41	− 0·74	Better not have sex before marriage
57	0·39	Pill should be universally available
64	− 0·66	Sex jokes disgust me
69	− 0·61	Would protect children from contacts with sex
76	0·30	Like to look at pictures of nudes
78	0·48	Pornographic writings should be freely published
79	0·38	Prostitution should be legally permitted
81	− 0·73	Too many immoral plays on T.V.
85	0·38	No censorship on sexual grounds of films and plays
87	− 0·72	Sexual permissiveness undermines civilised society
91	− 0·36	Preoccupation with sex created by T.V., films, newspapers
93	0·37	Sex among young children is harmless
134	− 0·44	Object to four-letter words in mixed company
149	− 0·31	Reading girlie magazines failure of adult attitude to sex
151	0·36	Blue films invitation accepted

Factor 2 is labelled 'Satisfaction', and again the meaning of the factor is quite unmistakable. The index of factor comparison is 0·92, which again suggests considerable agreement in structure of attitudes between men and women.

Factor 2: Satisfaction

Item	Loading	Item
Males		
4	0·85	Satisfied with sex life
11	− 0·48	Have been deprived sexually
16	0·32	Sex contacts have never been a problem
19	− 0·82	Something lacking in sex life

Item	Loading	Item
Males		
21	− 0·73	Love life has been disappointing
56	− 0·36	Worry a lot about sex
105	− 0·32	Don't always know for sure when had an orgasm
108	0·64	Partner satisfies all physical needs
113	0·52	Find easy to tell partner like/dislike about love-making
114	− 0·45	Like partner to be more expert, experienced
118	− 0·51	Feel sexually less competent than friends
139	− 0·41	Cannot discuss sexual matters with wife/partner
Females		
4	0·78	Satisfied with sex life
11	− 0·69	Have been deprived sexually
16	0·32	Sex contacts never a problem
19	− 0·84	Something lacking in sex life
20	0·30	Sex behaviour never caused any trouble
21	− 0·63	Love life been disappointing
56	− 0·36	Worry a lot about sex
108	0·77	Sex partner satisfies all physical needs
113	− 0·59	Would like partner to be more expert, experienced
114	0·37	Easy to tell partner what I like/don't like about love-making
117	− 0·50	No one been able to satisfy sexually
118	− 0·36	Sexually less competent than friends
147	− 0·32	Right that male should be dominant sex partner
155	− 0·33	Suffered frigidity

Factor 3 has been called 'Neurotic sex', and the very high index of factor comparison suggests that the items characterising this factor are very similar for both sexes. Another name for this factor might have been 'Conflict over sex'; the items are suggestive of a conflict between strong sex drives and conscience or some other factor holding back the person from indulgence.

Factor 3:   Neurotic sex

Item	Loading	Item
Males		
7	0·57	A problem to control sex feeling
18	0·54	Sexual feelings unpleasant
20	− 0·43	Sex behaviour never caused trouble
24	0·57	Felt guilt about sex experience
26	0·60	Afraid for what might do sexually
32	0·38	Sex disturbs more than it should
44	0·52	Conscience bothers too much
46	0·45	Sexual feelings overpower
56	0·34	Worry a lot about sex

90

Item	Loading	Item
Males		
60	0·64	Perverted thoughts have sometimes bothered
68	0·61	Sometimes felt like humiliating partner
75	0·57	Sometimes felt hostile to partner
84	0·37	Had some bad sex experience when young
100	0·32	Sexual fantasy often involves flogging
155	0·33	Suffered impotence
Females		
7	0·54	Problem to control my sexual feelings
18	0·41	Sexual feelings sometimes unpleasant
23	0·42	Try to keep sex thoughts out of mind
24	0·47	Guilty about sex experiences
26	0·64	Afraid for what might do sexually
32	0·38	Thoughts of sex disturbs
44	0·35	Conscience bothers too much
46	0·59	Sexual feelings overpower
48	0·40	Sex thoughts drive crazy
56	0·32	Worry lot about sex
59	0·39	Thinking about sex makes nervous
60	0·33	Perverted thoughts sometimes bother
84	0·45	Bad sex experiences when young

Factor 4, called 'Impersonal sex', is equally clear as the previous three factors, and has the highest index of factor comparison, 0·97. Very similar items load this factor in the case of men and women, respectively.

Factor 4: Impersonal sex

Item	Loading	Item
Males		
2	− 0·50	'Impersonal sex' highly unsatisfactory
40	− 0·37	Sex orgy disgusting
42	0·34	Thought of coloured partner particularly exciting
65	0·46	Believe in taking pleasures where found
83	0·37	Should do away with marriage entirely
89	0·55	Faithfulness is nearly as silly as celibacy
92	0·75	Enjoy watching partner have intercourse with someone else
95	0·57	Would vote for law permitting polygamy
97	0·37	Prefer new partner every night
119	0·73	Group sex appeals
120	0·45	Illicit relationship excites
135	−0·65	'Wife-swapping' is distasteful
144	0·77	Would not be disturbed if partner had sex with someone else
153	0·67	Accept an invitation to an orgy

91

Item	Loading	Item
Females		
2	−0·35	Sex without love unsatisfactory
46	−0·39	Sexual feeling overpowers
65	0·35	Take pleasures where found
83	0·42	Do away with marriage
89	0·51	Faithfulness as silly as celibacy
92	0·60	Enjoy watching partner have intercourse with another
95	0·53	Vote for law permitting polygamy
102	0·37	Sex more exciting with a stranger
119	0·70	Group sex appeals
120	0·38	Illicit relationships excite
135	−0·67	'Wife-swapping' distasteful
144	0·60	Not disturbed overmuch if partner had relations with someone else
153	0·75	Accept invitation to an orgy

Factor 5 contains largely items dealing with pornography, and has accordingly been so named. The index of factor comparison is 0·91, which is quite satisfactory.

Factor 5: Pornography

Item	Loading	Item
Males		
10	0·30	Get pleasant feelings from touching sexual parts
43	0·76	Like to look at sexy pictures
58	−0·40	Seeing a person nude doesn't interest
76	0·70	Like to look at pictures of nudes
77	0·54	If had chance to see people making love, would take it
83	−0·30	We should do away with marriage entirely
141	0·32	Naked body is a pleasing sight
151	0·59	Accept an invitation to 'blue film'
152	0·61	Accept if offered a highly pornographic book
Females		
10	0·44	Pleasant feelings from touching sexual parts
13	0·30	Need neither love nor respect to enjoy petting/intercourse
40	−0·31	Thought of sex orgy disgusting
43	0·77	Like sexy pictures
58	−0·38	Seeing a nude doesn't interest
76	0·72	Like pictures of nudes
77	0·69	Would take chance to see people making love unseen
96	0·42	Masturbation good for a change
151	0·44	Accept an invitation to 'blue film'
152	0·55	Accept if offered pornographic book

Factor 6, like the preceding ones, is largely self-explanatory; it has been called 'Sexual shyness'. The index of factor comparison is 0·89, which is reasonable.

Factor 6:   Shyness

Item	Loading	Item
Males		
22	0·42	Never had many dates
29	0·43	Have had strong sex feeling but can't express
47	0·81	Feel nervous with opposite sex
50	− 0·83	Feel at ease with opposite sex
52	0·79	Hard to talk with opposite sex
59	0·30	Thinking about sex makes nervous
61	0·39	Am embarrassed to talk about sex
124	0·35	Afraid of sexual relationships
Females		
47	0·81	Nervous with opposite sex
50	− 0·87	Feel at ease with opposite sex
52	0·78	Hard to talk with opposite sex

These six factors constitute the backbone, as it were, of this analysis; the remainder, although not difficult to interpret, have somewhat lower indices of factor comparison, and there is consequently a suggestion that men and women may not entirely agree on the nature of the factor in question. Nevertheless, they are similar to factors unearthed in earlier analyses, and are sufficiently clear-cut to make it permissible to introduce them here. Factor 7 is called 'Prudishness', and has an index of factor comparison of 0·76.

Factor 7:   Prudishness

Item	Loading	Item
Males		
15	0·41	Prefer people of own sex
51	0·57	Don't like to be kissed
55	− 0·48	Enjoy petting
58	0·50	Seeing a nude person doesn't interest
64	0·31	Sex jokes disgust
71	− 0·33	Get excited when touching woman's breast
76	− 0·30	Like to look at pictures of nudes
124	0·33	Afraid of sexual relationships
126	0·55	Can't stand being touched
141	− 0·43	Naked body is a pleasing sight

93

Item	Loading	Item
Females		
51	0·48	Don't like to be kissed
55	−0·48	Enjoy petting
97	−0·34	Prefer a new partner every night
112	−0·41	Enjoy lengthy pre-coital love-play
122	−0·51	Sexual activities are average
126	0·41	Can't stand being touched

Factor 8, labelled 'Dominance–submission', has an index of factor comparison of 0·75, but the label is applied only very tentatively; the items leave open many other interpretations, particularly of the male factor.

Factor 8 : Dominance–submission

Item	Loading	Item
Males		
31	−0·36	Parents' influence inhibited sexually
65	0·30	Believe in taking pleasures where found
93	−0·50	Sex among children is harmless
99	0·61	Prefer partners several years older
110	0·31	Most men sex-mad
158	0·33	Strength of sexual desire great
Females		
10	0·30	Pleasant feelings from touching sexual parts
82	−0·39	Dual standards of morality should continue
128	−0·36	Prefer partner to dictate rules of the sex game
147	−0·51	Right that males should dominate in sex relations

Factor 9, entitled 'Sexual disgust', is much more clear-cut although the index of factor comparison is only 0·71. Nevertheless, the items defining it are similar for the two sexes, and their meaning is unmistakable.

Factor 9 : Sexual disgust

Item	Loading	Item
Males		
9	−0·54	If loved a person could do anything with her
34	0·58	Some things wouldn't do with anyone
104	0·37	Some things do only to please partner
133	0·33	Female genitals are aesthetically unpleasing
146	0·58	Some forms of love-making are disgusting

Item	Loading	Item
Females		
9	− 0·35	Love a person, could do anything with them
34	0·31	Some things wouldn't want to do with anyone
48	− 0·36	Sex thoughts drive crazy
105	− 0·30	Don't know whether had an orgasm
112	− 0·33	Enjoy pre-coital love-play
121	− 0·37	Usually feel aggressive with partner
129	− 0·47	'Straight sex' unsatisfactory
146	0·35	Some forms love-making disgusting

Factor 10, too, is very explicit; it is called 'Sexual excitement', and has an index of factor comparison of 0·07. There is little doubt about the meaning of this factor.

Factor 10 : Sexual excitement

Item	Loading	Item
Males		
3	− 0·61	Conditions have to be right to get excited sexually
30	0·72	Doesn't take much to get excited sexually.
39	0·68	Excited sexually easily
155	− 0·36	Not suffered from impotence
158	0·33	Strength of sexual desire great
Females		
3	− 0·41	Conditions have to be right to get sexually excited
6	− 0·43	Think rarely about sex
9	0·64	Love a person, could do anything
18	− 0·37	Sexual feelings sometimes unpleasant
30	0·79	Doesn't take much to get sexually excited
34	− 0·58	Some things wouldn't want to do
37	0·46	Think about sex every day
39	0·78	Sexually excited easily
58	− 0·30	A person nude doesn't interest
61	− 0·32	Embarrassed to talk of sex
71	0·40	Excited when men touch breasts
86	·0·48	Sex greatest pleasure
109	− 0·56	Sex not all that important
125	− 0·33	Wish men were less sexually demanding
133	− 0·53	Male genitals aesthetically unpleasing
141	0·30	Naked human body is pleasing
146	− 0·61	Some love-making is disgusting
154	0·60	Preference for having intercourse often
157	0·64	Strength of sexual desire great

Factor 11 is one of 'Physical sex', and has an index of factor comparison of 0·66; this is rather low, but the items leave little doubt about the interpretation of the factor.

Factor 11: Physical sex

Item	Loading	Item
Males		
48	0·30	Sex thoughts drive nearly crazy
49	0·36	Excited, can think of nothing but satisfaction
71	0·32	Get excited touching a woman's breast
72	0·32	Have been in more than one sex affair at a time
86	0·54	Sex is greatest pleasure
106	0·57	Few things more important than sex
109	− 0·32	Sex not all that important
111	0·62	Being good in bed terribly important in partner
121	0·36	Usually feel aggressive to partner
127	0·60	Sex is the important part of marriage
131	0·52	Physical attraction important
145	0·31	Men more selfish in love-making than women
158	0·30	Habitual strength of sexual desire great
Females		
31	− 0·30	Parents' influence inhibited sexually
53	0·36	Learnt facts of life quite old
86	0·46	Sex greatest pleasure
103	0·47	Never discuss sex with parents
106	0·62	Few things more important than sex
111	0·39	Good in bed with marriage partner important
127	0·66	Sex most important part of marriage
131	0·39	Physical attraction important

Factor 12, the last of the interpretable factors, is called 'Aggressive sex'; it has an index of factor comparison of only 0·52, but the items having the highest loadings are sufficient similar to make the interpretation possible.

Factor 12: Aggressive sex

Item	Loading	Item
Males		
13	0·33	No need to respect/love a woman to enjoy petting/intercourse
68	0·34	Sometimes felt like humiliating partner
88	0·32	Sex should be for purpose of reproduction
101	0·41	Make lots of vocal noises during intercourse

ADULT POPULATIONS

Item	Loading	Item
Males		
116	0·50	Sometimes feel like biting, scratching during intercourse
121	0·44	Usually feel aggressive with partner
132	−0·33	In sex, tenderness important quality
Females		
68	0·53	Felt like humiliating sex partner
75	0·54	Felt hostile to sex partner
91	0·41	Preoccupation with sex created by T.V., films and newspapers
116	0·46	Feel like scratching, biting partner
121	0·30	Feel aggressive to partner
145	0·35	Men more selfish in love-making

These twelve factors, being oblique, are of course not uncorrelated and table 3.3 shows the actual correlations between the factors, for males and females separately. It will be seen that these correlations are similar for the two sexes, but not identical; particularly in the case of sexual excitement are there quite marked differences between males and females in the pattern of correlations with the other factors. However, there is clearly a tendency for the correlations in the table to fall into two groups, which are largely independent of each other. The first group, for men and women alike, is made up of factors of permissiveness, impersonal sex, pornography, dominance, physical sex and aggressive sex; for the women sexual excitement also falls into this cluster. The second group of correlations joins dissatisfaction, neurotic sex, shyness, prudishness and disgust; for the women, again, sexual excitement is (negatively) correlated with this cluster. For the men sexual excitement is correlated with the other factors in much the same direction, but correlations are all much lower. This is the only difference between the two sexes that stands out from the analysis; apart from this, the two patterns are quite similar.

When higher-order factors were extracted in the next stage of the Promax programme, two terminal factors were found for both men and women, and these bear a close relationship to the two clusters identified by simple study of the matrices of factor intercorrelations. We shall call the first of these factors 'Sexual Libido' and the second 'Sexual Satisfaction', again without wishing to preempt any discussion about the true nature of these factors. Loadings

97

Table 3.3 Correlations between twelve factors for males and females separately

	1	2	3	4	5	6	7	8	9	10	11	12
1 Permissiveness	–	-0·06	-0·06	0·43	0·25	-0·03	0·01	0·30	-0·04	0·02	0·15	0·19
2 Satisfaction	0·09	–	-0·31	-0·18	-0·08	-0·32	-0·25	0·00	-0·05	0·09	-0·01	0·01
3 Neurotic sex	-0·15	-0·29	–	0·02	-0·05	0·38	0·01	-0·04	-0·20	0·10	0·03	-0·19
4 Impersonal sex	0·37	-0·01	-0·04	–	0·30	-0·02	-0·06	0·25	-0·02	0·06	0·20	0·25
5 Pornography	0·33	0·01	0·14	0·28	–	0·00	-0·04	0·15	-0·06	0·17	0·19	0·26
6 Sexual shyness	-0·22	-0·26	0·22	-0·11	-0·05	–	0·02	-0·18	-0·18	0·07	-0·12	-0·19
7 Prudishness	0·10	-0·04	-0·06	0·04	-0·07	-0·01	–	-0·08	0·21	-0·14	0·08	0·00
8 Dominance–submission	0·07	-0·25	0·10	-0·04	0·14	-0·20	0·18	–	-0·17	0·14	0·24	0·13
9 Sexual disgust	-0·08	-0·16	0·11	0·01	-0·09	-0·08	0·25	-0·07	–	-0·16	0·02	0·02
10 Sexual excitement	0·47	0·26	-0·09	0·28	0·28	-0·30	-0·01	-0·08	0·04	–	0·16	0·08
11 Physical sex	-0·08	-0·12	0·21	-0·01	0·08	0·17	-0·09	0·06	0·03	-0·08	–	0·11
12 Aggressive sex	0·09	-0·09	0·05	0·21	-0·06	-0·04	0·03	-0·10	0·12	0·01	0·13	–

of more than 0·3 again are used to sort out those items that best
characterise the factors and items and loadings are printed below.

Superfactor 1: Sexual libido

Item	Loading	Item
Males		
1	−0·34	Opposite sex will respect more if not too familiar
2	−0·45	'Impersonal love' highly unsatisfactory
5	−0·34	Virginity is a girl's most valuable possession
6	−0·32	Think rarely of sex
10	0·30	Get pleasant feelings from touching sexual parts
17	−0·30	Disturbing to see necking in public
25	0·38	Would not bother if person married was not a virgin
30	0·30	Doesn't take much to get me sexually excited
34	−0·35	There are some things I wouldn't do with anyone
37	0·45	Think of sex almost every day
38	−0·48	One shouldn't experiment with sex before marriage
39	0·37	Get excited sexually easily
40	−0·57	Thought of sex orgy disgusts
41	−0·62	Better not to have sex until married
42	0·38	Coloured sex partner particularly exciting
43	0·43	Like to look at sexy pictures
46	0·42	Sometimes sexual feelings overpowering
48	0·40	Sex thoughts nearly drive crazy
49	0·32	When excited can think of nothing but satisfaction
55	0·32	Enjoy petting
57	0·35	'Pill' should be universally available
64	−0·41	Sex jokes disgust
65	0·55	Believe in taking pleasure where found
72	0·38	Have been involved with more than one affair at time
74	0·55	All right to seduce a person old enough to know
76	0·33	Like to look at pictures of nudes
77	0·48	Chance to see people making love, would take it
78	0·49	Pornographic writing should be allowed to be freely published
79	0·37	Prostitution should be legally permitted
81	−0·35	Too many immoral plays on T.V.
85	0·40	There should be no censorship on sex grounds of plays and films
86	0·38	Sex far and away greatest pleasure
87	−0·34	Sexual permissiveness threatens to undermine civilised society
89	0·47	Faithfulness to partner is as silly as celibacy
92	0·32	Enjoy watching partner have intercourse with someone else
95	0·35	Would vote for a law permitting polygamy
96	0·35	Though having regular intercourse, masturbation is good for a change
97	0·31	Prefer a new partner every night

99

Item	Loading	Item
Males		
106	0·37	Few things more important than sex
109	−0·31	Sex not all that important
119	0·53	Group sex appeals
120	0·45	Thought of illicit relationship excites
125	0·39	Wish women more forthcoming sexually
127	0·31	Physical sex important part of marriage
134	−0·37	Object to four-letter words in mixed company
135	−0·51	'Wife-swapping' extremely distasteful
146	−0·37	Some forms of love-making are disgusting
151	0·54	Accept invitation to see 'blue-film'
152	0·54	Accept pornographic book if offered
153	0·60	Accept invitation to orgy if offered
154	0·40	Preference for having intercourse frequently
158	0·50	Strength of sexual desire great
Females		
1	−0·43	Opposite sex will respect more if not too familiar
2	−0·55	Sex without love unsatisfactory
3	−0·33	Conditions just right to get excited sexually
5	−0·41	Viriginity a girl's most valuable possession
6	−0·32	Think rarely about sex
10	0·37	Pleasant feelings from touching sex parts
25	−0·44	Not bother if person married not a virgin
30	0·33	Doesn't take much to get sexually excited
36	0·31	Understand homosexuals
37	0·40	Think of sex everyday
38	−0·43	Should not experiment with sex before marriage
39	0·39	Get sexually excited easily
40	−0·52	Thought of sex orgy disgusting
41	−0·58	Better not to have sex until married
42	0·40	Coloured partner exciting
43	0·44	Like to look at sexy pictures
46	0·31	Sexual feelings overpower
58	−0·42	A nude person doesn't interest
63	0·32	Sometimes a woman should be sexually aggressive
65	0·53	Believe in taking pleasure where found
69	0·32	Protect children from sex contacts
72	0·52	Have been involved in more than one sex affair at time
74	0·37	All right to seduce a person old enough
76	0·40	Like to look at pictures of nudes
77	0·31	If chance to see people making love, would take it
78	0·48	Pornographic writing should be allowed to be freely published
79	0·43	Prostitution should be legally permitted
81	−0·32	Too many immoral plays on T.V.
83	0·32	Do away with marriage entirely
85	0·41	No censorship on sexual grounds of plays and films
87	−0·39	Sexual permissiveness threatens to undermine civilisation

100

Item	Loading	Item
Females		
89	0·54	Faithfulness in partner is as silly as celibacy
92	0·31	Enjoy watching partner have intercourse with someone else
95	0·32	Would vote for law permitting polygamy
96	0·35	Though having regular intercourse, good to masturbate for a change
108	− 0·34	Partner satisfies all physical needs
113	0·30	Like partner to be more expert/experienced
116	0·34	Feel like scratching and biting partner
119	0·42	Group sex appeals
120	0·55	Illicit relationship excites .
132	− 0·37	In sex, tenderness important quality
134	− 0·41	Object to four-letter words in mixed company
135	− 0·54	Idea of 'wife-swapping' distasteful
144	0·45	Not disturbed if partner has sex with someone else
151	0·47	Accept invitation to blue film
152	0·45	Accept pornographic book if offered
153	0·39	Accept invitation to take part in an orgy
154	0·36	Preference for having intercourse frequently
158	0·34	Strength sexual desire great

Superfactor 2: Sexual satisfaction

Item	Loading	Item
Males		
4	0·52	Am satisfied with sex life
11	− 0·47	Have been deprived sexually
15	− 0·32	Prefer people of my own sex
18	− 0·30	Sex feelings are sometimes unpleasant
19	− 0·51	Something lacking in sex life
21	− 0·51	Love life disappointing
31	− 0·37	Parents' influence has inhibited sexually
32	− 0·31	Thoughts about sex disturb more than should
44	− 0·31	Conscience bothers more than should ·
47	− 0·43	Feel nervous with opposite sex
50	0·31	Feel at ease with opposite sex
51	− 0·32	Don't like to be kissed
56	− 0·34	Worry a lot about sex
58	− 0·34	Seeing a person nude doesn't disturb
60	− 0·30	Perverted thoughts have sometimes bothered
65	− 0·30	Believe in taking pleasures where found
108	0·32	Partner satisfies all physical needs
113	0·33	Easy to tell partner if like/dislike her love-making
117	− 0·37	No one has satisfied sexually
118	− 0·39	Feel less sexually competent than friends
124	− 0·35	Afraid of sexual relationships
126	− 0·37	Can't stand being touched
133	− 0·34	Female genitals are aesthetically unpleasant

101

Item	Loading	Item
Males		
139	−0·35	Can't discuss sexual matters with wife
141	0·30	Naked body pleasing sight
149	−0·34	'Girlie' magazines suggests failure of adult attitudes
159	−0·34	Inhibiting sexual influences
Females		
4	0·57	Satisfied with sex life
11	−0·51	Have been deprived sexually
15	−0·40	Prefer people of own sex
18	−0·32	Sexual feelings sometimes unpleasant
19	−0·62	Something lacking in sex life
20	0·42	Sex behaviour never caused trouble
21	−0·58	Love life disappointing
24	−0·32	Felt guilty about sex experiences
31	−0·44	Parents' influence inhibited sexually
32	−0·36	Sex thoughts disturb more than should
44	−0·32	Conscience bothers too much
55	0·39	Enjoy petting
56	−0·34	Worry about sex
64	−0·33	Sex jokes disgust
68	−0·31	Sometimes felt like humiliating partner
75	−0·39	Sometimes felt hostile to partner
86	0·34	Sex is greatest pleasure
108	0·57	Partner satisfies all physical needs
109	0·31	Sex is not all
112	0·34	Enjoy lengthy pre-coital love play
113	0·34	Easy to tell partner like/dislike about love-making
114	−0·45	Like partner to be more experienced and expert
117	−0·33	No one has satisfied sexually
118	−0·41	Feel sexually less competent than friends
124	−0·33	Afraid sexual relationships
125	−0·37	Often wish men less demanding sexually
133	−0·37	Male genitals aesthetically unpleasing
144	−0·30	Not disturbed overmuch if partner had sex with someone else
145	−0·39	Men more selfish in love-making
146	−0·38	Some forms of love-making disgusting
150	−0·34	In sex, women come off second-best
155	−0·54	Suffered frigidity
157	0·39	Strength sexual desire great
158	−0·42	Influences inhibited sexually

When it comes to the correlation between the two superfactors, there is a large difference between the sexes. For the men the correlation is very small ($r=0·09$) and essentially unimportant; it accounts for less than 1 per cent of the variance. For the women, however, the correlation is much larger ($r=0·31$) and certainly not negligible;

it accounts for 10 per cent of the variance. This difference may be connected with the 'excitement' variable mentioned above; for women satisfaction and libido are much more closely connected than for men, for whom there is practically no connection at all. It would not be helpful to speculate on the reasons for this difference; obviously further work is required before any confident interpretation can be given. Here we merely note the fact of this difference; it is of importance in trying to assess the contribution of genetic factors to both libido and satisfaction.

It is possible to devise scales for the measurement of both the primary factors and also the superfactors. To take the primary factors first, scales have been devised for eleven out of the twelve;

Table 3.4 *Reliabilities, means and standard deviations for eleven sexual attitudes scales*

	Reliability		Means	
	M	F	M	F
1 Permissiveness	0·84	0·83	11·69 ± 2·66	10·92 ± 2·84
2 Satisfaction	0·82	0·83	8·03 ± 2·90	8·79 ± 2·84
3 Neurotic sex	0·74	0·72	2·87 ± 2·35	2·75 ± 2·30
4 Impersonal sex	0·85	0·81	5·91 ± 3·56	3·43 ± 2·86
5 Pornography	0·78	0·78	6·82 ± 1·71	5·14 ± 2·25
6 Sexual shyness	0·72	0·66	0·81 ± 1·21	0·61 ± 0·99
7 Prudishness	0·58	0·61	1·09 + 1·18	1·64 ± 1·43
8 Dominance–submission	—	—		
9 Sexual disgust	0·54	0·65	1·88 ± 1·32	2·20 ± 1·56
10 Sexual excitement	0·66	0·77	7·00 ± 1·69	5·47 ± 2·35
11 Physical sex	0·65	0·61	5·23 ± 2·01	4·61 ± 1·97
12 Aggressive sex	0·47	0·51	2·36 ± 1·42	2·62 ± 1·40

there were not sufficient common items for males and females on the dominance–submission factor to make construction of a scale possible. Items for the scales were selected in such a way that both size of loading and common loading for men and women were considered important. The actual items for the various scales, with key, are given in Appendix A to this chapter. Table 3.4 shows the reliabilities of the scales (alpha coefficients), and the means and standard deviations for men and women separately. Half of the reliabilities are in excess of 0·7; half the scales have reliabilities too low for serious consideration, except perhaps for group comparison. It is interesting to note that scales 1 to 6, which were put in this order in accordance with the factor comparison indices, also have the highest reliabilities; thus we have two different reasons for considering our first six factors to be better established than the second set of six.

The means of the various scales show interesting sex differences. Males clearly have higher scores on permissiveness, impersonal sex, pornography, excitement and physical sex; this is very much what popular wisdom (and previous studies) would have led one to expect. Women have higher scores on satisfaction, disgust and prudishness; these too accord with previous work, although the high satisfaction scores of the women, as compared with the men, would not perhaps form part of the popular wisdom (Eysenck 1971a).

Table 3.5 *Means and standard deviations of masculinity–femininity scale, and personality scales* P, E, N *and* L. *In brackets: standardisation data for personality scales*

	Males	Females
Mean: M–F scale	$32\cdot93\pm5\cdot93$	$24\cdot05\pm6\cdot33$
P	$2\cdot26\pm1\cdot77(\ 2\cdot74)$	$1\cdot60\pm1\cdot62(\ 1\cdot57)$
E	$10\cdot83\pm4\cdot46(12\cdot67)$	$12\cdot04\pm3\cdot87(12\cdot43)$
N	$9\cdot17\pm4\cdot92(\ 9\cdot59)$	$11\cdot48\pm4\cdot66(12\cdot31)$
L	$5\cdot76\pm3\cdot66(\ 6\cdot74)$	$6\cdot68\pm3\cdot47(\ 7\cdot84)$

Scales were also constructed for the superfactors of sexual libido and sexual satisfaction; the items and keys are given in Appendix B. Yet another scale was constructed to measure masculinity–femininity, based on the items showing the largest differences between the sexes; this scale and key is given in Appendix C. This scale is very similar to an earlier one based on our original sample of item (Eysenck 1971b). To take the M/F scale first, table 3.5 records the means and standard deviations of the scale for men and women separately; it will be seen, as of course was inevitable, that men are more 'masculine', their scores being on the average well over one standard deviation (S.D.) higher than those of the women. The reliability of the scale is 0·8 for both sexes; this is very satisfactory as the scale was constructed by taking items giving the largest differences between the sexes; there is no *a priori* reason why such a method should produce a scale that would be reliable *within* either sex. Also given in the table are the means and standard deviations of the four personality scales used, i.e. psychoticism (P), extraversion (E), neuroticism (N) and the Lie or dissimulation scale (L). The instrument used was an earlier form of the E.P.Q. and is reprinted in Appendix D, together with a key. The scale was standardised on a fairly random sample of the population obtained through a market research firm and is not likely to differ substantially from a true sample. The reliabilities of the personality scales on the standardisation group, for males and females separately, were 0·74 and 0·57 for P, 0·79 and 0·78 for E, 0·84 and 0·82 for N and 0·78 and 0·74 for L.

It will be seen that the sample tested with the sex questionnaire ✓ is not very different, in point of personality, from the standardisation sample, although because of the large size of both samples almost all the differences are statistically significant. For P differences are minimal. For E, males and to a lesser extent females are somewhat less extraverted than the standardisation group. For N, males and even more so females are somewhat less neurotic than the standardisation group. For L, both males and females have lower scores than the standardisation group. Our experimental group consequently contains more stable introverts than would be found by chance; its members also seem to dissimulate somewhat less (or are more conformist!). None of these differences is large in absolute amount.

Table 3.6 shows the correlations between the M/F scale and the four personality scales. It will be clear that these correlations are not very large. Masculinity correlates with P for both men and women (0·10 and 0·20, respectively). Correlations with E are positive but very small, while correlations with N are contradictory. Masculinity correlates negatively with L ($-0·15$ and $-0·18$). This is interesting in view of the fact that men usually have lower L scores than women (see table 3.5). The direction of these correlations is therefore in the expected direction, even though the size of the correlations is rather small. The intercorrelations between the personality variables are small throughout, although E and P clearly show a negative correlation ($-0·19$ and $-0·19$), with E and N also showing a negative correlation ($-0·06$ and $-0·20$) and N and P a positive correlation (0·07 and 0·11). Correlations of L with the other three variables are all negative. Again, these values are statistically significant but do not amount to much psychologically; it is the large number of subjects that accounts for the statistical significance.

Table 3.6 *Correlations between masculinity–femininity scale and personality scales: males above leading diagonal, females below*

	M–F	P	E	N	L
M–F	–	0·10	0·07	0·12	– 0·15
P	0·02	–	– 0·19	0·07	– 0·11
E	0·06	– 0·19	–	– 0·06	– 0·25
N	– 0·03	0·11	– 0·20	–	– 0·11
L	– 0·18	– 0·22	– 0·11	– 0·12	–

We may now turn to the Libido and Satisfaction scales. The reliabilities of these scales are very satisfactory: for the males, they are 0·90 and 0·82, while for the females they are 0·89 and 0·81. Correlations are −0·11 and 0·03 respectively.(1) Means on the Libido scale, as one might have expected, are higher for the males: 24·47, S.D. 6·82, as compared with 19·11, S.D. 6·84 for the females. This difference is of course fully significant. On the Satisfaction scale there is no meaningful difference, although the females have a slightly higher score: the mean for the males is 12·40, S.D. 3·06; that for the females is 12·70, S.D. 3·02. These results agree well with our previous work.

Table 3.7 reports the intercorrelations of eleven of our twelve scales (scale 8, it will be remembered, showed too little agreement between males and females to make proper construction possible) with each other, and with the Libido and Satisfaction scales. It will be seen that both sexes give very similar results, and that the pattern of correlations makes perfectly good sense. Scales for permissiveness, pornography, impersonal sex, excitement, physical sex and aggressive sex correlate positively together, and negatively with prudishness, sexual disgust and sexual shyness, to form the factor of Libido. Satisfaction, physical sex and sexual excitement correlate positively together, and negatively with neurotic sex, sexual shyness, sexual disgust and prudishness to form the factor of Satisfaction. Figure 3.1 shows the pattern of correlation of these eleven scales with the two superscales, Libido and Satisfaction. It is noteworthy that the two sexes show very similar patterns, without any marked discrepancies between the positions of the scales in the two-dimensional framework. Correction for attenuation would give even higher correlations, but would not change the pattern.

There were 239 pairs of subjects who were married or were living together on a semi-permanent basis. It seemed of interest

Table 3.7 *Intercorrelations between sexual attitude scales: males above leading diagonal, females below*

	1	2	3	4	5	6	7	9	10	11	12	Satisfaction	Libido
	–	-0·08	0·03	0·47	0·45	0·04	-0·22	-0·27	0·28	0·15	0·21	-0·06	0·76
2	0·04	–	-0·48	-0·20	-0·04	-0·46	-0·21	-0·17	0·11	0·01	-0·04	0·91	-0·14
3	0·00	-0·48	–	0·15	0·01	0·29	0·05	0·09	0·03	0·18	0·25	-0·60	0·15
4	0·44	0·14	0·15	–	0·47	0·10	-0·14	-0·20	0·33	0·30	0·26	-0·18	0·84
5	0·51	0·01	0·08	0·39	–	0·01	-0·44	-0·24	0·40	0·28	0·15	0·02	0·71
6	-0·09	-0·37	0·33	0·47	0·02	–	0·18	0·10	-0·11	0·03	0·01	-0·52	0·06
7	-0·42	-0·17	0·05	-0·18	-0·48	0·09	–	0·40	-0·45	-0·35	-0·18	-0·28	-0·29
9	-0·34	-0·23	0·10	-0·19	-0·28	0·20	0·50	–	-0·62	-0·27	-0·10	-0·23	-0·31
10	0·42	0·20	0·04	0·24	0·43	-0·16	-0·51	-0·72	–	0·43	0·19	0·16	0·49
11	0·24	0·20	0·06	0·20	0·35	-0·06	-0·39	-0·36	0·51	–	0·24	0·06	0·38
12	0·28	-0·06	0·24	0·27	0·28	0·01	-0·17	-0·18	0·24	0·13	–	-0·07	0·32
Satisfaction	0·08	0·90	-0·58	-0·12	0·06	-0·40	-0·25	-0·34	0·26	0·26	-0·03	–	-0·10
Libido	0·79	-0·02	0·16	0·75	0·78	-0·06	-0·41	-0·37	0·54	0·36	0·38	0·03	–

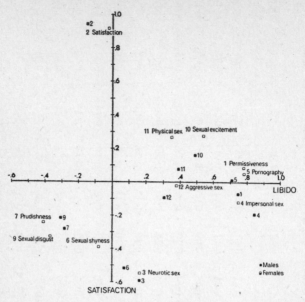

Figure 3.1   *Position of primary sexual attitudes factor scales on two super-factors: libido and satisfaction*

to study the degree of homogamy present for the eleven scales constructed to measure the primary factors, and also for the two scales measuring the two higher-order factors, Libido and Satisfaction. Table 3.8 gives the correlations for the pairs for these scales. Also included are correlations for the factor scores on the two super-factors; this was done to compare the observed relationships for scales and factor scores. It will be seen that factor scores give very similar information to that obtained from the scales. There is clearly a considerable range of assortative mating,(2) with correlations between spouses ranging from 0·58 to a low of between 0·13 and 0·15, there being three scales at the low level. Both Satisfaction and Libido seem to give rise to similar degrees of homogamy; there is a low degree of homogamy for neurotic sex, sexual shyness, prudishness, sexual disgust and sexual excitement. These low correlations between spouses may be of interest to marriage guidance counsellors; they are likely to provoke difficulties in a close sexual relationship.(3)

Our data make it possible for us to determine also the degree of assortative mating for personality demonstrated by our subjects.

Table 3.8 *Intercorrelations between 239 spouses for scores on sex factor scales*

1	0·58	Permissiveness
2	0·47	Satisfaction
3	0·22	Neurotic sex
4	0·42	Impersonal sex
5	0·36	Pornography
6	0·14	Sexual shyness
7	0·13	Prudishness
8	—	Dominance–submission
9	0·15	Sexual disgust
10	0·20	Sexual excitement
11	0·47	Physical sex
12	0·40	Aggressive sex
Satisfaction	0·46	Satisfaction
Libido	0·51	Libido
F 1	0·50	Factor satisfaction
F 2	0·42	Factor libido

As this feature is of great importance in genetic analysis, a brief review of what is known about assortative mating for personality will be given before we discuss our own results. (See Eysenck 1974 for more detailed analysis.) There are two main lines of thought, each supported by some data. Early investigators favoured a theory of homogamy (Burgess and Wallis 1944). In contrast, Winch (1958) elaborated a theory of complementary needs in the marital relationship. The heterogamy position has received some support (Schellenberg and Bee 1960, Gray 1949, Tharp 1963, Roos 1956, Reiter 1970); the homogamy position has equally received some support, usually indicating that 'there is homogamy for psychopathology'. Kallman and Mickey (1946), Kreitman (1964, 1968), Murstein (1971) and Yom and others (1976) may be cited here. Other writers again find that their data are not in conflict with a theory of panmixia: Udry (1967), Bowerman and Day (1956), Hill (1968) and Gottesman (1965) might be quoted in this connection. Cattell and Nesselroade (1967) and Pickford and others (1967) cite data in support of the contention that happy marriages are characterised by homogamy – a point that is interesting but not relevant to the genetic aspects of assortative mating unless happy marriages produce more children (Eysenck 1974). A consideration of all the available data suggests no departure from panmixia, except with respect to psychiatrically abnormal persons where a small amount of homogamy appears to be present.

Studies with the *P*, *E*, *N* and *L* have on the whole supported this view. In our Department, Nias (1974) studied 700 pairs of parents who had 1,200 children, and Insel (1971) made a thorough study of 98 families, including 589 subjects in all, involving in every case three generations. The correlations found by them were quite insignificant (and indeed opposite in sign) for *E* (0·06 and −0·10) and *N* (0·12 and −0·09). For *P*, however, both report significant positive correlations (0·22 and 0·36, respectively). The data from the present study are as follows: *P*, 0·142; *E*, 0·061; *N*, 0·223; *L*, 0·174. The correlations for the two psychiatric variables (*P* and *N*) are both significant, as is that for *L*. (*L* is usually negatively correlated with both *P* and *N*; this may account for the observed small positive correlation.) For *E* the correlation is quite insignificant. There is thus the suggestion of a very mild degree of homogamy in normals for *P* and possibly *N*.

We may turn to a discussion of the relationship between sexual attitudes and personality. In the previous chapter we have shown that there are consistent and predictable differences in sexual attitudes between subjects having certain personality scores on the personality dimensions *P* (psychoticism), *E* (extraversion) and *N* (neuroticism). These studies, as well as the German study by Giese and Schmidt (1968), were carried out on students, many of whom had only very little experience of sexual matters; it seemed important to investigate in our present older and much more experienced sample whether similar results to those observed in the earlier study could be found. The method used in this study is rather different from that used previously, when factors were correlated with personality scale scores. The reason for preferring a different method in the present study is simply that not all the items could be used in factor-analysing our results, owing to limitations imposed by the capacity of the computer; consequently there would have been a considerable waste of information had we correlated the factors with the personality variables. What was done instead was to correlate each item, for males and females separately, with scores on the *P*, *E*, *N* and *L* questionnaire variables; in this way all items could be considered. We also correlated all attitude items with social class, occupation, age and marital status; in this way it was hoped to discover attitude differences between different class and age groups. The detailed findings are recorded in table 3.9, this should be consulted for all details. However, in order to give a more cohesive account of attitude differences relevant to individual personality factors, and to age and social class, a verbal picture will be given below of the highest correlations in each column. No correlations below the value of ± 0.12 have been used, although in cases where there were very many items exceeding this value we put the lower limit of acceptance slightly higher. Correlations are low on the whole, but this is not remarkable in view of the fact that single items are always rather unreliable; no very high correlations could have been expected. With the numbers of subjects involved the correlations included would nearly all be significant, although of course in view of the large numbers of items involved ordinary standards of significance cannot reasonably be applied to single items.

Table 3.9 *Sex inventory item correlations with personality, class, occupation, age and marital status*

Item	Class	Occupation	Age	Marital Status	P	E	N	L
Males								
1	−0·003	−0·059	0·198	0·002	−0·131	0·007	0·036	0·210
2	0·125	−0·149	0·078	0·067	−0·102	−0·076	0·065	0·105
3	−0·030	0·032	0·096	−0·072	−0·010	−0·026	0·089	0·039
4	0·005	−0·016	−0·084	−0·200	0·013	0·017	−0·221	−0·029
5	−0·047	0·015	0·088	0·157	−0·054	0·004	0·169	0·113
6	0·064	0·031	0·115	0·102	0·111	0·018	−0·016	0·064
7	−0·025	0·022	−0·051	−0·004	−0·074	0·149	0·218	−0·169
8	−0·055	0·038	0·118	−0·050	0·039	−0·055	0·093	0·084
9	0·009	0·196	−0·039	−0·079	−0·009	0·011	0·065	0·014
10	−0·039	0·037	−0·151	−0·092	−0·001	0·051	−0·011	−0·212
11	−0·021	−0·055	0·150	0·008	0·144	−0·075	0·173	0·024
12	0·020	0·017	0·003	0·074	−0·169	0·014	0·118	0·020
13	−0·050	−0·100	0·003	−0·068	0·097	0·026	−0·015	−0·142
14	−0·092	0·030	0·030	−0·092	0·080	−0·086	0·133	0·081
15	0·023	−0·011	0·016	0·158	0·088	−0·076	0·007	−0·062
16	−0·028	0·065	−0·062	0·026	−0·038	0·209	−0·071	−0·005
17	0·008	−0·175	0·140	0·125	−0·162	−0·113	0·114	−0·016
18	−0·045	−0·111	0·009	0·048	−0·027	−0·091	0·108	−0·049
19	−0·061	0·001	0·080	0·070	0·027	−0·107	0·230	0·027
20	−0·066	0·181	−0·079	−0·095	−0·049	−0·063	−0·120	0·237
21	−0·056	−0·025	0·129	0·130	0·085	−0·096	0·221	0·015
22	0·013	0·021	0·076	−0·059	0·012	−0·317	0·087	0·264
23	0·009	0·033	0·042	−0·030	−0·079	0·035	0·010	0·087
24	0·017	−0·232	0·105	0·032	−0·028	−0·021	0·238	−0·126
25	0·068	0·023	−0·071	−0·223	0·109	0·015	−0·051	−0·139
26	−0·030	0·032	−0·075	−0·033	0·026	0·097	0·261	−0·119
27	0·010	0·006	0·000	0·096	−0·032	0·094	0·014	−0·132

Item	Class	Occupation	Age	Marital Status	P	E	N	L
Males								
28	−0·082	0·012	0·055	0·078	−0·033	0·297	0·048	−0·124
29	−0·026	0·046	0·063	−0·041	0·115	−0·160	0·094	0·112
30	−0·152	0·030	−0·168	−0·068	−0·010	0·068	0·039	−0·042
31	0·055	−0·105	0·259	0·030	0·110	−0·128	0·185	0·077
32	−0·028	0·001	0·071	−0·079	−0·031	−0·028	0·340	0·085
33	−0·054	0·102	0·083	−0·021	−0·078	0·049	−0·059	−0·128
34	0·019	−0·196	0·124	0·054	−0·020	−0·013	0·062	0·028
35	0·031	0·067	−0·005	−0·120	−0·069	0·112	0·015	0·017
36	0·006	0·058	−0·099	−0·088	−0·034	0·090	0·018	−0·017
37	−0·016	−0·015	−0·233	−0·098	−0·010	0·173	0·043	−0·092
38	−0·012	−0·106	0·148	0·129	−0·057	−0·063	−0·012	0·212
39	−0·179	0·033	−0·217	−0·077	−0·055	0·217	0·166	−0·096
40	−0·097	−0·167	0·185	0·214	−0·143	−0·068	−0·059	0·209
41	−0·087	−0·133	0·185	0·132	−0·137	−0·137	−0·026	0·239
42	−0·119	0·218	−0·074	−0·020	0·043	0·059	0·204	−0·048
43	−0·009	0·115	−0·066	−0·118	0·021	−0·099	0·118	−0·110
44	0·021	−0·060	0·027	0·088	−0·060	−0·016	0·275	−0·097
45	0·073	−0·073	0·142	−0·006	0·113	−0·170	0·099	0·130
46	−0·070	0·091	−0·215	−0·038	0·048	0·155	0·267	−0·193
47	0·043	−0·053	−0·035	−0·058	0·129	−0·187	0·233	0·032
48	−0·072	0·071	−0·040	0·020	−0·071	0·013	0·227	0·042
49	−0·057	0·162	−0·051	0·009	−0·024	0·009	0·260	0·011
50	−0·007	−0·018	0·038	−0·031	−0·041	0·199	−0·121	−0·073
51	0·009	0·067	0·120	0·149	0·083	−0·079	0·056	0·093
52	−0·006	0·071	−0·038	0·081	−0·026	−0·200	0·021	0·113
53	0·011	0·032	0·081	−0·055	−0·001	−0·127	0·158	0·005
54	0·003	0·126	−0·017	0·072	−0·001	−0·092	0·075	0·111
55	−0·066	0·066	−0·161	0·006	−0·042	−0·144	0·092	−0·028
56	0·121	−0·003	0·003	0·025	−0·073	−0·044	0·330	0·039
57	0·006	0·163	−0·093	−0·082	0·083	0·017	0·062	−0·136
58	−0·037	0·013	0·136	0·085	0·104	0·051	−0·031	−0·005
59	−0·142	0·174	−0·003	0·055	−0·074	0·059	0·234	−0·068
60	0·020	−0·034	0·027	0·016	0·000	−0·011	0·185	−0·094
61	0·110	−0·103	−0·079	−0·088	−0·021	−0·175	0·029	−0·013
62	−0·106	0·048	−0·120	−0·095	0·066	−0·001	0·053	−0·156
63	−0·061	0·067	−0·081	0·028	0·067	0·056	0·031	−0·157
64	−0·019	−0·079	0·082	0·128	−0·032	−0·065	−0·002	0·102
65	−0·080	0·222	−0·013	−0·158	0·143	0·199	0·177	−0·158
66	−0·077	0·014	−0·018	0·025	0·016	0·024	0·122	−0·090
67	−0·023	0·118	−0·137	−0·149	0·028	0·066	−0·087	−0·161
68	0·060	0·051	0·023	0·002	0·011	0·095	0·229	−0·202
69	−0·061	0·089	0·050	0·112	−0·069	0·063	0·171	0·156
70	0·052	−0·154	0·032	−0·082	0·021	−0·047	−0·020	0·067
71	−0·091	0·061	0·060	−0·037	−0·137	0·112	0·118	0·004
72	−0·008	0·049	0·163	−0·056	0·091	0·186	0·086	−0·262
73	−0·015	0·045	−0·044	−0·058	−0·044	0·086	−0·000	−0·056
74	−0·039	0·118	−0·177	−0·107	0·141	0·060	0·108	−0·210
75	0·021	0·000	−0·065	−0·043	−0·000	0·048	0·311	−0·225
76	0·105	−0·037	−0·042	−0·123	0·004	−0·078	0·028	−0·012

Item	Class	Occupation	Age	Marital Status	P	E	N	L
Males								
77	−0·082	0·113	−0·103	−0·141	0·063	−0·036	0·095	−0·092
78	−0·027	0·090	−0·114	−0·084	0·192	−0·011	0·093	−0·194
79	−0·151	0·092	0·029	−0·073	0·082	0·025	0·039	−0·121
80	0·055	0·200	0·206	0·005	−0·033	−0·026	0·045	−0·002
81	−0·081	−0·115	0·110	0·131	−0·111	0·018	−0·033	0·071
82	−0·127	0·187	−0·079	−0·014	0·011	0·160	0·086	−0·061
83	0·044	−0·033	−0·095	−0·016	0·281	0·117	0·058	−0·092
84	0·062	0·163	−0·019	−0·069	0·106	0·117	0·211	−0·057
85	0·005	0·055	0·027	−0·108	0·107	−0·031	0·030	−0·131
86	−0·156	0·196	−0·025	−0·102	−0·082	0·070	0·251	0·034
87	0·014	−0·024	0·137	0·208	−0·054	−0·060	0·044	0·200
88	−0·092	−0·028	−0·009	−0·024	−0·073	0·045	−0·053	0·044
89	−0·033	0·122	−0·004	−0·079	0·129	0·168	0·094	−0·139
90	−0·035	−0·014	0·013	0·042	0·099	−0·055	0·000	−0·041
91	0·003	−0·025	−0·062	0·045	−0·094	0·031	0·121	0·060
92	−0·065	0·212	0·077	0·000	−0·019	0·046	0·043	−0·025
93	−0·046	−0·013	0·102	−0·044	0·143	−0·028	−0·180	−0·010
94	−0·102	−0·002	0·069	−0·026	−0·024	−0·019	−0·012	0·143
95	0·046	0·099	−0·001	−0·031	0·142	0·097	0·001	−0·055
96	−0·005	0·212	−0·097	0·029	0·036	−0·017	0·094	−0·082
97	−0·007	0·125	−0·002	0·024	−0·006	0·098	0·104	0·047
98	0·000	0·000	0·000	0·000	0·000	0·000	0·000	0·000
99	−0·089	0·250	−0·158	−0·086	0·128	0·072	0·178	−0·012
100	0·018	0·085	0·011	−0·041	−0·086	−0·105	0·141	0·010
101	−0·009	−0·042	0·007	−0·033	−0·090	0·145	0·140	0·088
102	0·019	0·144	−0·006	−0·027	−0·034	−0·022	0·099	0·000
103	0·005	0·001	0·118	−0·012	−0·022	−0·186	0·129	0·120
104	0·104	−0·149	−0·093	−0·069	0·032	0·099	0·174	−0·055
105	0·000	−0·070	0·063	−0·097	−0·057	−0·020	0·022	0·058
106	0·186	0·054	−0·019	−0·070	0·006	0·004	0·183	0·029
107	0·027	0·011	−0·049	0·114	−0·067	0·058	0·107	0·090
108	−0·019	−0·064	−0·030	−0·059	0·040	0·089	−0·142	0·046
109	0·111	−0·021	0·114	0·112	0·108	−0·125	−0·149	0·039
110	−0·121	0·060	−0·164	0·002	0·136	0·044	0·083	−0·206
111	0·046	0·103	0·133	0·028	−0·045	0·017	0·092	0·080
112	−0·072	0·116	0·076	0·008	−0·105	0·144	0·101	0·062
113	−0·069	0·088	−0·188	−0·233	0·070	0·120	−0·015	−0·026
114	−0·054	0·112	0·040	0·060	0·078	−0·013	0·048	0·068
115	−0·023	−0·163	−0·093	0·056	−0·012	−0·093	0·009	−0·034
116	0·070	−0·048	−0·249	−0·113	0·041	0·216	0·094	−0·219
117	−0·063	0·082	−0·075	−0·086	0·094	−0·097	0·102	0·030
118	−0·076	0·117	−0·045	−0·089	0·019	−0·006	0·116	−0·008
119	−0·163	0·324	−0·034	−0·060	0·061	0·129	−0·033	−0·132
120	−0·131	0·117	0·048	−0·040	0·009	0·025	0·230	−0·083
121	−0·123	0·158	−0·144	−0·086	−0·018	0·250	0·170	−0·151
122	0·037	0·015	0·003	−0·021	−0·066	0·076	−0·021	−0·040
123	0·040	−0·151	0·145	0·128	−0·072	−0·002	0·099	0·049
124	0·006	−0·068	−0·014	0·003	0·048	−0·152	0·153	0·050
125	−0·058	0·138	0·033	0·073	0·083	0·122	0·198	−0·026

113

Item	Class	Occupation	Age	Marital Status	P	E	N	L
Males								
126	− 0·043	− 0·015	0·078	0·026	0·169	− 0·159	0·101	− 0·016
127	− 0·066	0·165	0·074	− 0·010	− 0·020	− 0·013	0·150	0·064
128	− 0·074	0·248	− 0·136	0·053	0·047	0·085	0·160	0·005
129	− 0·109	0·138	− 0·067	− 0·042	0·061	0·050	0·144	0·063
130	0·057	− 0·022	0·119	− 0·106	0·082	− 0·019	− 0·129	0·087
131	0·012	0·041	0·087	0·098	0·020	0·105	0·239	0·029
132	0·003	− 0·087	0·076	0·109	− 0·132	− 0·048	0·101	0·114
133	0·153	− 0·112	0·047	− 0·069	0·044	− 0·115	0·113	0·031
134	− 0·100	− 0·078	0·075	0·046	− 0·194	− 0·078	0·001	0·206
135	0·152	− 0·196	0·053	0·152	− 0·056	− 0·017	0·045	0·055
136	− 0·040	0·120	0·106	0·010	0·146	− 0·038	0·096	0·099
137	0·025	− 0·036	0·139	0·208	− 0·014	0·013	0·169	0·051
138	− 0·022	0·045	− 0·035	− 0·124	0·071	0·015	0·064	− 0·090
139	0·041	− 0·088	0·104	− 0·012	0·080	− 0·036	0·175	0·061
140	0·046	− 0·089	0·208	0·083	− 0·002	0·032	− 0·093	0·039
141	− 0·041	0·104	− 0·107	− 0·071	− 0·057	− 0·034	0·054	− 0·006
142	− 0·018	0·028	0·122	− 0·001	− 0·012	0·049	− 0·123	0·069
143	− 0·059	0·066	0·031	− 0·051	− 0·073	0·094	0·050	0·001
144	− 0·016	0·137	− 0·005	− 0·041	0·120	− 0·014	− 0·019	− 0·048
145	− 0·063	0·011	0·003	− 0·032	− 0·122	0·087	0·065	0·005
146	0·041	− 0·201	0·080	− 0·009	0·056	− 0·076	0·025	0·003
147	0·080	− 0·127	0·155	0·001	− 0·088	0·041	− 0·098	0·135
148	− 0·060	0·121	0·031	− 0·044	0·003	0·022	0·202	0·055
149	0·158	− 0·172	0·307	0·140	0·064	− 0·175	− 0·005	0·254
150	− 0·075	− 0·015	0·091	0·067	0·001	0·014	0·100	0·062
151	0·010	0·093	− 0·171	− 0·155	0·044	0·028	0·100	− 0·186
152	− 0·008	0·089	− 0·196	− 0·109	− 0·006	− 0·001	0·088	− 0·177
153	− 0·056	0·193	0·016	− 0·094	0·108	0·148	0·091	− 0·127
154	− 0·083	0·065	− 0·300	− 0·107	0·036	0·121	− 0·036	− 0·129
155	0·129	− 0·064	0·055	0·077	0·103	0·085	0·101	− 0·100
156	0·119	− 0·239	0·351	0·106	− 0·065	− 0·310	0·056	0·305
157	− 0·168	0·211	− 0·265	− 0·106	− 0·085	0·227	0·212	− 0·033
158	0·033	0·091	0·162	0·090	− 0·016	− 0·058	0·102	0·132
Females								
1	0·033	− 0·021	0·107	0·066	− 0·144	− 0·076	0·184	0·180
2	0·010	− 0·041	0·201	0·014	− 0·109	− 0·051	− 0·010	0·138
3	0·152	− 0·066	0·153	0·042	− 0·087	− 0·050	0·244	0·152
4	− 0·091	0·041	− 0·040	− 0·130	− 0·030	0·025	− 0·137	0·084
5	− 0·005	0·026	0·252	0·177	− 0·117	− 0·065	0·062	0·269
6	− 0·029	0·061	0·275	0·094	− 0·011	− 0·004	− 0·017	0·101
7	0·043	− 0·092	− 0·127	− 0·053	0·079	0·096	0·104	− 0·068
8	0·079	− 0·119	0·099	0·023	− 0·010	− 0·035	0·024	0·060
9	− 0·028	− 0·018	− 0·201	− 0·057	0·139	0·156	− 0·079	− 0·011
10	− 0·061	0·115	0·033	0·007	0·044	− 0·079	− 0·027	− 0·051
11	0·055	− 0·140	0·244	0·091	0·042	− 0·074	0·139	− 0·029
12	− 0·054	0·116	0·039	0·113	0·107	− 0·107	0·173	0·127

114

Item	Class	Occupation	Age	Marital Status	P	E	N	L
Females								
13	−0·101	0·134	0·002	0·064	0·015	−0·035	0·051	−0·045
14	0·064	−0·007	0·007	−0·061	0·109	−0·203	0·135	0·084
15	−0·019	0·057	0·069	0·012	0·042	0·008	0·101	−0·031
16	−0·129	0·095	−0·059	0·004	−0·060	0·199	−0·178	0·133
17	−0·045	−0·041	0·140	0·127	0·068	−0·136	0·139	0·010
18	0·047	0·015	−0·042	0·071	0·012	−0·057	0·263	−0·101
19	0·140	−0·085	0·143	0·218	0·039	−0·033	0·192	−0·101
20	−0·087	0·052	−0·056	−0·100	−0·066	0·095	−0·130	0·092
21	0·097	−0·014	0·100	0·032	0·092	−0·092	0·142	−0·049
22	0·094	−0·137	0·072	−0·122	0·028	−0·197	0·040	0·055
23	−0·107	0·045	0·205	0·075	0·034	−0·051	0·101	−0·003
24	−0·024	−0·067	−0·019	0·013	0·137	−0·080	0·208	−0·066
25	−0·024	0·054	−0·180	−0·182	0·179	−0·054	0·126	−0·182
26	0·023	−0·041	−0·097	−0·017	0·100	0·101	0·121	−0·089
27	−0·072	0·017	−0·067	0·021	0·101	−0·028	0·071	−0·074
28	0·014	−0·147	−0·041	0·104	−0·108	0·345	−0·117	−0·044
29	−0·135	0·103	−0·002	0·033	0·047	−0·102	0·260	−0·095
30	−0·064	0·054	−0·159	−0·075	0·076	0·128	0·050	−0·068
31	0·075	−0·148	0·128	−0·068	0·058	−0·171	0·203	0·018
32	−0·099	0·048	0·057	0·005	0·106	−0·048	0·148	0·027
33	−0·044	0·050	−0·096	0·019	0·193	0·021	0·063	0·029
34	−0·007	0·094	0·174	0·073	−0·171	−0·193	0·167	0·050
35	−0·099	0·055	0·090	0·019	−0·009	−0·036	0·018	−0·059
36	−0·140	−0·023	−0·102	−0·114	0·038	0·070	−0·069	−0·153
37	−0·067	0·039	−0·216	−0·014	0·000	0·098	0·010	−0·160
38	0·101	−0·036	0·269	0·164	−0·091	−0·088	0·064	0·080
39	−0·102	0·096	−0·215	−0·034	0·132	0·166	0·082	−0·101
40	0·027	−0·062	0·209	0·045	0·007	−0·054	−0·030	0·195
41	0·049	−0·132	0·331	0·158	−0·163	0·071	0·075	0·158
42	−0·087	0·182	−0·143	−0·049	0·022	0·057	0·036	−0·084
43	−0·152	0·260	−0·195	−0·060	0·043	−0·096	0·156	−0·052
44	−0·003	0·092	0·090	−0·029	0·047	−0·042	0·295	0·065
45	−0·084	0·046	−0·057	−0·003	−0·015	−0·022	0·133	−0·001
46	0·003	0·022	−0·108	−0·123	0·067	0·053	0·100	−0·138
47	0·068	0·109	0·044	−0·015	0·142	−0·170	0·232	−0·032
48	0·094	0·030	−0·139	−0·004	−0·023	0·098	0·089	0·022
49	−0·160	0·112	0·076	0·017	−0·124	0·047	0·200	0·110
50	0·020	−0·169	0·003	−0·012	−0·106	0·176	−0·144	0·066
51	0·026	−0·039	0·064	−0·034	0·114	−0·110	0·095	−0·007
52	−0·034	0·171	−0·017	0·003	0·100	−0·232	0·190	0·037
53	0·063	0·095	0·110	0·068	0·019	−0·096	0·200	0·074
54	−0·092	0·123	0·108	−0·025	0·089	−0·098	0·101	−0·012
55	−0·005	−0·134	−0·190	0·026	−0·024	0·124	−0·033	−0·112
56	0·067	−0·030	−0·030	−0·006	0·008	−0·114	0·246	−0·002
57	−0·006	0·025	−0·069	0·048	0·010	0·027	0·059	−0·135
58	0·103	−0·160	0·171	0·037	−0·070	0·104	−0·050	0·091
59	0·025	−0·015	0·019	0·068	0·066	−0·003	0·272	−0·121
60	0·010	0·060	0·051	0·036	0·097	−0·115	0·181	0·014
61	0·116	0·009	0·153	0·185	0·027	−0·131	0·158	0·014

Item	Class	Occupation	Age	Marital Status	P	E	N	L
Females								
62	− 0·074	− 0·039	− 0·122	− 0·160	0·079	0·122	− 0·118	− 0·185
63	− 0·114	0·032	− 0·136	− 0·049	− 0·068	0·129	− 0·090	− 0·052
64	0·035	− 0·125	0·157	0·086	0·032	− 0·130	0·020	0·107
65	− 0·135	0·135	− 0·143	− 0·027	0·109	0·121	− 0·014	− 0·054
66	− 0·102	− 0·046	− 0·149	− 0·025	0·045	0·097	− 0·063	− 0·120
67	− 0·008	0·027	− 0·026	0·016	− 0·078	0·094	− 0·127	0·043
68	0·047	0·037	− 0·109	0·055	0·208	− 0·058	0·261	− 0·233
69	− 0·005	− 0·057	0·228	0·089	− 0·067	− 0·002	0·065	0·134
70	− 0·021	− 0·138	− 0·046	− 0·144	− 0·164	0·108	− 0·187	0·004
71	− 0·034	− 0·061	− 0·039	0·060	0·049	0·042	0·050	0·002
72	− 0·042	0·038	0·047	0·080	0·091	0·069	− 0·026	− 0·068
73	− 0·099	0·007	− 0·100	− 0·025	− 0·036	0·049	0·007	− 0·096
74	− 0·054	0·032	− 0·177	0·021	− 0·059	0·076	0·026	− 0·049
75	0·070	− 0·115	0·018	− 0·014	0·111	− 0·069	0·250	− 0·193
76	− 0·148	0·237	− 0·118	− 0·073	0·003	− 0·019	0·105	− 0·008
77	− 0·132	0·277	− 0·220	0·023	0·017	− 0·061	0·048	− 0·015
78	− 0·029	0·033	− 0·187	− 0·082	0·063	0·053	0·043	− 0·248
79	− 0·011	− 0·073	0·099	− 0·058	0·077	0·024	− 0·127	− 0·119
80	− 0·065	0·136	0·103	− 0·002	− 0·007	− 0·008	− 0·038	0·167
81	0·076	− 0·152	0·288	0·128	− 0·041	− 0·001	− 0·004	0·082
82	− 0·003	0·200	− 0·015	− 0·007	− 0·051	− 0·068	0·056	0·279
83	− 0·038	0·097	− 0·050	− 0·009.	0·385	0·059	0·217	− 0·079
84	− 0·023	0·087	− 0·113	− 0·016	0·084	0·007	0·181	− 0·152
85	− 0·044	0·018	− 0·048	− 0·042	0·088	− 0·029	− 0·034	− 0·192
86	− 0·158	0·099	− 0·027	− 0·095	− 0·057	0·017	− 0·034	0·049
87	− 0·009	− 0·044	0·229	0·101	− 0·062	− 0·012	0·103	0·169
88	− 0·090	− 0·026	0·058	0·153	− 0·165	− 0·032	0·082	− 0·036
89	− 0·137	0·124	− 0·027	0·047	0·088	0·098	0·038	− 0·077
90	0·028	− 0·051	0·226	0·087	0·010	− 0·130	0·040	0·128
91	0·019	− 0·028	0·078	0·017	− 0·028	− 0·048	− 0·022	0·069
92	− 0·029	0·190	− 0·046	0·001	0·046	− 0·044	0·012	0·003
93	0·028	− 0·003	0·024	− 0·069	0·032	0·049	− 0·094	0·000
94	− 0·006	0·041	0·186	0·047	− 0·151	− 0·053	0·039	0·243
95	0·083	0·077	− 0·048	0·044	0·281	0·046	0·027	− 0·178
96	− 0·104	0·154	− 0·029	− 0·038	0·004	− 0·024	0·093	− 0·061
97	− 0·128	0·070	− 0·044	− 0·045	0·037	0·032	0·119	− 0·063
98	− 0·013	− 0·019	0·181	0·136	− 0·014	− 0·107	0·070	0·093
99	− 0·078	0·111	− 0·044	− 0·006	0·036	− 0·024	0·175	0·027
100	0·047	0·145	− 0·039	− 0·003	0·052	0·055	0·093	− 0·089
101	− 0·138	0·013	− 0·175	− 0·078	0·104	0·139	0·052	− 0·131
102	0·009	0·102	− 0·031	− 0·006	0·063	0·125	0·107	− 0·086
103	− 0·058	0·000	0·257	− 0·021	0·061	− 0·114	− 0·021	0·133
104	0·024	0·056	0·097	0·084	− 0·120	− 0·139	0·178	0·140
105	− 0·014	0·037	− 0·011	0·005	0·040	0·032	0·000	− 0·129
106	− 0·121	− 0·002	− 0·061	− 0·062	− 0·048	0·082	− 0·106	0·064
107	0·101	− 0·030	0·036	− 0·088	− 0·170	− 0·024	0·005	0·110
108	− 0·134	0·115	− 0·043	− 0·123	− 0·073	0·094	− 0·115	0·138
109	0·093	− 0·052	0·185	0·099	− 0·017	− 0·050	0·094	0·150
110	0·009	0·132	− 0·007	− 0·005	0·075	− 0·037	0·181	0·048

116

Item	Class	Occupation	Age	Marital Status	P	E	N	L
Females								
111	− 0·072	0·094	0·169	− 0·025	− 0·088	0·067	0·095	0·100
112	− 0·120	0·018	− 0·145	0·047	− 0·060	0·095	− 0·046	− 0·071
113	− 0·022	− 0·010	− 0·018	− 0·015	0·029	− 0·003	0·118	− 0·123
114	− 0·078	0·094	− 0·185	− 0·019	0·043	0·050	− 0·143	0·029
115	0·151	− 0·266	0·063	− 0·075	0·060	− 0·044	− 0·121	0·005
116	− 0·112	0·058	− 0·357	− 0·164	0·115	0·051	0·142	− 0·199
117	0·064	− 0·066	− 0·009	0·104	0·050	− 0·168	0·088	− 0·084
118	0·040	− 0·107	0·098	0·045	0·040	− 0·246	0·240	0·004
119	0·020	0·114	− 0·091	0·070	0·047	0·017	0·032	− 0·172
120	− 0·137	0·058	− 0·105	0·038	0·106	0·135	0·144	− 0·136
121	− 0·101	0·132	− 0·161	− 0·081	0·093	− 0·071	0·204	0·005
122	− 0·020	− 0·122	0·000	0·025	0·013	0·050	0·055	− 0·102
123	− 0·015	− 0·018	0·134	0·204	0·014	− 0·020	0·038	0·023
124	− 0·024	− 0·011	0·060	− 0·007	0·108	− 0·091	0·191	− 0·069
125	0·094	0·101	0·167	0·004	0·025	− 0·090	0·225	0·055
126	0·030	− 0·038	0·006	0·007	0·053	− 0·162	0·113	0·094
127	− 0·067	0·047	0·042	− 0·152	− 0·040	0·000	0·096	0·161
128	− 0·021	0·058	0·226	0·011	− 0·074	− 0·018	0·008	0·097
129	0·006	0·124	− 0·110	− 0·073	0·089	− 0·013	0·143	0·006
130	0·030	− 0·013	0·037	0·020	0·032	0·136	− 0·046	0·143
131	− 0·072	− 0·005	− 0·025	0·004	− 0·020	0·111	0·111	0·045
132	0·014	− 0·014	0·106	- 0·055	− 0·062	0·018	0·161	0·144
133	0·157	− 0·019	0·208	0·125	− 0·023	0·046	0·069	0·119
134	0·013	0·185	0·141	0·125	− 0·145	− 0·090	− 0·039	0·249
135	0·002	− 0·088	0·101	− 0·009	− 0·051	− 0·063	0·070	0·114
136	− 0·069	− 0·010	0·083	− 0·019	0·216	0·010	0·034	0·097
137	− 0·049	0·120	0·143	0·064	0·016	0·118	0·026	0·012
138	− 0·068	0·022	− 0·036	0·012	− 0·022	0·184	0·023	− 0·079
139	0·058	0·110	0·151	0·136	0·058	− 0·048	0·109	0·010
140	0·111	0·058	0·251	0·077	0·024	0·011	0·029	0·046
141	− 0·061	0·093	− 0·041	− 0·034	− 0·032	0·142	− 0·148	0·014
142	0·040	0·048	0·267	0·169	− 0·082	0·036	− 0·012	0·059
143	0·048	0·042	0·062	0·042	− 0·121	− 0·041	0·146	0·138
144	− 0·025	0·036	− 0·032	0·030	0·130	0·061	− 0·012	− 0·095
145	− 0·048	0·054	0·171	0·155	− 0·004	− 0·029	0·124	− 0·016
146	0·008	0·034	0·251	0·110	− 0·124	− 0·100	0·110	0·053
147	0·122	− 0·047	0·115	0·039	− 0·024	− 0·070	0·084	0·129
148	0·144	− 0·041	0·106	0·001	0·009	− 0·094	0·034	0·052
149	0·113	− 0·214	0·278	0·030	0·073	0·012	− 0·029	− 0·067
150	0·035	0·013	0·192	0·055	− 0·009	− 0·106	0·209	− 0·066
151	− 0·069	0·062	− 0·143	− 0·053	0·105	0·097	− 0·005	− 0·150
152	− 0·110	0·090	− 0·126	− 0·080	0·115	0·007	0·022	− 0·160
153	− 0·023	0·093	− 0·126	0·034	0·047	0·140	− 0·002	− 0·064
154	0·015	− 0·057	− 0·389	− 0·098	0·026	0·131	− 0·056	− 0·163
155	0·133	− 0·105	0·101	− 0·034	0·150	− 0·109	0·255	− 0·203
156	0·104	− 0·165	0·513	0·139	− 0·247	− 0·112	− 0·180	0·167
157	− 0·062	0·109	− 0·196	− 0·116	− 0·066	0·225	− 0·015	− 0·062
158	0·126	− 0·023	0·234	0·022	0·013	− 0·073	0·164	0·015

In order to demonstrate that the patterns of correlations are meaningful, the following method was adopted. Extraverted men and women should show similar patterns of correlations over the items; so should introverted men and women. The same argument applied to the other columns; if men and women agree on the pattern of item correlations, then we may confidently assume that the results are significant and probably meaningful. Accordingly, product–moment correlations were run between men and women for each of the eight columns in table 3.9, with results shown in table 3.10.

Table 3.10 *M–F correlations for personality scales, social class, occupation, age and marital status over columns in table 3.9*

	M–F correlation
Social class	0·52
Occupation	0·47
Age	0·71
Marital status	0·44
Psychoticism	0·74
Extraversion	0·57
Neuroticism	0·55
Lie scale	0·64

It will be seen that all the correlation coefficients are highly significant, indicating that men and women of given personality have similar attitude patterns. This seems to justify our procedure, and we will next proceed to give a coherent picture of the sexual attitudes characteristic of different personality types. By 'coherent' in this connection is meant simply that an attempt has been made to put together similar items, even though in order of correlation they might not be very close together; all details are, of course, contained in table 3.9, to which serious readers are referred. Many of the conclusions are borne out by items having correlations slightly below the arbitrary value of 0·12 which was chosen to exclude items with lower coefficients; while inclusion of these items would have strengthened our case, no effort has been made to round out the picture in this manner.

Let us consider first of all subjects with high *P* scores, as opposed to subjects with low *P* scores. Male high scorers, first of all, are clearly opposed to current morality and customs. They wish to

118

do away with marriage;(4) they favour polygamy; they believe it is all right to seduce a person old enough to know what she is doing; they consider premarital sex all right. High scorers have a realistic, not an idealistic, view of sex. They believe that romantic love is an illusion; they don't think it disgusting to see animals having sex; they believe in taking pleasure where they can find it; they believe that tenderness in sex is not important, and that faithfulness in marriage is silly; they would not be disturbed if their sex partner had sex with someone else. High scorers are very permissive. They believe that pornography should be freely available; they don't object to four-letter swear words being used in mixed company; they are not disturbed by seeing necking in public; they don't think sex orgies are disgusting; they consider sex play among children to be harmless; they do not believe that the opposite sex will respect you more if you are not too familiar with them; they do not believe that men are more selfish in their love-making than women – although they also believe that most men are sex-mad. When it comes to personal history and feelings, however, there is a curious contrast with this tough-minded façade. High scorers can't stand people touching them; they claim to have been deprived sexually; they prefer sex partners several years older; they feel nervous with the opposite sex.

Females have similar patterns. They too wish to do away with marriage, opt for polygamy, and consider premarital sex all right. They too believe that romantic love is an illusion, don't object to the use of four-letter swear words in mixed company and are not disturbed by their sex partner having sex with someone else; they don't believe that the opposite sex will respect you more for being not too familiar. In addition, they hold certain other views which help to round off the picture. They do not consider virginity important; they are not keen on babies; they had their first intercourse early; they believe that sex is for personal pleasure, not only for reproduction, and that females have equally strong sex drives as males; they get excited sexually very easily. These items all refer to impersonal, physical sexual satisfaction. In agreement with this preference is their endorsement of so-called 'perverted' practices. There is nothing they would not do with anyone; they could do anything with the person they love; there is nothing they do only to please their sex partner; no form of love-making is disgusting to them. Interestingly enough, such women have felt like humiliating their sex partners, and are attracted by people of their own sex. They have not suffered from frigidity, but have felt guilty about sex experiences, and feel nervous with the opposite sex; here again we find this curious contradiction between strong permissive sexuality and personal feeling. All in all, high P scorers emerge as advocates of impersonal, permissive sexual practices, the abandonment of social rules and laws concerning marriage and the other aspects of sexual behaviour, and an 'all's fair in love and war' attitude; one might be tempted to call this the Don Juan syndrome. It is interesting to note the absence of items signifying satisfaction; if anything there is some indication of nervousness and even guilt. The total picture is very similar to that found in our previous research, and confirms results there reported on a quite different sample.

We next turn to the attitudes endorsed by male extraverts, as opposed to introverts. First of all, they are clearly able to get on well with the opposite sex. Extraverts have many dates; have many friends of the opposite sex; sex contacts have never been a problem for them; they feel at ease with the opposite sex and don't find it hard to talk to women; they are not nervous with the opposite sex. Extraverts are highly sexed. They had intercourse early; have strong sexual desires; get sexually excited very easily; think about sex almost every day; are sometimes overpowered by sexual feelings; are not afraid of sexual relationships; have no difficulty in expressing strong sexual feelings. The sexual attitude of extraverts is rather aggressive and overt. They usually feel aggressive with their sex partner; they sometimes feel like scratching and biting their sex partner; they have been involved with more than one sex affair at the same time; they consider the dual standard of morality natural; they consider absolute faithfulness in marriage silly and would take part in an orgy if invited; hedonistic to the last, they believe in taking their pleasures where they find them. Their sexual development has clearly been rather more healthy than that of the high P scorers. They have discussed sex with their parents; they are not embarrassed to talk about sex; their religious beliefs are not against sex; they don't mind people touching them; they don't consider reading 'girlie' magazines to be a sign of failure to achieve adult sex attitudes.

Female extraverts show a very similar pattern. They have strong sexual desires; don't feel sexually less competent than their friends; consider themselves sexually attractive; have had many dates, many

120

friends of the opposite sex, and for them sex contacts have never been a problem. They love physical contact with people of the opposite sex, feel at ease with them, and there is nothing they would not do with anyone. They get excited sexually very easily, have not been inhibited by their parents, are not nervous with the opposite sex, don't mind being touched by people, and don't do things only to please their sex partner. Extraverted women clearly have no inhibitions; they always make love in the nude, consider the human body a pleasing sight, would take part in an orgy, prefer to have intercourse often, make lots of vocal noises during intercourse, are not disturbed by seeing necking in public, and could do anything with a person they love. They are not embarrassed to talk about sex, do not consider sex jokes disgusting, feel that sometimes a woman should be sexually aggressive and prefer to make love with the lights on and not under cover. Extraverts, both male and female, are clearly of the 'healthy animal' type, unembarrassed and uninhibited, but without the anti-social, somewhat abnormal, conflictful admixture shown by the high P scorer.

When we turn to the high N males, there is clear evidence of considerable abnormality and disturbance. They find thoughts about sex disturbing, they worry a lot about sex, feel nervous with the opposite sex, have felt guilty about sex experiences and cannot discuss sexual matters with their wives. Yet they are highly sexed. They confess to strong sexual desires, declare that sometimes sexual feelings overpower them, have sometimes been afraid of themselves for what they might do sexually, can think of nothing but satisfaction when excited, and consider sex far and away their greatest pleasure. Physical attraction is extremely important to them, sex thoughts almost drive them crazy, yet thinking about sex makes them very nervous. They get excited sexually very easily, believe in taking pleasures where they find them and consider few things more important than sex. However, there is also considerable dissatisfaction with their love life. Conscience bothers them too much; they are not satisfied with their sex life; something is lacking in their sex life; their love life has been disappointing; they have had some bad sexual experiences; parents' influence has inhibited them sexually; they have been deprived sexually. There is an aura of abnormality about their desires. They have sometimes felt hostile to their sex partner; are excited by the thought of an illicit relationship; have sometimes felt like humiliating their

121

sex partner; sometimes have problems in controlling their feelings; find the thought of a coloured sex partner particularly exciting; have been bothered by perverted thoughts; prefer a sex partner several years older; usually feel aggressive about their sex partner; consider that the need for birth control upsets love-making because it makes everything so cold-blooded and planned. In addition, they believe that women often use sex to gain all sorts of advantages; wish that women would be more forthcoming sexually; would protect children from contact with sex; consider virginity a girl's most important possession and do some things only to please sex partner.

Women show a very similar pattern of conflict between strong sexual desires and equally strong inhibitions. Conscience bothers them too much; thinking about sex makes them nervous; they have strong sexual feelings but can't express them satisfactorily; sexual feelings are sometimes unpleasant and they often wish that men would be less demanding sexually. Yet when excited they think of nothing but satisfaction; consider physical sex the most important part of marriage; like to look at sexy pictures. They find straight sex unsatisfactory; sometimes feel like humiliating their sex partners; feel hostile to their sex partners; usually feel aggressive with their sex partner; consider most men sex-mad; prefer a partner several years older; are bothered by perverted thoughts; are embarrassed to talk about sex; find thoughts about sex disturbing; and consider the naked body not a pleasing sight. They are afraid of sexual relationships; prefer their partner to dictate the rules of the sexual game; had some bad sexual experiences when young; have suffered from frigidity; have felt guilty about sex experiences; have been inhibited by parents' influence; and didn't learn facts of life until late. They worry a lot about sex, feel nervous with the opposite sex, feel sexually less competent than their friends, are afraid of sexual relationships, find it hard to talk to people of the opposite sex, and admit to strong inhibiting influences. Something is lacking in their sex life; sex contacts have usually been a problem; there are some things they would not do with anyone, and some things which they do only to please their sex partners. They did not learn the facts of life until quite old; they are disgusted by seeing animals having sex in the street; consider self-relief dangerous; consider tenderness the most important quality in sex; and believe that in matters of sex women always seem to come off second best. The word that comes to mind in characterising high N scorers is 'crazy mixed up kids' – although of course these are not kids, but grown-up people demonstrating their conflicts and complexes.

Little is known about the personality patterns associated with high and low L scorers respectively, although one would expect high L scorers to have very orthodox, socially approved views and attitudes, and to deny any thoughts of perverted practices and other socially undesirable habits. Taking the male high L scorers first, we find that this is precisely what they show. They are not overpowered by sexual feelings; they have no problems in controlling sexual feelings; they don't believe in taking pleasures where they find them; they would be bothered if the woman they married were not a virgin; they had their first intercourse late; they have not been involved in more than one sex affair at any one time; they never had many dates and sex behaviour never caused them any trouble; the strength of inhibiting influences is high. They never felt like humiliating their sex partners; never felt hostile to them; never felt like biting and scratching their partner during intercourse; have never suffered from impotence; don't get pleasant feelings from touching their sexual parts. They would refuse to see a blue film, read a pornographic book or take part in an orgy; they would also object to the use of four-letter swear words in mixed company. They oppose premarital sex, believe that pornographic writings should be censored, that young people should not learn about sex through their own experience, that women should not be sexually aggressive and that young people should not be allowed out all night without being closely checked. They would protect children from contact with sex, consider absolute faithfulness in marriage not silly, do not believe that females have such strong sexual desires as males and consider it right that the man should be the dominant partner in a sex relationship. They would need to love a woman in order to have intercourse, consider the reading of 'girlie' magazines to suggest a failure to achieve adult attitudes to sex and believe that we should not experiment with sex before marriage. They find the thought of a sex orgy disgusting, do not consider it all right to seduce a person old enough to know what she is doing and believe that sexual permissiveness threatens to undermine the foundations of society. They do not believe that most men are sex-mad, and do not agree that the pill should be universally available.

123

The women share this highly conservative pattern. Female high L scorers approve of the 'double standard' of sexual morality; they believe that virginity is a girl's most valuable possession; they would prohibit pornographic writings; they object to the use of four-letter swear words in mixed company. They deny that females have as strong a sex drive as males, find the thought of a sex orgy disgusting and believe there should be censorship of plays and films. They feel that the opposite sex will not respect you if you are too familiar, would be bothered if the person they married were not a virgin and would oppose a law in favour of polygamy. Group sex does not appeal to them, and they believe that sexual permissiveness undermines the foundations of civilised society. They would reject a highly pornographic book, would refuse to see a blue film and believe that the pill should not be universally available. Sex without love is considered highly unsatisfactory; they do not understand homosexuals; the thought of an illicit sexual relationship does not excite them. They have never felt like humiliating their sex partner; don't feel like scratching and biting their sex partners; have never suffered from frigidity; never feel hostile to their sex partner; had first intercourse at a late age; do not think about sex every day. They do not think that physical sex is the most important part of marriage; would prefer to have intercourse only rarely; consider sex not all that important to them; did not have bad sex experiences when young; are not overpowered by sex feelings and need conditions to be just right to get excited sexually. Their sex partners satisfy all their physical needs completely and there are some things they only do in order to please their sex partners. Tenderness is the most important quality in a sex relationship to them and they feel that it is better not to have sex relations until you are married. These views are very conservative and this is in good agreement with the fact that Wilson (1973) has reported positive correlations between conservatism and L scores. He also found a positive correlation between L scores and tender-mindedness and the attitudes summarised above agree with this finding too. In the sexual realm, high L scorers are tender-minded conservatives, which puts them into the religious quadrant (people with positive religious beliefs tend to collect in this quadrant). In agreement with this, Wilson found the highest correlation with L in his religious–puritanical factor.

In looking at these brief and pictorial descriptions of the main results of this study, it should be borne in mind that the statements made are relative, not absolute. When it is said that 'extraverts believe ...', this simply means that more extraverts than introverts hold this belief; it is quite possible that the belief is not in fact held by a majority of extraverts. Thus if 25 per cent of extraverts and 10 per cent of introverts believe that big-breasted women are more attractive, then this belief would have been cited as characteristic of extraverts, although, in fact, only one extravert in four might hold it. This is therefore, strictly speaking, an inaccurate way of describing the results, but it obviates considerable complexities of description that would otherwise be needed, and this warning, together with the actual figures given in table 3.9, will, it is hoped, make it unlikely that any misunderstanding will arise.

In addition to correlating the four personality scales with each of the items in the questionnaire, correlations were calculated between these items and the age of the subjects, their married status, their social class (working class v. middle class) and their occupation. Subjects were asked whether their family was working-class or middle-class and they were asked to give their occupation (housewives giving that of their husbands); in addition, they were asked to classify the occupation as higher professional/administrative, lower professional/administrative, clerical, skilled manual, semi-skilled manual or unskilled. A positive correlation in the table indicates that the 'Yes' answer to an item is positively related to older age, married status, middle class, low occupational status. As a result, the signs of the correlations for social class and for occupational status are opposite to each other; this should not prove confusing as in the table the heading of each column indicates the direction of the correlation.

The correlations are not large, rarely exceeding 0·5; this is of course only to be expected by virtue of the low reliability of single questions. Statistical significance is not very helpful in view of the fact that the numbers of subjects are so large as to make even quite small values of coefficients significant, and the additional fact that, with so many items being correlated with so many social indicants, the total number of correlations is so large that many would be apparently 'significant' by chance. We will lay emphasis, as before, on congruence of values from different items tapping the same general attitude. In addition, we have correlated the various columns

125

SEX AND PERSONALITY

in table 3.9; the results of this calculation are given in table 3.11, with results for males being given above the leading diagonal and those for females below the leading diagonal. The leading diagonal itself is made up of the correlations for each of the indicants between males and females; this set of figures shows to what extent high correlations for a given item and a particular indicant are produced by both men and women, and to what extent low correlations are produced by both sexes. (These correlations have already been abstracted in table 3.10.) The table has been extended to do the same thing for our four personality scales.

Table 3.11 *Correlations between columns in table 3.9 for four social indicants and four personality traits: values above the leading diagonal are for males, those below for females; values in the leading diagonal (in italics) are correlations between corresponding columns for males and females*

	1	2	3	4	5	6	7	8
1 Working class	*0·52*	−0·53	0·36	0·22	0·03	−0·35	−0·14	0·20
2 Middle-class occupation	−0·55	*0·47*	−0·43	−0·38	0·20	0·39	0·18	−0·24
3 Age	0·50	−0·35	*0·71*	0·58	−0·14	−0·44	0·10	0·59
4 Married status	0·35	−0·14	0·61	*0·44*	−0·28	−0·26	0·06	0·45
5 P	−0·07	0·14	−0·38	−0·24	*0·74*	−0·02	−0·02	−0·35
6 E	−0·37	0·04	−0·49	−0·28	−0·03	*0·57*	0·03	−0·55
7 N	0·20	0·15	0·11	0·22	0·27	−0·52	*0·55*	−0·15
8 L	0·20	−0·04	0·60	0·30	−0·56	−0·28	−0·09	*0·64*

Let us first look at the leading diagonal. Clearly values for men and women correlate reasonably highly together; in other words, what is true of men is mostly also true of women. The highest values are obtained by the P scale, among the personality measures, and by age among the social indicants. Marital status, occupation and social class give less clear-cut evidence for male–female agreement, but the other three personality scales show reasonably high male–female agreement. As regards the values in the body of the table, we have divided this up into four quadrants. Two of these represent the intercorrelations between the social indicants and the personality scales, respectively; the other two represent the cross-correlations between indicants and scales for men and women respectively. Taking the personality scales first, we see that P and E show opposite patterns for both sexes; so do E and N for the women, but not for the men. L and E show opposite patterns for both

126

sexes, but more so for the men. When we turn to the indicants we find the expected negative relation between class and occupation, owing to the reverse labelling of the two columns. Higher social class goes with older age, and slightly with marital status. Age and marital status are, of course, also quite highly correlated.

Looking at the cross-correlations, we find that E shows a pattern of answering similar to that of the working class, and to that of young people. P too shows this tendency to respond like young people. N shows no noteworthy correlations, but L clearly produces responses similar to those of older and married people. These results are not unexpected. Scores on E and P decline with age, while those on L increase (Eysenck and Eysenck 1975); so far, the results in our table are predictable. However, N usually declines with age, too; yet the correlations with age in the table, while very low, are positive instead of negative. This table demonstrates the complexity of the interweaving of causal factors in the production of attitudes towards sex; in interpreting our data, this complexity must always be kept in mind.

We will now turn to a discussion of the attitudes that characterise old as opposed to young subjects, working-class as opposed to middle-class subjects and married as opposed to single subjects. In this discussion, it should always be borne in mind that we are dealing with the results of correlational procedures, i.e. that comparisons are strictly relative. When we say that old people prefer to have intercourse less frequently, this statement is true (and meaningful) only in comparison with the younger groups in this study. On an absolute scale, older subjects might still prefer to have intercourse quite frequently; it is only by comparing them with the younger people who wish to have intercourse even more frequently that we arrive at our conclusion. Similarly, the fact that older subjects find orgies more frequently 'disgusting' than do younger subjects does not mean that a majority of older subjects holds this view; it may merely mean that a larger minority can be found among the older than among the younger subjects.

With this proviso in mind, we will first look at the attitudes of the older subjects, as compared with the younger ones. We would expect the libido of older subjects, both men and women, to be weaker than that of younger subjects, and this is indeed the case. They prefer to have intercourse less frequently; their habitual sex desire is weaker; they do not think about sex every day; they do not get excited sexually very easily; sexual feelings do not overpower them; they do not feel like scratching and biting their partner during intercourse; it takes a lot to get them excited sexually; they do not enjoy petting; they can take sex and they can leave it alone; they think only rarely about sex. In addition, we would expect older people to hold less 'permissive' and more conservative, 'old fashioned' views concerning morality and sexual behaviour; this too is what is found. Older subjects disapprove of blue films and pornographic books, and find orgies disgusting; they consider the reading of 'girlie' magazines to indicate a failure to achieve adult attitudes towards sex. Similarly, people who attend 'strip-tease' shows are considered sexually abnormal. They deplore premarital sex, consider it right that the man should be the dominant partner in the sexual relationship, believe that there are too many immoral plays on television, consider virginity a girl's most valuable possession, believe that sexual permissiveness undermines the entire foundation of civilised society, consider impersonal sex highly unsatisfactory, don't feel it would be right to seduce a person old enough to know what he or she is doing and believe that females do not have such strong sexual desires as males. In addition, older people seem to be more 'inhibited' than younger ones. They were older at first intercourse, consider that their parents' influence has inhibited them, do not find it easy to tell sex partners what they like and do not like about their love-making; they admit to strong inhibitions, find some forms of love-making disgusting, prefer intercourse under bedclothes and with the lights off, don't think they could do anything with a person, even if they loved that person, consciously try to keep sex thoughts out of their minds, don't like to look at sexy pictures, would particularly protect their children from contacts with sex, get sexually aroused at night, never in the daytime, and do not make lots of vocal noises during intercourse. Sex is not all that important to them; they believe that the opposite sex will respect you more if you are not too familiar with them; there is a feeling that they have been deprived sexually. The men do not prefer a sex partner several years older and they do not believe that most men are sex-mad. Women find male genitals aesthetically unpleasing; prefer the partner to dictate the rules of the sexual game; wish that men would be less demanding sexually; consider that men are more selfish in their love-making than women; and believe that in matters of sex women always seem to come off second-best. Most of these attitudes fit in pretty well with the stereotype of the 'square', inhibited, non-swinging type of person the young 'swingers' imagine their parents to be; it is noteworthy, however, that there is little hint of any less satisfaction with their sex lives among the older subjects. It would be interesting to discover whether the differences between the generations are due to age by itself, i.e. whether attitudes of the older subjects have actually changed as they grew older, or whether the attitudes of the older subjects simply mirror a different generation's patterns of upbringing. If the former hypothesis is true, then the 'young' subjects of our experiment would be expected to grow into the typical attitude patterns of our 'old' subjects in the course of time. If the latter hypothesis is true, then no change would be expected. Only a longitudinal study can answer questions of this type.

Married people (as contrasted with unmarried people not living together with any particular person, but having had sexual experience) do not differ on very many items from unmarried people and the few items that do show significant correlations do not make any very clear pattern, other than duplicating some of the features of the comparison between old and young subjects. They do not find it easy to tell sex partners what they like and do not like about their love-making, and they cannot discuss sexual matters with their husbands; the women are embarrassed to talk about sex. The need for birth control upsets their love-making, but they do not consider physical sex the most important part of marriage. The men are not satisfied with their sex life, and the women feel that something is lacking in their sex life – this would sound like a vote of lack of confidence in the institution of marriage, were it not for the fact that the correlations in question are not very large! Married people are non-permissive, oppose orgies, wife-swapping, blue films, voyeurism, sexy pictures, premarital intercourse, masturbation and the young learning about sex through their own experience. Virginity is important and sex should be for purposes of reproduction, not for personal pleasure. Marriage being a traditional institution, it is not unexpected that those who are married tend towards traditional values and attitudes; it is perhaps somewhat unexpected that the correlations found are not larger and more numerous.

The class and occupational comparisons show the working-class groups as more 'earthy' and the middle-class groups as more 'moral' in their attitudes, which is perhaps not surprising in view of the general finding of greater degrees of 'tough-mindedness' in working-class groups and of 'tender-mindedness' in middle-class groups (Eysenck 1954, Wilson 1973). Working-class groups are not averse to group sex, wife-swapping, masturbation, perversions, orgies; they consider physical sex the most important part of marriage. They would not mind if sex partner had sexual relations with someone else, consider sex more exciting with strangers, consider sex far and away their greatest pleasure and believe that physical factors in their sex partners are far more important than psychological ones. They have strong sex drives, believe in taking their pleasures where they find them, enjoy pornography, would watch people making love, don't object to the use of four-letter swear words in mixed company, would find a coloured sex partner particularly exciting, have sexual fantasies involving flogging, don't mind seeing necking in public and would enjoy watching their usual sex partner having intercourse with someone else. Permissiveness clearly is not a middle-class invention, although it should be borne in mind that many of these items have very low incidence, so that our caveat about the interpretation of correlations as purely relativistic indicators applies doubly in connection with such items as watching one's usual sex partner having intercourse with someone else or finding a coloured sex partner particularly exciting.

This concludes our discussion of the correlations between sex attitudes and our various social indicants. There is very little in the literature with which to compare our findings. There are data in Kinsey's work on the incidence of certain types of behaviour in relation to age and class, but Kinsey was not concerned with attitudes as such, and attitudes may be something very different from actual behaviour. Women may take part in fellatio, but may not enjoy it at all and have very negative attitudes towards such practices (Eysenck 1971b); in such cases, knowledge of only the attitudes or only the actual behaviour gives information that is essentially one-sided, and such information should be complemented by knowledge of those aspects of the total situation that tap a different class of components. Our data provide a beginning of information in this complex and difficult field. The data tend to form meaningful patterns, and we have tried to indicate the sorts of patterns that are suggested by the figures in the table. These patterns cut across those discussed in relation to personality variables, and to obtain a general picture both sets of data should be borne in mind. The facts so disclosed may suggest testable hypotheses to future workers in this field which may admit of a simple design to test their adequacy or otherwise; while several hypotheses were put forward for testing in this study, the whole field is so new that these 'hypotheses' would perhaps better be called 'hunches' than anything deriving from a well-established theory permitting of quantitative deductions.

Another scale was administered to the same population, namely the Reiss Permissiveness Scale. This premarital sexual permissiveness scale constructed by Reiss (1967) has the properties of a Guttman-type scale, and has twelve items. In this study we have used the shorter five-item 'universal scale' consisting of items 5, 7, 10, 11 and 12; it appears from the original book that little is lost by thus shortening the scale. The items deal respectively with the following questions to which the subject is required to answer on a six-point scale, from strongly agree (1) through medium (2) and slight agreement (3) to slight (4) and medium disagreement (5) to strong disagreement (6). Item 1 states that petting is acceptable before marriage when the subject is engaged to be married; item 2 states that petting is acceptable when subject has strong affection for the partner; item 3 states that sexual relations are acceptable before marriage when subject is in love; item 4 states that sexual relations are acceptable before marriage when subject feels strong affection for the partner; and item 5 states that sexual relations are acceptable before marriage even if subject does not feel particularly affectionate towards the partner. Each subject answers the scale only for himself/herself, and not from both the male and female points of view, as in Reiss's original study.

Table 3.12 reports the means and standard deviations of male and female subjects separately for the five permissiveness scales and the four personality scales. From the nature of the scale, we would expect that scores would increase monotonically (implying greater disagreement with the permissive wording of the question from the first to the fifth item), and this is indeed so. We would expect males to be more permissive than females, and again this is so on all items; all the comparison show differences that are highly significant statistically. Women clearly are less permissive than men on this inventory. (Women also seem to be less agreed on their opinions; the standard deviations of the women are significantly greater on all items except the last than the standard

131

deviations of the men. This may be an artefact of the different scale positions; values around the 3 and 4 positions are more likely to have larger standard deviations.)

Table 3.12 *Means and standard deviations of five permissiveness scales from the Reiss Courtship Inventory*

Item	Males	Females
1	1·17 ± 0·53	1·38 ± 1·00
2	1·28 ± 0·74	1·51 ± 1·10
3	1·49 ± 1·23	1·71 ± 1·41
4	1·79 ± 1·41	2·41 ± 1·67
5	2·82 ± 1·80	4·01 ± 1·83

The correlations between the five items in the Reiss scale are given in table 3.13 as are their correlations with P, E, N and L. As expected, the intercorrelations of the five Reiss items follow the superdiagonal form; i.e., correlations decrease the further they are from the superdiagonal. This is true for both men and women, and is a necessary property of a scale that has Guttman properties. All the intercorrelations are of course fully significant statistically. The correlations with personality scales are similar for males and females and give a clear picture. P correlates positively with permissiveness, with correlations much higher for the questions involving premarital sexual intercourse; the correlations quoted are negative because high scores on the scales signify disagreements with the permissive content of the item. L correlates negatively with permissiveness, with correlations much higher for the questions involving premarital sexual intercourse. N shows hardly any correlations at all and correlations with E are slight but on the whole indicate a permissive attitude. These correlations are all in good agreement with predictions to be derived from our previous work.

Of the subjects questioned, 241 were married to each other, or in a number of cases were living with each other without being married. The existence of these couples enables us to provide some evidence for or against assortative mating. It is well known that assortative mating with respect to intelligence is quite marked, approximating a correlation of 0·6 between spouses; with respect to personality, the evidence suggests little or no assortative mating, except for spouses with some degree of psychiatric disability

(Eysenck 1975a). There is little evidence regarding attitudes, but it might be surmised that as attitudes are easier to change than largely innate personality qualities, higher correlations between spouses would be found with respect to sexual permissiveness, although of course it would not be clear whether these correlations were due to true assortative mating, or whether they were due to a tendency towards agreement consequent upon marriage. The correlations between spouses for the five permissiveness scales are as follows: 0·11, 0·22, 0·44, 0·27; all except the first of these are statistically significant at the ⟨0·01 level. There clearly is evidence for homogamy here with items 3 and 4 providing the highest figures.

Table 3.13 *Intercorrelations of five courtship scales and correlations with four personality scales. A single asterisk indicates statistical significance at the 5 per cent level and double asterisks at the 1 per cent level*

	1	2	3	4	5	P	E	N	L
			Females						
Males									
1	–	0·69	0·32	0·32	0·26	−0·07	0·03	−0·01	0·06
2	0·71	–	0·56	0·54	0·36	−0·09*	0·01	−0·04	0·14**
3	0·48	0·58	–	0·85	0·51	−0·15**	−0·09*	−0·05	0·19**
4	0·39	0·59	0·78	–	0·66	−0·21**	−0·11*	−0·06	0·20**
5	0·26	0·38	0·47	0·65	–	−0·20**	−0·11*	−0·05	0·18**
P	0·03	−0·05	−0·22**	−0·23**	−0·25**				
E	−0·09	−0·09*	−0·01	−0·04	−0·08				
N	0·10*	0·02	−0·02	−0·02	−0·02				
L	0·08	0·13**	0·22**	0·19**	0·17**				

In addition to the Sex Attitudes Scale and the Permissiveness Scale, a Sexual Behaviour Scale was also applied to the subjects of the experiment. This scale is reproduced below; it differs from an earlier version (Eysenck 1972), which contained more 'low-level' sexual behaviour items, because in this sample all subjects had sexual experience with intercourse, and would therefore not have been discriminated from each other by these items. The twelve items included are not in ascending order; this arrangement was intentional as an ascending order might produce artificial conformity with the construction of the scale. The scale here printed is that for females; that for males requires suitable alteration.

Sexual Behaviour Scale

Here are brief descriptions of sexual behaviour patterns in which people indulge. There are three possible answers for each item; please put a cross (x) in the appropriate category.

Column 1 means: 'I have done this and enjoyed it'
Column 2 means: 'I have done this, but didn't like it'
Column 3 means: 'I have never done this, but would like to do it'

If you do *not* endorse any of these three categories, we would take this to mean that you have *not* done this, and *don't* think you would enjoy doing it.

	Have done and enjoyed	Have done and didn't like	Have not done but would like to do
1 One-minute continuous lip kissing	———	———	———
2 Having genitals kissed by a male	———	———	———
3 Sexual intercourse, man above woman	———	———	———
4 Having naked breasts fondled	———	———	———
5 Kissing male genitals	———	———	———
6 Sexual intercourse, man behind woman	———	———	———
7 Having nipples kissed and/or bitten by male	———	———	———
8 Mutual handling of genitals	———	———	———
9 Mutual kissing of genitals ('69')	———	———	———
10 Sexual intercourse in positions other than 3 or 6	———	———	———
11 Intercourse with more than one person present	———	———	———
12 Intercourse with several people around ('group sex')	———	———	———

Table 3.14 gives the results of the study; it shows means and standard deviations on the three parts of the scale for men and women separately, as well as correlations of scores on the three parts with the eleven sexual attitude factors, with the two sexual attitude superfactors, with masculinity–femininity, and with the personality scales (P, E, N, L). The mean value of the 'Have done and enjoyed' column is slightly higher for men than women.

Table 3.14 *Means and standard deviations of sexual behaviour scale for males and females; also correlations with sexual attitudes scale*

	Have done and enjoyed (1)		Have done and disliked (2)		Would like to do (3)	
	M	F	M	F	M	F
1 Permissiveness	0·18	0·36	−0·04	−0·20	0·10	0·08
2 Satisfaction	0·31	0·33	−0·06	−0·20	−0·33	−0·20
3 Neurotic sex	−0·15	−0·03	−0·02	0·03	0·22	0·04
4 Impersonal sex	0·26	0·23	−0·09	−0·02	0·19	0·20
5 Pornography	0·33	0·40	−0·18	−0·17	0·08	0·10
6 Sexual shyness	−0·26	−0·20	0·09	0·10	0·25	0·18
7 Prudishness	−0·39	−0·44	0·20	0·31	0·06	−0·02
9 Disgust	−0·36	−0·51	0·24	0·44	0·02	0·04
10 Excitement	0·40	0·51	−0·28	−0·38	0·02	0·01
11 Physical sex	0·29	0·36	−0·11	−0·23	0·00	0·01
12 Aggressive sex	0·21	0·32	−0·04	−0·15	−0·03	−0·04
SF1 Libido	0·38	0·45	−0·14	−0·24	0·16	0·13
SP2 Satisfaction	0·49	0·52	−0·17	−0·39	−0·32	−0·15
Masculinity–Femininity	0·32	0·38	−0·17	−0·17	0·20	0·17
P	−0·04	0·09	0·06	−0·02	−0·12	0·08
E	0·18	0·09	−0·01	−0·05	0·10	−0·01
N	−0·03	−0·06	0·01	0·08	0·02	0·03
L	−0·14	−0·06	0·03	0·08	0·20	−0·07

Means
| Males | 8·92±2·16 | | 0·21±0·60 | | 1·37±1·71 | |
| Females | 8·53±2·13 | | 0·76±1·21 | | 0·56±1·08 | |

Figure 3.2 gives the actual percentage values for men and women for the items in the 'have done and enjoyed' column. Items 1, 3, 4, 7 and 8 are all around the 95 per cent level, and there seemed little point in separating them out; none of the differences are statistically significant. Consequently, they have been designated as 'Base level: Intercourse', and grouped together at the 95 per cent level for both men and women. (There are no meaningful sex differences on these items.) Of interest in the curves shown in figure 3.2 are the sex differences for later items, which, although not large in absolute terms, are quite meaningful and mostly significant statistically. Thus it seems that women have done and enjoyed cunnilingus more than fellatio, while for men the position is reversed. It is not perhaps surprising that passive oral activity is more pleasurable than active, although other explanations of the finding may be possible. For all the later items (6, 9, 11, 12) men have a higher percentage than women; this again is not perhaps surprising. These

figures are of interest mainly on two accounts. They extended earlier work which has mostly concentrated on students and other adolescent and very young groups, to adult men and women. And secondly, they characterise our sample by sexual activity; this descriptive function takes its place beside the description by personality already given.

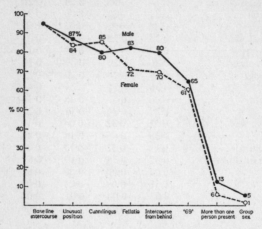

Figure 3.2 *Frequency of different sexual behaviours for male and female participants in experimental study*

There are no English norms with which this figure could be compared. If the random sample of French adults by Simon (1972) can be used as a rough guide for present-day European adults, and if we can accept the veridical nature of their responses, then our sample gives rather similar responses to those of the French group. For mutual kissing of genitals, 60 and 55 per cent respectively of French males and females answer 'Yes', as compared with our 65 and 61 per cent. (These are only for those respondents in the French sample who actually answered the questions; if it is reasonable to assume that most of those refusing to answer had had no experience with this type of conduct, the 'true' figures would be somewhat lower.) For the question regarding intercourse with others present, 10 per cent of males and 1 per cent of females answered in the affirmative, again of those who answered the question at all. Granted that there are many difficulties in making such a comparison, it nevertheless becomes clear that the figures are not too dissimilar to those of our own inquiry.

136

As regards activities which our subjects 'have done and disliked', the distributions are very abnormal and indeed J-shaped; this is clearly brought out by the fact that the standard deviations are much larger than the means. However, clearly there are important sex differences; women have done almost four times as many things they disliked as men; and they are much more variable in this respect. This result is not surprising in view of the fact that it is men who mainly dictate what is to be done in sexual intercourse. As regards things our subjects 'would like to do', again we note a J-shaped distribution, with the men listing almost three times as many items as the women. This result does not seem unexpected, in view of the traditionally greater sexual libido of men, which we have also found in our own work. In view of the abnormal distributions involved statistical tests of significance may be misleading; for the sake of interest, however, we may note that the differences between men and women on all three scales are statistically significant.(5)

When we turn to the correlations of the three scales (which we shall refer to as B.S.$_1$, B.S.$_2$ and B.S.$_3$ (B.S. for behaviour scale) with personality, we find only low correlations (table 3.14). B.S.$_1$ correlates positively with E, negatively with N and L; these correlations are consistent for the two sexes and may therefore, in spite of the low values of the coefficients, represent some factual relationship. B.S.$_2$ does not show any meaningful correlations with the personality scales. B.S.$_3$ has a positive correlation with L, but only for the men; for the women the correlation is very small and negative. This may represent a genuine sex difference, or else a statistical artefact. For P, too, the coefficients for the two sexes have opposite signs; they are probably too low to require interpretation. Altogether, therefore, there is little evidence for any involvement of personality with sexual behaviour as here indexed.

Correlations of the three scales with the attitude scales are congruent for the two sexes and reach quite reasonable values. Taking B.S.$_1$ first, we find that this correlates (positively) with permissiveness, satisfaction, impersonal sex, pornography, excitement, physical sex, aggressive sex, libido, satisfaction and masculinity (in both sexes!). There are negative correlations with neurotic sex, sexual shyness, prudishness and disgust. These correlations all make perfectly good sense if we postulate some general form of sex drive which, if strong, leads to varied sexual performance, as well as attitudes favouring diverse forms of sexual expression. The results contradict an often expressed hypothesis that liking for pornography represents an outlet for sexual desire which is chosen *instead of* more direct sexual activity; our results suggest that pornography represents such an outlet *in addition to* more direct sexual activity.

$B.S._2$ produces much lower correlations; this may in part be due to the small number of positive endorsements in this scale. It does appear, however, that dislike of some sexual activities indulged in is positively correlated with sexual shyness, prudishness and disgust; negative correlations appear with excitement, physical sex, libido, satisfaction, masculinity, pornography, impersonal sex and permissiveness. Again these correlations are easy to understand.

$B.S._3$ shows few even medium-sized correlations. The most marked are perhaps a negative correlation with sexual satisfaction and a positive one with sexual shyness; there is also a positive one with impersonal sex and another with masculinity. On the whole, people who are satisfied with their sex lives have no 'hang-ups' about what they would like to do, whereas shy people do. Here too, the results do not seem to contradict common sense.

It should be noted that the correlations between sexual attitudes and sexual behaviour are not likely to have been caused by personality traits; the correlations between personality and sexual behaviour, as we have noted, are uniformly low and certainly much lower than those between attitudes and behaviour. Even if personality were partialled out from the correlations between attitudes and behaviour, the resulting partial correlations would only be marginally different from those actually found.

It is interesting to note the relationship between sexual behaviour and the two independent superfactors we found in our analysis of the attitude scales. Libido and satisfaction are uncorrelated, but subjects who had done and enjoyed more than their fair share of the activities mentioned in our behaviour scale have high scores on both libido and satisfaction. On the contrary, those who have done some of the things described and disliked them have low scores on both the libido and the satisfaction scales – the women more markedly so than the men. Only with respect to things subjects had not done but would like to do do libido and satisfaction part company; subjects high on libido would, those high on satisfaction would not, want to indulge in these activities.

A special analysis was made of the 'perverted' sex attitudes (11 and/or 12), relating to group sex (Eysenck 1976). Participation of subjects in such perverted practices was significantly correlated with P in females and with E in males; there was also a significant correlation with L (negative) in males. (All the observed differences mentioned above were significant at $p < 0.01$. All other comparisons gave non-significant differences between perverts and non-perverts.) Participation in perverse practices also correlated with the libido factor ($p < 0.001$) and with the masculinity factor ($p < 0.001$) for both males and females, but not with satisfaction. There was also a significant correlation with tough-mindedness (0·05 and 0·01 respectively for men and women). (The meaning of this term is explained in some detail in the next chapter.)

The major finding of interest is that relating to the personality variables. It is not unexpected that perversity relates to P in women, but to E in men; such practices are more usually regarded as 'typically masculine'; a woman would have to be rather 'abnormal' (high P) to behave in a manner regarded as unfeminine. For men, such behaviour being regarded as more nearly normal, indulgence would only require a certain amount of extraversion. There is evidence from other types of conduct (criminality, V.D., etc.) that women who behave in a 'masculine' fashion tend to be characterised by particularly high P scores (Eysenck 1976).

1. Note that while the *factors* of libido and satisfaction correlated significantly for the women, the *scales* did not. We shall take the scale intercorrelations more seriously because of statistical doubts about the accuracy of inter-factor correlation estimates (Guilford 1975).

2. This is possibly the wrong term; scores at the time of 'mating' may have been different from those after years of association.

3. Byrne (1971) has reviewed the evidence on husband–wife similarity, concluding that spouses indicate congruence on a wide variety of ideals and attitudes. Byrne and others (1973) also report a study that is directly relevant to our discussion. Using forty-two married couples, they exposed their subjects to a variety of erotic stimuli (pictorial, verbal, imaginal) and recorded their reactions. Total arousal scores correlated 0·47 between spouses; pornographic judgements (i.e. degree of pornography judged for each stimulus) correlated 0·32. Restrictiveness scores were obtained by summing the pro-censorship responses to questions that advocated forbidding the sexual materials in question to various groups; the correlation for this index was 0·39. Authoritarianism scores were also obtained, and showed a strong correlation ($r = 0.64$). In addition, authoritarians reported greater arousal, and advocated greater restrictiveness. These results are relevant to our own work, as reported in a later chapter, dealing with social attitudes;

authoritarianism correlates positively with both tough-mindedness and conservatism, and it will be seen that the relations reported by Byrne and others are similar to those found by us.

4. This item also figures in the P scale, and its high correlation with that scale is, therefore, partly spurious. However, it is only one item in twenty, and hence only a small part of the correlation is due to this overlap. The same caution applies to one or two of the E items later.

5. The statistical assumption underlying t tests are of course well known, and so are the effects of deviating from these assumptions. Boneau (1959), Havlicek and Peterson (1974) and Welch (1937) have investigated the results of such violations, and on the whole the departures from the conditions for which t tests are appropriate are not such as to make the use of the test contra-indicated here. In particular, it appears that when sampling from two non-normal distributions, it is important for the use of t that *both sets of scores should be skewed in the same direction* and that *variances should not be too dissimilar.* As t values obtained in the present comparisons have p values of <0.01 and <0.001 attached to them, there seems little doubt that the differences are, in fact, replicable.

APPENDIX A

ITEMS AND KEYS FOR PRIMARY FACTOR SCALES

1 Permissiveness

5 −
17 −
25 +
38 −
41 −
57 +
64 −
78 +
79 +
81 −
85 +
87 −
93 +
134 −

2 Satisfaction

4 +
11 −
16 +
19 −
20 +
21 −
56 −
108 +
113 +
114 −
118 −
139 −

3 Neurotic sex

7 +
18 +
20 −
23 +
24 +
26 +
32 +
44 +
46 +
56 +
59 +
60 +
84 +

4 Impersonal sex

2 −
40 −
65 +
83 +
89 +
92 +
95 +
97 +
102 +
119 +
120 +
135 −
144 +
153 −

5 Pornography

10 +
43 +
58 —
76 +
77 +
141 +
151 —
152 —

6 Sexual shyness

47 +
50 —
52 +
59 +
61 +
124 +

7 Prudishness

51 +
55 —
58 +
64 +
71 —
112 —
122 —
126 +
141 —

9 Sexual disgust

9 —
34 +
104 +
112 —
133 +
146 +

10 Sexual excitement

3 —
6 —
9 +
30 +
34 —
37 +
39 +
71 +
146 —

11 Physical sex

31 —
48 +
49 +
71 +
86 +
106 +
109 —
111 +
127 +
131 +

12 Aggressive sex

68 +
75 +
101 +
116 +
121 +
132 —

APPENDIX B

ITEMS AND KEYS FOR SUPERFACTOR SCALES

Sexual satisfaction			Sexual libido		
Item	Key	Item	Key	Item	Key
4	+	1	−	76	+
11	−	2	−	77	+
15	−	5	−	78	+
18	−	6	−	79	+
19	−	10	+	81	−
20	+	25	+	85	+
21	−	37	+	87	−
31	−	38	−	89	+
32	−	39	+	92	+
44	−	40	−	95	+
56	−	41	−	96	+
108	−	42	+	119	+
117	−	43	+	120	+
118	−	46	+	134	−
124	−	65	+	135	−
133	−	72	+	151	+a
		74	+	152	+a
				153	+a
				154	+efg

APPENDIX C

MASCULINITY–FEMININITY SCALE KEY

Item	Key	Item	Key	Item	Key
2	−	64	−	96	+
3	−	65	+	97	+
7	+	67	+	101	−
10	+	69	−	102	+
13	+	76	+	106	+
16	−	77	+	109	−
18	−	78	+	113	+
22	+	79	+	114	−
30	+	80	−	116	−
37	+	84	−	119	+
39	+	85	+	120	+
40	−	86	+	128	−
42	+	89	+	135	−
43	+	91	−	145	+
44	−	92	+	146	−
55	+	95	+	147	−
58	−				
63	+				

APPENDIX D

PERSONALITY QUESTIONNAIRE

INSTRUCTIONS

Please answer each question by putting a circle around the 'Yes' or the 'No' following the question. There are no right or wrong answers, and no trick questions. Work quickly and do not think too long about the exact meaning of the question.

REMEMBER TO ANSWER EACH QUESTION

1	Do you often long for excitement?	YES	NO
2	Does your mood often go up and down?	YES	NO
3	Would parachute jumping appeal to you?	YES	NO
4	Have you ever taken the credit for something you knew someone else had really done?	YES	NO
5	Are you a talkative person?	YES	NO
6	Do you ever feel 'just miserable' for no good reason?	YES	NO
7	Do most things taste the same to you?	YES	NO
8	Were you ever greedy by helping yourself to more than your share of anything?	YES	NO
9	Are you usually carefree?	YES	NO
10	Do you often worry about things you should not have done or said?	YES	NO
11	Would it upset you a lot to see a child or an animal suffer?	YES	NO
12	If you say you will do something, do you always keep your promise no matter how inconvenient it might be?	YES	NO
13	Can you usually let yourself go and enjoy yourself a lot at a gay party?	YES	NO
14	Are your feelings rather easily hurt?	YES	NO

145

15 Do you think that marriage is old-fashioned and should be done away with? YES NO

16 Have you ever blamed anyone for doing something you knew was really your fault? YES NO

17 Are you an irritable person? YES NO

18 Do you have many different hobbies? YES NO

19 Do you love your mother? YES NO

20 Are *all* your habits good and desirable ones? YES NO

21 Do you often do things on the spur of the moment? YES NO

22 Are you often troubled about feelings of guilt? YES NO

23 Do fast roundabouts and swings at funfairs give you a thrill? YES NO

24 Have you ever taken anything (even a pin or button) that belonged to someone else? YES NO

25 Do you like going out a lot? YES NO

26 Would you call yourself tense or 'highly-strung'? YES NO

27 Do you read the Bible every day? YES NO

28 Do you sometimes talk about things you know nothing about? YES NO

29 Do you have many friends? YES NO

30 Do you worry about awful things that might happen? YES NO

31 Do you enjoy hurting people you love? YES NO

32 Do you always say you are sorry when you have been rude? YES NO

33 Do you hate being with a crowd who play harmless jokes on one another? YES NO

34 Would you call yourself a nervous person? YES NO

35 Can you easily understand the way people feel when they tell you their troubles? YES NO

36 As a child, did you do as you were told immediately and without grumbling? YES NO

37 Do you like talking about sex? YES NO

38 Do you worry about your health? YES NO

39 Would you like to learn to fly an aeroplane? YES NO

40 Have you ever broken or lost something belonging to someone else? YES NO

41 If there is something you want to know about, would you rather look it up in a book than talk to someone about it? YES NO

42 Do you suffer from sleeplessness? YES NO

43 Would you like to think that other people are afraid of you? YES NO

44 Are you always quiet when other people are talking? YES NO

45 Are you rather lively? YES NO

46 Do you very easily feel bored? YES NO

47 Would you like to see blood sports like fox hunting forbidden because they are cruel? YES NO

48 Do you throw waste paper on the floor when there is no waste paper basket handy? YES NO

49 Can you easily get some life into a rather dull party? YES NO

50 Do you sometimes sulk? YES NO

51 Do you find it hard to trust anyone? YES NO

52 Do you sometimes boast a little? YES NO

53 Do you like doing things in which you have to act quickly? YES NO

54 Do you often feel life is very dull? YES NO

55 Would you take drugs that may have strange or dangerous effects? YES NO

56 Have you ever written your name in a school or library book? YES NO

57 Do you prefer reading to meeting people? YES NO

58 Have you often felt listless and tired for no good reason? YES NO

59 Do you usually note the number of a car you think is being driven too fast and tell the police? YES NO

60 Have you ever said anything bad or nasty about anyone? YES NO

61 Are you mostly quiet when you are with other people? YES NO

62 Do you often feel 'fed up'? YES NO

63 Do you enjoy practical jokes that can sometimes really hurt people? YES NO

64 As a child were you ever cheeky to your parents? YES NO

65 Do you like having long chats on the telephone? YES NO

66 Are you touchy about some things? YES NO

67 Are you slow and unhurried in the way you move? YES NO

68 Do you always wash before a meal? YES NO

69 Would you rather plan things than do things? YES NO

70 Are you sometimes bubbling over with energy and sometimes very sluggish? YES NO

71 Do you give something to every beggar you see? YES NO

72 Have you ever cheated at a game? YES NO

73 Do you often take on more activities than you have time for? YES NO

74 Do you worry too long after an embarrassing experience? YES NO

75 Is your mother a good person? YES NO

76 Have you ever 'played sick' to get out of something? YES NO

77 Would you say that you were fairly self-confident? YES NO

78 Have you always been known as a loner? YES NO

79 Do you get nervous in places like lifts, trains or tunnels? YES NO

80 Have you ever taken advantage of someone? YES NO

81 Do you like cracking jokes and telling funny stories to your friends? YES NO

82	Do your friendships break up easily without it being your fault?	YES	NO
83	Do you like mixing with people?	YES	NO
84	Do you suffer from 'nerves'?	YES	NO
85	Are you always polite even to unpleasant people?	YES	NO
86	Would you feel very sorry for an animal caught in a trap?	YES	NO
87	Do you nearly always have a 'ready answer' when people talk to you?	YES	NO
88	Do you daydream a lot?	YES	NO
89	Are you always specially careful with other people's things?	YES	NO
90	Have you ever insisted on having your own way?	YES	NO
91	Would you call yourself happy-go-lucky?	YES	NO
92	Do you have many nightmares?	YES	NO
93	When you are in a crowd, do you worry about catching germs?	YES	NO
94	Would you dodge paying taxes if you were sure you would never be found out?	YES	NO
95	Do you mind selling things or asking people for money for some good cause?	YES	NO
96	Do you try not to be rude to people?	YES	NO
97	Have you ever deliberately said something to hurt someone's feelings?	YES	NO
98	Are you easily hurt when people find fault with you or the work you do?	YES	NO
99	Would you rather be on a desert island than in the middle of a bustling city crowd?	YES	NO
100	Do you sometimes get cross?	YES	NO
101	Do you sometimes feel life is just not worth living?	YES	NO
102	Before taking decisions do you generally ask someone's advice?	YES	NO
103	Do you always practise what you preach?	YES	NO
104	Do you always keep smiling even when things go wrong?	YES	NO
105	Are you troubled by aches and pains?	YES	NO
106	Have you ever told a lie?	YES	NO
107	Do you prefer to have few but special friends?	YES	NO
108	Do good manners and cleanliness matter much to you?	YES	NO
109	Do you go for things you want rather than wait for them to come to you?	YES	NO
110	Did you mind filling in this questionnaire?	YES	NO

Key to personality scale

P	E	N	L
7	5	2	— 4
— 11	13	6	— 8
15	18	10	12
— 19	21	14	—16
31	25	17	20
— 35	29	22	—24
43	— 33	26	—28
— 75	45	30	32
55	49	34	—40
63	— 57	38	—52
78	— 61	42	—60
82	65	50	—64
— 86	— 69	54	68
— 89	73	58	—72
93	81	62	—80
— 96	83	66	85
—100	87	70	—90
—106	91	74	—94
—108	— 95	84	—97
110	—107	98	103

4

Social attitudes and sexual behaviour

In addition to the questionnaires mentioned already, and discussed in some detail (sexual attitudes, sexual behaviour, permissiveness, personality), the subjects of our main inquiry, as described in chapter 3, were also administered a social attitudes inventory. The purpose of this additional inquiry was of course to see to what extent social attitudes might be related to sexual attitudes and behaviour. The inventory was a revision and extension of the questionnaire used in *The Psychology of Politics* (Eysenck 1954); it contains eighty-eight items, as well as questions regarding the social class and voting intentions of the subject. It was expected that the main factors to emerge from this inventory would be conservatism and toughmindedness; these two major factors originally appeared in the analyses reported in *The Psychology of Politics*, and have been duplicated several times since (cf. Wilson 1973). More recently we have found that a third factor, capitalism *v.* socialism, could be isolated; this factor was sufficiently independent of conservatism (with a small c!) to deserve separate measurement, and consequently the questionnaire here used contained several more questions on socialism and capitalism than did the original one.

Our expectation to find relations between social attitudes and sexual ones was heightened by the fact that

1 there is a strong genetic factor in the causation of social attitudes
2 social attitudes are related to personality factors
3 these relations themselves have a genetic rather than an environmental basis (Eaves and Eysenck 1974).

The heritability of the conservatism–radicalism factor was 0·65, and that of toughmindedness 0·54; toughmindedness was significantly associated with personality factors E and P on a genetic basis. In

150

this study no separate factor of capitalism–socialism was looked for or found, the original Social Attitude Inventory being used (Eysenck 1954). A later study (Eysenck 1975b) was designed to investigate the possibility that this might be an additional, third, major factor in the social attitudes field. The choice of items in this study was similar to that used in the present study, and may therefore be worthy of discussion.

First of all a thorough survey was made of published articles and books dealing with social attitudes, and each item listed that seemed in any way related to the three putative factors of conservatism, capitalism or toughmindedness. Duplicates and similar-to-each-other items were eliminated, and the remaining 176 items randomly assigned to one of two sets, A and B. One of these sets constitutes the present groups of items, while the other was used in the published study. It cannot of course be claimed that in this way we have succeeded in procuring a truly random sample of all relevant social attitude statements or questions, but this procedure seems to cut subjectivity down to a certain minimum. The questionnaire was administered to a reasonably random sample of subjects ($n=368$), and factor-analysed; three effectively independent factors corresponding to conservatism, capitalism and toughmindedness were extracted (Eysenck 1975b). This finding suggested that similar factors would emerge from the present study, using the second set of items.

The Public Opinion Inventory is given below (table 4.1), together with instructions. Given after each question is the percentage of males and females giving a positive answer to each question. It will be seen that, although men and women do differ on many items, their differences are on the whole much smaller than were those on the sexual attitudes inventory. It would seem that it is particularly with respect to sexual matters that men and women disagree, whereas with respect to general social attitudes their disagreements remain rather muted.

Table 4.1 *Public Opinion Inventory, together with percentage 'yes' answers of men and women*

Sex _____ Age _____ Name _____ (optional)

It is hoped you will be interested in this survey of public opinion. Below are given 88 statements which represent widely held opinions on various social questions, selected from speeches, books, newspapers and other sources. They were chosen in such a way that most people are likely to agree with some, and to disagree with others.

After each statement, you are requested to record your personal opinion regarding it. You should use the following system of marking:

++ if you strongly agree with the statement
+ if you agree on the whole
0 if you can't decide for or against, or if you think the question is worded in such a way that you can't give an answer
− if you disagree on the whole
−− if you strongly disagree

Please answer frankly. Remember this is not a test; there are no 'right' or 'wrong' answers. The answer required is your own personal opinion. Be sure not to omit any questions.

Do not consult any other person while you are giving your answers.

Opinion statements	Your opinion	Social attitudes % yes answers	
		M	F
1 Our treatment of criminals is too harsh; we should try to cure them, not punish them	————	58	61
2 It will always be necessary to have a few strong, able people actually running everything	————	72	78
3 The United Nations Organisation is useless and does not deserve our support	————	9	9
4 Pacifism is simply not a practical philosophy in the world today	————	39	28
5 The idea of God is an invention of the human mind	————	63	44
6 We should not restrict immigration into this country as we have done in the past	————	30	26
7 Private profit is the main motive for hard work	————	61	60
8 There is very little discipline in today's youths	————	36	39
9 It is the moral responsibility of strong nations to protect and develop weaker and poorer nations	————	75	75
10 Sex crimes, such as rape and attacks on children, deserve more than mere imprisonment; such criminals ought to be flogged or worse	————	25	31
11 Communists should not be allowed to hold jobs in government service	————	33	31
12 We spend too little money on foreign aid	————	39	33
13 An occupation by a foreign power is better than war	————	28	32
14 The average man can live a good enough life without religion	————	82	77
15 In capitalist countries there is an inevitable conflict between workers and employers	————	72	68
16 Great wealth should be shared much more than at present	————	71	67
17 A white lie is often a good thing	————	79	85
18 The great increase in drug-taking by the young is another example of how far our society has deteriorated	————	31	37
19 The death penalty is barbaric, and its abolition right and proper	————	64	61

SOCIAL ATTITUDES AND SEXUAL BEHAVIOUR

		M	F
20	The police should have the right to listen in on private telephone conversations when investigating crime	32	32
21	The so-called underdog deserves little sympathy or help from successful people	13	12
22	We have never, as a nation, fought an unjust war	11	14
23	We should believe without question all that we are taught by the Church	2	3
24	In this country, the most able rise to the top	36	37
25	A firm should produce what is most profitable, not what the government believes to be in the national interest	32	23
26	The practical man is of more use to society than the thinker	18	20
27	Even though the masses behave pretty stupidly at times, I have a lot of faith in the common sense of the ordinary man	59	68
28	The maintenance of internal order within the nation is more important than ensuring that there is complete freedom for all	53	43
29	Poverty, mental illness and other problems are a responsibility for the whole community	95	95
30	The dropping of the first atom bomb on a Japanese city, killing thousands of innocent women and children, was morally wrong and incompatible with our kind of civilisation	56	72
31	Life is not perfect nowadays but it is much better than it used to be	82	77
32	Sunday observance is old-fashioned and should cease to govern our behaviour	77	71
33	Capitalism is immoral because it exploits the worker by failing to give him full value for his productive labour	34	35
34	Nowadays more and more people are prying into matters which do not concern them	51	49
35	There are many advantages to having a king or queen to govern the country, provided they do not have too much power	56	56
36	Most modern art is pretentious nonsense	32	26
37	The 'welfare state' tends to destroy individual initiative	39	34
38	A person should be free to take his own life, if he wishes to do so without any interference from society	62	65
39	On the whole workers in this country are fairly treated by their employers	62	69
40	If you start trying to change things very much, you usually make them worse	19	20
41	Christ was divine, wholly or partly, in a sense different from other men	29	40

153

		M	F
42	The nationalisation of the great industries is likely to lead to inefficiency, bureaucracy and stagnation	56	51
43	People should realise that their greatest obligation is to their family	49	49
44	Business competition is necessary for national welfare		
45	Most strikes are caused by bad management	36	36
46	We ought to have a world government to guarantee the welfare of all nations irrespective of the rights of any nation	50	46
47	Sex relations except in marriage are always wrong	5	7
48	The way wealth is distributed at the moment is unsound and unjust	57	56
49	It is always a good idea to look for new ways of doing things	96	93
50	There are no such things as 'supernatural powers'	37	22
51	Economic security for all is impossible under capitalism	37	36
52	The less government the better	33	22
53	There are many responsible positions for which women are unsuited, such as judgeships, ministerial office and high positions in banking and industry	18	12
54	Trade unions do more harm than good to industrial progress	30	37
55	I would support my country even against my convictions	17	15
56	Free love between men and women should be encouraged as a means towards mental and physical health	46	39
57	Scientific inventions have carried us too far too fast; we should be given a resting pause now	26	33
58	Government nowadays is too centralised	55	52
59	Negroes are often denied opportunities for good jobs and promotions that are given to white people	82	86
60	Our nation is more democratic than any other nation	37	37
61	Housing will never be adequate until the government acquires ownership of all land	19	12
62	It is wrong that men should be permitted greater sexual freedom than women by society	77	81
63	The government should do a lot more to regulate the activities of labour unions	52	49
64	In taking part in any form of world organisation, this country should make certain that none of its independence and power is lost	36	50

154

	M	F
65 The practice of birth control should be discouraged	2	2
66 Modern adolescents are no more immoral than were their parents or grandparents at their age	77	73
67 There may be a few exceptions, but in general Jews are pretty much alike	20	21
68 Workers should take part in the running of businesses in which they are employed	71	69
69 Women are not really the equals of men, and never will be	24	28
70 Teachers have no business to take an active part in politics	17	14
71 Censorship of books and films should be completely abolished	74	57
72 A national health service does not give doctors an opportunity to do their best for their patients	25	33
73 Most politicians can be trusted to do what they think is best for the country	37	34
74 Conscientious objectors are traitors to their country, and should be treated accordingly	5	6
75 The laws restricting abortion should be abolished	63	66
76 The permissive modern ways of bringing up children are an improvement on older methods	69	68
77 All kinds of discrimination against the coloured races, the Jews etc. should be made illegal, and subject to heavy penalties	65	70
78 Democracy depends fundamentally on the existence of free business enterprise	36	42
79 Slumps and unemployment are the inevitable consequences of capitalism	33	28
80 The government must ensure *above everything else* that unemployment is kept very low	28	36
81 The school leaving age should be raised as much as possible, whether young people want to stay on or not	27	21
82 It seems to me that, whoever you vote for, things go on pretty much the same	64	66
83 This country is just as selfish as any other nation	77	77
84 In the interest of peace the private manufacture of arms and ammunition must be abolished	50	60
85 The nation exists for the benefit of the individual, not the individual for the benefit of the nation	62	61
86 When it comes to the things that count, all races are certainly not equal	43	42
87 Stable peace will be possible only in a socialist world	20	23
88 Morals in this country are pretty bad, and getting worse	14	18

If you had to choose, would you vote for:

89 A Conservative candidate ————

155

90 A Labour candidate ————
91 A Liberal candidate ————
92 Other (specify) ————

Would you say that your family was:
93 Working-class ————
94 Middle-class ————
95 Other (specify) ————

What is your occupation? (housewives please give occupation of husband)

Would you clarify this as:
Higher professional/administrative ————
Lower professional/administrative ————
Clerical ————
Skilled manual ————
Semi-skilled manual ————
Unskilled manual ————

Previous work (Eysenck 1954) had shown women to be less tough-minded and more conservative; the few differences in our table that exceed ten points bear this out. Women are more in favour of pacifism, opposed to the private manufacture of arms, and consider the dropping of the atom bomb immoral; they are more religious, emphasising belief in God, the divinity of Christ and the existence of supernatural powers. They favour government, censorship and world organisations as opposed to nationalism; in other words, they are on the side of law and order, even in the international sphere. None of these differences is large, and they are all in the expected direction. It would not be very useful to construct a masculinity–femininity scale from these items, as was done with our sexual attitudes inventory; there simply are too few differences between men and women in the field of general attitudes to make this possible.

Table 4.2 gives the main results from a factor analysis of the inter-correlations (product–moment) of the eighty-eight items of the Public Opinion Inventory. Three factors were extracted from the matrix of intercorrelations and rotated by Promax to oblique simple structure; the table gives the loadings resulting from this analysis, which was carried out separately for men and women. The resulting factors are very similar for the two sexes, and are identified as

1 conservatism
2 capitalism
3 toughmindedness.

Table 4.3 shows the intercorrelations between the three factors; capitalism and conservatism show a moderate to high correlation, and both correlate negatively and not at all highly with toughmindedness. For all practical purposes toughmindedness is independent of both capitalism and conservatism.

Table 4.2 *Factor loadings of items on conservatism, capitalism and toughminded factors*

	Conservatism		Capitalism		Toughmindedness	
	M	F	M	F	M	F
1	−0·57	−0·58	−0·25	−0·20	0·01	0·00
2	0·33	0·42	0·30	0·11	0·00	0·01
3	0·53	0·37	−0·01	−0·12	0·28	0·16
4	0·31	0·37	0·12	0·16	0·07	0·04
5	−0·07	0·04	−0·05	−0·11	0·63	0·72
6	−0·42	−0·36	−0·25	−0·35	−0·04	0·07
7	0·61	0·45	0·04	0·08	0·15	0·23
8	0·57	0·53	−0·09	−0·06	−0·07	−0·08
9	−0·15	−0·28	−0·34	−0·21	−0·30	−0·25
10	0·67	0·74	−0·05	−0·12	−0·04	0·01
11	0·46	0·48	0·18	0·17	−0·12	−0·15
12	−0·57	−0·34	−0·24	−0·31	−0·26	−0·14
13	−0·22	−0·02	−0·19	−0·24	−0·01	0·10
14	0·16	0·15	−0·11	−0·09	0·65	0·71
15	0·25	0·16	−0·57	0·47	0·14	0·16
16	−0·17	−0·09	−0·60	−0·69	−0·03	−0·09
17	0·15	0·24	0·10	0·06	0·28	0·41
18	0·54	0·44	−0·14	−0·13	−0·29	−0·34
19	−0·56	−0·61	−0·22	−0·19	−0·04	−0·17
20	0·18	0·30	0·14	0·09	−0·12	−0·02
21	0·40	0·45	0·09	0·08	0·14	0·16
22	0·52	0·57	−0·02	−0·15	−0·14	0·08
23	0·34	0·36	0·23	−0·16	−0·38	−0·38
24	0·20	0·35	0·20	0·18	−0·09	0·05
25	0·37	0·43	0·25	0·21	0·08	0·03
26	0·50	0·54	−0·26	−0·19	0·04	0·03
27	0·30	0·17	−0·35	−0·19	−0·32	−0·14
28	0·19	0·42	0·30	0·06	−0·20	−0·02
29	−0·29	−0·30	−0·24	−0·21	−0·07	−0·08
30	−0·24	−0·28	−0·35	−0·32	−0·12	−0·17
31	−0·03	0·09	0·09	0·04	0·08	0·18
32	−0·02	0·06	0·07	−0·08	0·67	0·67
33	0·07	0·25	−0·82	−0·84	0·06	0·07
34	0·44	0·40	−0·28	−0·17	0·09	0·05
35	0·03	0·18	0·40	0·22	−0·21	−0·23
36	0·56	0·51	−0·02	−0·11	0·01	−0·07
37	0·42	0·40	0·19	0·22	0·02	0·03
38	0·13	0·12	−0·08	−0·09	0·45	0·44
39	0·15	0·10	0·57	0·55	−0·06	−0·10

	Conservatism		Capitalism		Toughmindedness	
	M	F	M	F	M	F
40	0·45	0·55	− 0·14	− 0·09	− 0·05	− 0·01
41	0·01	− 0·02	0·05	0·06	− 0·68	− 0·70
42	0·34	0·25	0·45	0·46	0·06	− 0·04
43	0·46	0·45	− 0·09	− 0·08	− 0·18	− 0·09
44	0·38	0·32	0·46	0·42	− 0·06	− 0·07
45	0·06	0·10	− 0·49	− 0·51	− 0·09	0·12
46	− 0·22	− 0·12	− 0·22	− 0·41	− 0·02	0·03
47	− 0·04	0·24	− 0·07	− 0·20	− 0·62	− 0·56
48	− 0·23	− 0·13	− 0·58	− 0·59	− 0·01	− 0·06
49	− 0·02	− 0·11	0·02	0·01	0·29	0·13
50	− 0·02	0·02	− 0·17	− 0·15	0·38	0·39
51	0·13	0·17	− 0·68	− 0·67	0·12	0·11
52	0·11	0·20	− 0·05	− 0·11	0·11	0·24
53	0·54	0·43	− 0·04	− 0·11	− 0·03	− 0·12
54	0·47	0·50	0·18	0·21	0·01	0·04
55	0·46	0·51	0·06	0·02	− 0·13	− 0·08
56	0·25	0·14	− 0·31	− 0·16	0·52	0·63
57	0·18	0·18	− 0·32	− 0·27	− 0·17	− 0·20
58	0·16	0·11	− 0·15	− 0·24	− 0·05	− 0·02
59	− 0·24	− 0·25	− 0·18	− 0·19	0·10	0·02
60	0·27	0·28	0·09	0·03	− 0·12	0·00
61	0·07	0·04	− 0·71	− 0·61	0·03	0·02
62	− 0·34	− 0·14	0·04	− 0·16	0·12	0·17
63	0·35	0·35	0·44	0·43	− 0·06	− 0·04
64	0·73	0·59	− 0·06	0·08	− 0·02	− 0·05
65	0·15	0·25	− 0·15	− 0·21	− 0·32	− 0·25
66	− 0·15	− 0·25	0·14	0·11	0·30	0·23
67	0·57	0·62	− 0·21	− 0·21	− 0·03	0·04
68	− 0·21	− 0·26	− 0·46	− 0·45	− 0·15	− 0·04
69	0·47	0·51	− 0·07	− 0·05	− 0·10	0·00
70	0·50	0·58	0·02	− 0·03	0·01	0·02
71	0·05	− 0·07	− 0·13	− 0·07	0·58	0·50
72	0·41	0·40	0·11	0·07	0·06	− 0·02
73	− 0·04	0·19	0·20	0·20	− 0·25	− 0·09
74	0·52	0·70	− 0·02	− 0·14	− 0·03	0·01
75	0·02	− 0·05	− 0·06	− 0·08	0·60	0·50
76	− 0·18	− 0·18	− 0·08	− 0·22	0·45	0·29
77	− 0·20	− 0·28	− 0·17	− 0·23	0·05	− 0·05
78	0·51	0·40	0·21	0·28	− 0·07	− 0·10
79	0·10	0·19	− 0·75	− 0·72	0·06	0·04
80	0·49	0·39	− 0·65	− 0·58	− 0·07	− 0·06
81	0·08	0·26	− 0·34	− 0·35	− 0·02	− 0·09
82	0·42	0·32	− 0·20	− 0·18	0·14	0·11
83	− 0·08	− 0·16	− 0·03	− 0·03	0·18	0·13
84	− 0·12	− 0·13	− 0·45	− 0·43	− 0·02	− 0·11
85	− 0·26	− 0·21	0·11	0·06	0·11	0·04
86	0·49	0·47	0·15	0·12	0·06	0·04
87	0·05	0·00	− 0·74	− 0·74	0·09	0·01
88	0·32	0·35	− 0·10	− 0·16	− 0·45	− 0·43

Table 4.3 *Intercorrelations of three superfactors for males (above leading diagonal) and females (below leading diagonal): in brackets, intercorrelations between corresponding scales*

	Conservatism	Capitalism	Tough-mindedness
Conservatism	——	0·48 (0·49)	−0·19 (−0·17)
Capitalism	0·43 (0·40)	——	−0·16 (−0·19)
Toughmindedness	−0·27 (−0·30)	−0·16 (−0·22)	——

Items with high loadings (above 0·35) clearly identify these three factors. The most clear-cut factor of all is perhaps capitalism *v.* socialism; the main items with high loadings on this factor are the following: capitalism does not mean conflict between classes (item 15); great wealth should not be shared (16); little faith in common man (27); capitalism not immoral (33); kings are advantageous to country (35); workers are treated fairly (39); nationalisation is inefficient (42); business competition is necessary (44); strikes are not caused by bad management (45); distribution of wealth is not unjust (48); economic security is not impossible under capitalism (51); housing will be adequate without nationalisation of land (61); the government should regulate the unions (63); workers should not have a part in the running of business (68); slums and unemployment are not the inevitable consequences of capitalism (79); low unemployment not absolute priority of government (80); the private manufacture of arms need not be abolished (84); and stable peace is not only possible under socialism (87). These are the major items for males; to these should be added the following from the females: immigration should remain restricted (6); we ought not to have a world government (46); and the school leaving age should not be raised (81). The nature of these items, and in particular the highest-loading items, leaves little doubt about the nature of this factor.

The conservatism factor is characterised by the following items having loadings above 0·35: Treatment of criminals is not too harsh (1); United Nations is useless (3); immigration should be restricted (6); private profit is the main motive (7); there is little discipline in modern youth (8); sex crimes deserve flogging (10); communists should not be allowed to hold office (11); foreign aid is not too little (12); drug-taking is an index of social deterioration (18); death penalty is not barbaric (19); the underdog deserves little sympathy

159

(21); our nation has never fought an unjust war (22); firms should be profitable (25); the practical man is worth more than the thinker (26); there are more people prying (34); modern art is nonsense (36); the welfare state destroys initiative (37); change is for the worse (40); one's greatest obligation is to the family (43); business competition is necessary for the nation's welfare (44); women are not suited for many positions (53); trade unions do harm (54); always support one's country (55); the government should regulate unions (63); preserve national independence (64); Jews are all pretty much alike (67); women are not the equals of men (69); teachers should keep out of politics (70); national service not good (72); conscientious objectors are traitors (74); democracy depends on free business enterprise (78); low unemployment not primary consideration, vote is useless (82); and all races are not equal (86). To these the women added the following items: few strong, able people to run everything (2); pacifism not practicable (4); believe all we are told by church (23); the most able rise to the top (24); order more important than complete freedom (28); morals in this country are pretty bad, and getting worse (88).

The third factor, toughmindedness, emerges less clearly than the other two, probably because the choice of items was directed more at getting capitalism and conservatism more closely identified. Nevertheless, the items overlap considerably with the usual ones that have defined this factor in the past. They are: God is an invention of the human mind (5); the average man can live a good life without religion (14); we should not believe what we are told by the church (23); Sunday observance is old-fashioned (32); euthanasia is a good thing (38); Christ was not divine (41); disagree that sex except in marriage is wrong (47); there are no superior powers (50); free love should be encouraged (56); censorship should be abolished (71); abortion laws should be abolished (75); permissive ways of bringing up children are good (76); morals nowadays are not bad (88). To which the females add the following: a white lie is sometimes a good thing (17); and the increase in drug-taking is not an index of social deterioration (18). It would clearly be possible to regard this factor as one opposing religion to permissiveness, or ethical to hedonistic ideals, or idealism to realism; however, there is little point in discussing at length the name of the factor when its nature is fairly clear. We shall continue to call it toughmindedness here, but bear in mind that the items making

160

up this factor provide little more than a skeleton of the larger number previously used to define this factor.

Three scales were drawn up to measure these three factors; the items contained in these scales, and their keying, are given in Appendix E. The reliabilities of these scales (alpha coefficients) were found to be as follows (males first, females second); capitalism: 0·84, 0·82; conservatism: 0·89, 0·89; toughmindedness; 0·76, 0·76. These are adequate for our purposes.

Sex differences on these scales are small or non-existent for conservatism and capitalism, but marked on toughmindedness. For conservatism, the scores of males and females are $14·09 \pm 7·08$ and $14·55 \pm 7·00$; for capitalism they are $11·32 \pm 4·50$ and $10·85 \pm 4·12$. Neither of these differences is significant. For toughmindedness the scores are $12·40 \pm 2·89$ and $11·60 \pm 2·95$; this difference is significant at the 0·001 level. The result, showing males to be more toughminded, is fully in line with earlier work. The difference for conservatism, while in the right direction according to earlier work, is much too small to be of any practical significance.

In addition to the three-factor solution just described, which essentially gives us the major or higher-order factors, it was also thought interesting to make a primary factor analysis, using twelve factors and rotating these by Promax into simple oblique structure. Seven of these factors were easily and clearly interpretable; loadings on the items above 0·35 are given below, in connection with a brief discussion of each factor. Factor 1 is clearly 'Capitalism', very similar in nature to the three-factor solution.

Factor 1: Capitalism

Item	Loading	Item
Males		
2	0·51	Few strong, able people to run government
15	− 0·52	Capitalist countries conflict between workers and employers
16	− 0·63	Share wealth
24	0·35	Most able rise to top
33	− 0·80	Capitalism immoral
35	− 0·52	Royalty an advantage
39	0·63	Workers treated fairly
42	0·55	Nationalisation inefficient
44	0·63	Business competition needed
48	− 0·56	Distribution of wealth not fair
51	− 0·72	Economic security impossible under capitalism

Item	Loading	Item
Males		
61	−0·69	Housing inadequate until land nationalised
63	0·47	Regulate labour unions
68	−0·35	Workers share running of business
78	0·39	Democracy depends on free business
79	−0·77	Slump result of capitalism
80	−0·59	Government must keep unemployment low
87	−0·79	Stable peace only in socialist world
Females		
6	−0·36	Restrict immigration
15	−0·60	Conflict workers and employers in capitalism
16	−0·65	Share wealth
33	−0·82	Capitalism immoral
37	0·35	Welfare state destroys initiative
39	0·64	Workers fairly treated
42	0·41	Nationalisation inefficient
44	0·40	Business necessary
48	−0·58	Wealth distribution unsound
51	−0·71	Economic security impossible under capitalism
61	−0·56	Ownership of land
63	−0·49	Government regulates unions
79	−0·80	Slumps consequence of capitalism
80	−0·44	Unemployment must be kept low
87	−0·69	Peace only in socialist world

Factor 2, at least for the males, is similar to the toughmindedness one already discussed; for the women, the religious part of this factor is overpoweringly strong, so that for them it might be better renamed 'Anti-religionism' or something of that kind.

Factor 2: Toughmindedness

Item	Loading	Item
Males		
5	0·70	God invention of human mind
14	0·70	Good life without religion
32	0·57	Sunday observance old-fashioned
38	0·36	Euthanasia
41	−0·72	Christ divine
47	−0·56	Sex outside marriage wrong
50	0·56	No supernatural powers
56	0·47	Free love good
71	0·53	Abolish censorship
75	0·55	Abortion laws abolished
76	0·45	Permissiveness in education good
88	−0·43	Morals bad in this country

Females		
5	0·79	God invention of human mind
14	0·72	Life without religion
23	− 0·41	Believe all we are taught by Church
32	0·54	Sunday observance old-fashioned
41	− 0·82	Christ divine
50	0·68	No supernatural powers

Factor 3 seems to be concerned with problems of discrimination, particularly discrimination against women; it is accordingly named 'Discrimination'.

Factor 3 : Discrimination

Item	Loading	Item
Males		
53	0·65	Women unsuited for responsible positions
62	− 0·61	Men should not be permitted greater sexual freedom
67	0·36	Jews pretty much alike
69	0·70	Women not equals of men
70	0·35	Teachers not in politics
77	− 0·38	Discrimination illegal
Females		
53	0·71	Women unsuited for responsible positions
62	− 0·49	Wrong that men have greater sexual freedom
65	0·53	Discourage birth control
69	0·72	Women not equals of men
70	0·40	Teachers not in politics
74	0·42	Conscientious objectors traitors

Factor 4 is concerned with pacifism (strictly, anti-pacifism); all the items are in accord with this interpretation.

Factor 4 : Anti-pacifism

Item	Loading	Item
Males		
4	0·62	Pacifism impracticable
13	− 0·66	Occupation by foreign power better than war
46	− 0·41	World government
84	− 0·36	Abolish private manufacture of arms
Females		
4	0·51	Pacifism no good
13	− 0·68	Occupation by foreign power better than war
55	0·37	Would support country against convictions
60	0·47	Our nation more democratic than others
82	− 0·42	Whoever you vote for, things much the same
83	− 0·61	This country just as selfish as others

Factor 5 is very well defined; it is the conservatism factor already encountered.

Factor 5: Conservatism

Item	Loading	Item
Males		
1	−0·42	Treatment of criminals too harsh
8	0·48	Little discipline in today's youth
10	0·46	Flogging for sex crimes
18	0·69	Drug-taking bad
19	−0·50	Death penalty barbaric
20	0·49	Police right to listen
36	0·67	Modern art pretentious nonsense
37	0·48	Welfare state destroys initiative
54	0·42	Trade unions do harm
63	0·45	Government should control unions
74	0·39	Conscientious objectors traitors
88	0·50	Morals bad in this country
Females		
7	0·65	Private profit motive
8	0·43	Little discipline in today's youth
24	0·42	Most able rise to top
34	0·62	Prying
35	0·52	Royalty advantage
40	0·69	Changing things makes them worse
42	0·43	Nationalisation inefficient
54	0·42	Trade unions do harm
60	0·43	Our nation more democratic than others
64	0·39	In world organisation, not lose independence
72	0·50	National health service not good
78	0·46	Democracy depends on free enterprise
82	0·48	Whoever you vote for, things much the same

Factor 6 might be labelled 'Idealism'; clearly the items suggest some such underlying attitude.

Factor 6: Idealism

Item	Loading	Item
Males		
9	−0·56	Moral responsibility of strong nations
21	0·45	Underdog deserves little sympathy
29	−0·60	Poverty responsibility of whole country
46	−0·47	World government
49	−0·44	Look for new ways of doing things
68	−0·51	Workers should take part in running business

Females
1	0·37	Treatment of criminals harsh
3	− 0·38	United nations useless
4	− 0·41	Pacifism no good
9	0·62	Strong nations protect weaker
10	− 0·38	Flogging
12	0·36	Spend too little on foreign aid
19	0·39	Death penalty barbaric
29	0·63	Poverty responsibility of community
30	0·45	Atom bomb immoral
49	0·41	New ways of doing things
77	0·41	Discrimination illegal
84	0·38	Nationalise arms industry

Factor 7 may be called 'Pro-government', in the sense that government is not distrusted and disliked.

Factor 7:   Pro-government

Item	Loading	Item
Males		
28	0·36	Internal order more important than freedom
34	− 0·47	People prying
52	− 0·76	The less government the better
58	− 0·65	Government too centralised
Females		
3	− 0·45	United Nations useless
52	− 0·56	The less government the better
57	− 0·58	Too much scientific invention
58	− 0·61	Government too centralised
73	0·41	Politicians can be trusted

The remaining factors are difficult or impossible to identify, and will not be listed.

Table 4.4 shows the correlations between the primary factors and superfactors in the social attitudes field on the one hand and the personality factors, social class and age on the other. Significant correlations have been italicised; these should be taken seriously only when there is agreement between males and females, at least on the direction of the correlation found. It may be useful to discuss the major findings by a consideration of the variables in each column. Beginning with P, we find that high P scorers are predominantly toughminded, and generally anti-minded; they are against conservatism, against the government, against capitalism, against idealism and against pacifism; most of these correlations are fairly

165

Table 4.4 *Correlations of primary and superfactors in the social attitude field with personality, class and age. Italicised correlations significant at p < 0·05 level*

	P		E		N		L		Middle class		Age	
	M	F	M	F	M	F	M	F	M	F	M	F
Capitalism	*-0·13*	*-0·24*	0·05	0·03	-0·08	-0·07	*0·10*	0·09	*0·11*	0·08	-0·01	0·09
Toughmindedness	0·27	0·16	-0·04	-0·04	0·02	0·07	*-0·13*	-0·08	0·02	0·05	-0·10	-0·01
Discrimination	0·05	*-0·12*	-0·04	-0·02	0·07	0·06	0·07	0·23	-0·03	0·01	0·04	0·22
Anti-pacifism	0·08	*0·26*	0·06	0·04	*-0·15*	-0·02	-0·02	0·22	0·05	-0·02	0·08	0·08
Conservatism	0·03	*-0·14*	-0·06	-0·01	0·02	0·25	*0·20*	0·14	0·04	-0·03	*0·21*	0·05
Anti-idealism	*0·18*	0·06	-0·03	*-0·10*	0·05	-0·06	-0·02	0·00	-0·01	-0·04	-0·09	-0·03
Pro-government	-0·09	-0·08	-0·08	0·07	*-0·12*	*-0·12*	*0·16*	0·03	0·04	0·04	0·06	-0·03
Conservatism	-0·02	*-0·18*	0·04	-0·04	0·06	*0·18*	*0·12*	0·20	-0·08	-0·08	0·06	0·07
Capitalism	-0·08	*-0·19*	0·02	-0·00	*-0·15*	-0·06	0·09	0·05	*0·13*	0·09	0·01	0·01
Toughmindedness	*0·33*	*0·31*	-0·01	0·02	0·01	-0·03	*-0·21*	*-0·20*	0·02	-0·04	*-0·18*	*-0·19*

low, with the exception of those linking P with toughmindedness. This is not an unexpected finding; in the *Manual of the E.P.Q.* (*Eysenck Personality Questionnaire*) (Eysenck and Eysenck 1975) we have already suggested as an alternative name for P the term 'toughminded'.

The personality factor E has hardly any significant correlations with the social attitudes, and does not seem to be related to any of the variables here considered. N shows some slight correlation with conservatism (particularly among the women), but this correlation is too small and uncertain to be readily interpreted. L is clearly opposed somewhat to toughmindedness, and positively correlated with conservatism. These correlations are not large, and should not be overinterpreted.

Class and age correlations are small throughout. Middle-class respondents are in favour of capitalism and slightly against conservatism (with a small c!); this is not unexpected (Eysenck 1975b). It is possible that the correlations are not larger because of the difficulty in determining social class from the answers given in a questionnaire; there is considerable inaccuracy involved, and it is possible that this unreliability has caused the observed correlations to be smaller than they would otherwise have been (particularly for women).

Age correlates slightly with conservatism, but perhaps much less so than one might have expected. It also appears that the young are more toughminded; this agrees with the observation that P scores decrease with age, and that P is correlated with toughmindedness.

We must now turn to a consideration of the interrelations (if any) between the social attitude variables and the sexual attitude variables. We would not expect much in the way of relationships for the capitalism factor; conservatism might be expected to show some correlations with such sex factors as permissiveness, but on the whole conservatism too is not likely to show any very close relationship. It is with respect to toughmindedness that our main expectations must lie; toughminded persons, as we have seen, are high P scorers, and the close relation between P and several of the sex scales has already been shown.

Let us consider first of all the primary social attitude factors. Conservatism does indeed, as expected, correlate negatively with permissiveness ($r = -0.22$), and also with physical sex ($r = -0.20$).

167

Toughmindedness correlates 0·70 with permissiveness, 0·28 with pornography, 0·40 with impersonal sex, 0·20 with aggressive sex and 0·55 with the Libido superfactor. Capitalism shows a correlation only with permissiveness ($r = -0.22$). Pacifism correlates with physical sex ($r = -0.22$) and with dominance ($r = -0.37$). For the social attitude superfactors the relationships are similar. Capitalism correlates only with permissiveness ($r = -0.22$); conservatism correlates with permissiveness ($r = -0.22$), physical sex ($r = -0.23$) and dominance ($r = -0.28$). Toughmindedness correlates with permissiveness ($r = 0.74$), pornography ($r = 0.24$), impersonal sex ($r = 0.41$) and the Libido superfactor ($r = 0.56$). These are the values for the males; those for the females are similar.

For the women, the primary factor of conservatism correlates with permissiveness ($r = -0.23$), physical sex ($r = -0.22$), and dominance ($r = -0.33$). Toughmindedness correlates with permissiveness ($r = 0.38$), impersonal set ($r = 0.20$) and the Libido superfactor ($r = 0.31$). Discrimination correlates with permissiveness ($r = 0.32$), physical sex ($r = 0.23$) and dominance ($r = 0.30$). Pacifism correlates with permissiveness ($r = -0.24$) and dominance ($r = -0.24$). The anti-government factor correlates with aggressive sex ($r = 0.20$). Turning now to the superfactors, we begin with conservatism; this correlates with permissiveness ($r = -0.34$), sexual excitement ($r = -0.22$), shyness ($r = 0.35$), pornography ($r = -0.25$), neurotic sex ($r = 0.42$) and the Libido superfactor ($r = -0.28$).(1) Capitalism correlates with physical sex ($r = -0.25$) and dominance ($r = 0.42$). Toughmindedness correlates with permissiveness ($r = 0.67$), and with excitement ($r = 0.25$); with the Libido superfactor the correlation is 0·58. Most if not all of these correlations make sense as they stand, and do not require much discussion.

It will be remembered that almost half the sample were constituted of matched pairs, i.e. men and women either married or living together on a semi-permanent basis. It is interesting to know to what extent the social attitude of such pairs are similar, i.e. to what extent there is assortative mating in this field. Table 4.5 shows the results; it will be noted that assortative mating is quite strong for the three superfactors, and rather less strong for the primary factors. It must of course be remembered that the values given in this table are not, strictly speaking, evidence for assortative mating; the attitudes of the couple may have changed towards greater conformity after they started living together. It is a moot point whether this fact would disqualify the values in the table from being considered evidence of assortative mating; in one sense of the term the time of greatest interest would be not that of beginning an association, but rather that of having offspring. We have no data on which to base such a comparison.(2)

Table 4.5 *Assortative mating: correlations between males and females married or living together*

1 Capitalism	0·59
2 Toughmindedness	0·50
3 Conservatism	0·42
4 Anti-idealism	0·36
5 Anti-pacifism	0·28
6 Pro-government	0·21
7 Discrimination	0·18
SF1 Conservatism	0·67
SF2 Capitalism	0·65
SF3 Toughmindedness	0·60
Class	0·40
Age	0·88

Also given in table 4.5 are values dealing with social class and age. It will be seen that for age homogamy is very clear; this is only to be expected. For social class the correlation is much lower; this may in part be due to the difficulties of ascertaining social class at all, and in particular of ascertaining it in women. The figure quoted is probably a lower limit; the true value is likely to be in excess of this figure. The table as a whole enables us to say that, as in the case of intelligence, and unlike the case of personality, like mates with like as far as social attitudes are concerned; this was our conclusion too in the case of sexual attitudes.

One last comparison requires to be made, namely that between people who state that they voted for one of the major parties (Conservative, Labour, Liberal) or for some other party (which in the context of the sample in question means for all practical purposes the Communist Party, or some other left-wing extremist group). (In Scotland or Wales, or in Northern Ireland, the term 'Other' would of course in the majority of cases refer to nationalist candidates, but as our sample was exclusively English this point does not arise. There may have been one or two National Front sympathisers in the 'Other' group, but remarks and comments written into the inventory suggest that this is not a likely con-

Table 4.6 Mean social attitude scale scores for conservative, labour, liberal and 'other' voters: males

Males	Conservative voters (126)	Labour voters (149)	Liberal voters (98)	Others (48)	p
P	2·02 ± 1·77	2·27 ± 1·85	2·10 ± 1·63	3·23 ± 1·55	0·001
E	11·28 ± 4·31	10·67 ± 4·37	10·57 ± 4·74	10·91 ± 4·56	N.S.
N	8·60 ± 4·70	9·81 ± 5·16	9·33 ± 4·76	8·16 ± 4·88	N.S.
L	6·18 ± 3·80	5·44 ± 3·55	5·97 ± 3·48	5·18 ± 3·90	N.S.
Conservatism	112·26 ± 18·43	88·34 ± 21·95	94·51 ± 17·58	83·83 ± 20·95	0·001
Capitalism	76·63 ± 8·18	56·72 ± 10·35	67·29 ± 9·00	54·15 ± 16·14	0·001
Toughmindedness	62·14 ± 9·42	64·72 ± 9·53	61·44 ± 9·72	67·99 ± 6·40	0·001
Permissiveness	11·25 ± 2·74	11·92 ± 2·47	11·45 ± 2·87	12·74 ± 1·77	0·01
Satisfaction	8·45 ± 2·79	7·92 ± 2·94	7·48 ± 3·04	8·12 ± 3·02	N.S.
Neurotic sex	5·47 ± 1·90	5·28 ± 2·05	4·87 ± 2·09	5·04 ± 1·98	N.S.
Impersonal sex	6·99 ± 1·62	6·78 ± 1·75	6·62 ± 1·81	6·79 ± 1·68	N.S.
Pornography	2·52 ± 2·21	3·11 ± 2·47	3·06 ± 2·50	2·88 ± 2·06	N.S.
Shyness	5·70 ± 3·65	5·87 ± 3·52	5·82 ± 3·47	6·54 ± 3·66	N.S.
Prudishness	1·05 ± 1·31	1·03 ± 0·95	1·27 ± 1·37	1·27 ± 1·55	N.S.
Disgust	7·20 ± 1·72	7·01 ± 1·57	6·62 ± 1·87	6·98 ± 1·68	N.S.
Excitement	1·82 ± 1·42	1·81 ± 1·26	2·15 ± 1·47	2·00 ± 1·36	N.S.
Physical sex	2·31 ± 1·56	2·53 ± 1·45	2·26 ± 1·26	2·21 ± 1·18	N.S.
Aggressive sex	1·02 ± 0·80	1·02 ± 0·78	1·18 ± 0·77	1·28 ± 0·93	N.S.
Sex Behaviour 1	9·15 ± 1·86	8·93 ± 2·09	8·20 ± 2·77	9·42 ± 1·80	0·01
Sex Behaviour 2	0·16 ± 0·46	0·17 ± 0·51	0·32 ± 0·78	0·70 ± 0·84	0·05
Sex Behaviour 3	1·20 ± 1·38	1·48 ± 1·74	1·70 ± 2·21	0·73 ± 0·84	0·01
Satisfaction ⎱ Super-	12·91 ± 2·94	12·23 ± 3·11	11·80 ± 3·26	12·34 ± 3·32	N.S.
Libido ⎰ factors	24·13 ± 7·16	29·76 ± 6·69	23·58 ± 6·94	26·00 ± 5·58	N.S.

tingency as far as the majority of respondents are concerned.) It is interesting, and reassuring as far as the representativeness of the sample is concerned, that the numbers 'voting' for each party are roughly in the same proportion as was found in the two general elections held in 1974. The actual numbers were (numbers for males precede numbers for females): Conservative, 126 and 134; Labour, 149 and 157; Liberal, 98 and 110; Others, 48 and 28. A few subjects who did not fill in the information on voting behaviour have been omitted.

Mean scores and standard deviations of voters for these four parties were calculated on the following scores: P, E, N and L; conservatism, capitalism and toughmindedness; the eleven primary sex factors (using questionnaire scores, not factor scores); the three sex behaviour scores; and the two sex superfactors, libido and satisfaction. The actual scores obtained are given in tables 4.6 and 4.7; also given are the p values resulting from analyses of variance for each score. The figure must speak for themselves, but a brief discussion may be of value. In this discussion we have concentrated on issues that are of interest, and where the significance values and the agreement between males and females suggest that the results are replicable.

As far as the personality scales are concerned, the following points seem worthy of mention. On P, for both males and females, 'other' voters are clearly much higher than voters for the orthodox majority parties; this agrees well with the findings of Eaves and Eysenck (1974) that there are genetic links between toughmindedness and P, and Eysenck's (1954) finding that extremist parties (fascists and communists) are high on toughmindedness. In agreement with this, we find that in our present study also 'other' voters have higher toughmindedness scores in both the male and female samples. Eaves and Eysenck (1974) also found E associated genetically with toughmindedness; in the present study 'other' voters have high E scores in both samples, but conservative voters also have high E scores, and are less toughminded than either 'other' or Labour voters. It is possible that these correlations are predicated on different aspects of extraversion; perhaps the correlation with conservative voting is related to sociability, that with 'other' voting with impulsiveness. Only further research can decide on this point. For N the two sexes give contradictory results, but for L Conservatives clearly have the highest, and 'other' voters the lowest scores.

Table 4.7 *Mean social attitude scores for conservative, labour, liberal and 'other' voters: female*

Females	Conservative voters (134)	Labour voters (157)	Liberal voters (110)	Others (28)	p
P	1·31 ± 1·35	1·51 ± 1·57	1·71 ± 1·59	2·52 ± 1·96	0·01
E	12·60 ± 3·50	12·06 ± 4·19	11·32 ± 3·74	12·79 ± 3·50	0·05
N	11·64 ± 4·53	10·81 ± 4·65	12·37 ± 4·79	11·43 ± 4·40	0·05
L	6·97 ± 3·84	6·68 ± 3·34	6·70 ± 3·26	5·02 ± 2·68	N.S.
Conservatism	112·40 ± 16·57	88·33 ± 19·00	97·65 ± 18·42	82·82 ± 25·68	0·001
Capitalism	72·81 ± 8·11	57·38 ± 9·83	62·71 ± 8·36	55·50 ± 17·83	0·001
Toughmindedness	57·60 ± 9·68	62·25 ± 9·54	60·67 ± 9·16	64·89 ± 6·14	0·001
Permissiveness	10·25 ± 3·01	11·39 ± 2·68	10·67 ± 2·94	11·91 ± 2·04	0·01
Satisfaction	9·03 ± 2·77	9·04 ± 2·79	8·21 ± 2·92	8·00 ± 3·23	0·05
Neurotic sex	4·66 ± 2·15	4·78 ± 1·81	4·34 ± 2·01	4·34 ± 1·57	N.S.
Impersonal sex	4·94 ± 2·28	5·39 ± 2·17	5·02 ± 2·39	4·64 ± 2·02	N.S.
Pornography	2·88 ± 2·28	2·40 ± 2·32	3·20 ± 2·42	2·84 ± 2·06	0·05
Shyness	2·90 ± 2·82	3·58 ± 2·69	3·62 ± 3·00	4·43 ± 3·14	0·05
Prudishness	1·84 ± 1·37	1·33 ± 1·26	2·05 ± 1·79	1·30 ± 1·18	0·001
Disgust	5·25 ± 2·35	5·82 ± 2·24	5·06 ± 2·51	5·54 ± 2·17	0·05
Excitement	2·38 ± 1·59	1·89 ± 1·53	2·60 ± 1·06	1·86 ± 1·12	0·001
Physical sex	2·59 ± 1·52	2·71 ± 1·29	2·43 ± 1·41	2·91 ± 1·43	N.S.
Aggressive sex	1·01 ± 0·67	1·14 ± 0·84	1·18 ± 0·79	1·20 ± 0·81	N.S.
Sex Behaviour 1	8·32 ± 2·37	8·86 ± 1·83	8·01 ± 2·55	8·82 ± 1·61	0·05
Sex Behaviour 2	0·90 ± 1·19	0·57 ± 1·10	1·09 ± 1·70	0·46 ± 0·69	0·01
Sex Behaviour 3	0·51 ± 1·11	0·62 ± 1·09	0·53 ± 1·07	0·61 ± 1·03	N.S.
Satisfaction	12·89 ± 3·14	13·08 ± 2·87	11·81 ± 3·25	12·11 ± 3·11	0·001
Libido	17·93 ± 7·18	20·11 ± 6·23	18·75 ± 7·35	19·70 ± 6·39	0·05

SOCIAL ATTITUDES AND SEXUAL BEHAVIOUR

The first of these two findings is in good agreement with the
findings of Wilson and Brazendale (1973), who found a correlation
of 0·26 between conservatism and L; they also found a correlation
of $-0·26$ between L and realism, which is their name for toughmindedness (Wilson 1973). Wilson and Brazendale found other
correlations which do not agree with our findings, e.g. a significant
correlation between P and conservatism and a negative correlation
between E and conservatism. They also found a positive correlation
between E and realism–toughmindedness, which is in agreement
with our general findings. Their results were based on ninety-seven
female student teachers, and it is possible that in such small and
rather unrepresentative groups population trends may be reversed;
thus student groups tend to be exceptionally 'progressive', and
it may need a high P to confess to conservative leanings! Similarly,
the high popularity of 'progressive' ideas may make conservatives
less popular (low E) and high 'realism' scorers more popular (high
E). Clearly the relationship between personality and social attitudes
requires much further study. It should perhaps be added that the
correlation between L and conservative voting is more likely to
be explained in terms of the conventionality–conformity aspect of
this scale than its dissimulation-measuring properties; the correlation between L and N is no higher in the conservatives than
the other groups, and as Michaelis and Eysenck (1971) have shown,
it is this correlation that indicates dissimulation.

The relationship between voting behaviour and the social attitude
variables is very much as one might have expected, with conservatives, liberals, labour and 'other' voters having scores on conservatism and capitalism which decline in that order. We have already
commented on the high toughmindedness scores of 'other' voters;
at the tenderminded end we find liberals (which agrees with
Eysenck's 1954 finding) and (for the women) conservatives; it is
not clear why women should be different from men in this respect.
With this one exception, however, results support the original
hypothesis suggested by Eysenck (1954), to the effect that political
parties can be arranged in the shape of a horseshoe in the two-
dimensional space generated by the conservatism–radicalism and
the toughmindedness–tendermindedness factors, with liberals intermediate on the former, and most tenderminded on the latter factor,
and conservatives and fascists diverging upward towards toughmindedness and right towards conservatism, and labour voters and

173

communists diverging upward towards toughmindedness and left towards radicalism.

When we turn next to the sexual attitudes variables, we find smaller differences between voters for the different parties; this is of course not unexpected in view of the fact that political party programmes seldom if ever contain proposals relevant to this field. On permissiveness the conservatives have the lowest scores, the 'other' voters the highest; this is not unexpected. On satisfaction conservatives come highest; this may be simply a display of conventional sentiments, or it may reveal the more satisfactory nature of old-fashioned family-based mores. Our data do not enable us to answer this question. On neurotic sex it is difficult to see any pattern in the responses of the two sexes; the same is true of impersonal sex. Pornography is regarded least unfavourably by liberal voters, on the whole. Sexual shyness is least among conservatives, greatest among 'other' voters; this may be linked with the high extraversion of the conservatives (sociability?), but does not go well with the high extraversion of the 'other' voters (unless we agree that this is produced by some other sub-trait of E than sociability). Prudishness, disgust and excitement do not convey a very dissimilar picture for voters for the different parties; neither does physical sex. Aggressive sex shows a slight trend for 'other' voters to have high scores; this agrees with Eysenck and Coulter's (1972) finding of greater aggressiveness among communists and fascists.(3) On the superfactor scores of satisfaction and libido, we note again that conservatives tend to have the higher satisfaction scores, although this finding is not strong enough to deserve much credence until replicated. For libido the results for the two sexes are too contradictory to make it possible to draw any conclusions. None of these sexual attitude differences is very large or compelling, and the findings must of course be accepted with particular caution in view of the small size and the not completely representative nature of the sample.

The sex behaviour data are also difficult to interpret. On sex behaviour 1 (Have done ...) the only consistent finding is the low position of the liberals; there is a tendency in this direction also in connection with the libido superfactor scores. This behaviour syndrome may in turn be related to the tenderminded attitudes of the liberals, i.e. their idealistic view of the world. Seen in this context the findings (which of course require confirmation) possibly

174

make some sense. They are partly confirmed by the high scores of the liberals on sex behaviour 2 (Have done and didn't like ...); conscience thus doth make cowards of us all. On sex behaviour 3 (Have not done and would like to do ...) the results are not at all clear, and do not agree for the two sexes; it is probably best not to try to interpret the results.

On the whole, we may perhaps say that such results as have come up in connection with political party preference do not show any strong relation with sexual attitudes and behaviour, and that such rather weak associations as could be observed are in line with common sense and with theoretical predictions based on previous work. Clearly, much further work will be necessary to establish the degree to which we can put any trust in these generalisations; at best they serve to formulate more detailed hypotheses for testing. The same caution should be applied to the interpretation of the apparent tendencies for females to show a much closer and more significant relationship between voting behaviour and sexual attitudes. Perhaps it is true, as is sometimes said, that women look upon everything from the point of view of sex, but these data are hardly sufficient to establish the truth of this ancient adage!

1. These results are very similar to those reported by Thomas (1975) in a study of 114 male and 223 female students. Using the Wilson Patterson scale of conservatism, he found a correlation between C and sexual experience of -0.41. C correlated -0.58 with attitudes towards premarital sex; correlations of C with church attendance were positive ($r=0.49$ for males, 0.58 for females); and church attendance correlated negatively with sexual experience ($r=-0.29$, -0.48 respectively). These correlations were obtained in New Zealand.

2. Homogamy for attitudes has been extensively documented in such papers as those by Kirkpatrick and Stone (1935), Morgan and Remmers (1935), Newcomb and Svehla (1937), Schiller (1932), Schooley (1936) and Schuster and Elderton (1906). All found sizeable correlations, comparable with those here reported.

3. See also the work of Jaffe and others (1974) demonstrating a link between sexual arousal and aggressiveness.

APPENDIX E

KEY FOR CONSERVATISM, CAPITALISM AND TOUGHMINDEDNESS SCALES

Conservatism		Capitalism	Toughminded
− 1	53	−13	5
2	54	−15	9
3	55	−16	14
− 6	64	−27	17
7	67	−30	32
8	69	−33	38
10	70	35	−41
11	72	39	−47
−12	74	42	49
18	78	44	50
−19	82	−45	56
20	86	−48	−65
21		−51	66
22		−57	71
23		−61	75
24		−68	76
25		−79	−88
26		−80	
28		−81	
34		−84	
36		−87	
37			
40			
43			

5

Sexual attitudes and behaviour in psychiatric patients

It seemed of interest to apply the attitude and behaviour scales used in our study of normal men and women to a particularly abnormal sample, in order to see to what extent the relationships between factors and personality, and even the very nature of the factors, could be replicated. The very abnormality of the sample of criminally insane males tested at Broadmoor makes it likely that, if our main findings could be replicated with them, then any lack of randomness in the selection of the original normal sample could not have been responsible for producing the results observed. Accordingly a sample of 186 Broadmoor patients was administered the personality questionnaires, the sexual attitudes inventory and the sexual behaviour scale described in chapter 4. The patients come from a population described in some detail by Tennent and others (1974); they were all male, with an average age slightly above that of our normal group, and were all judged intelligent enough to understand the questions, and not so disturbed as to fail to respond properly to the situation. Each test was administered personally by Miss Gloria Bragança (1972), who gives a detailed description of the sample and the method of testing. The sample does not differ significantly from the total group of patients with respect to offender category: 16 per cent are sex offenders; 11 per cent have been committed for arson;' 26 per cent for murder and manslaughter; 28 per cent for attempted murder and wounding; 16 per cent for other violence, assault and property offences; and 3 per cent were admitted under Section 26 of the Mental Health Act. Patients volunteered to undergo the test, but of those approached over thirty failed to complete the inventory.

Table 5.1 lists the percentage of 'Yes' answers of the patients, and

177

also gives for the sake of comparison the percentage of 'Yes' answers of our normal sample, quoted from the preceding chapter. Questions 155 and 159 were omitted by too many patients to make it possible to include them in any of our analyses.

Table 5.1 *Percentage of 'yes' answers of Broadmoor patients and normal males to sex inventory items. Asterisked items omitted from factor analysis*

Question	Broadmoor	Normal	Question	Broadmoor	Normal
1	60	49	78	55	74
2	58	43	79	69	82
3	52	15	80	57	56
4	49	64	81	23	9
5	51	8	82	51	19
6	37	5	83	12	8
7	48	50	84	25	13
*8	18	4	85	53	73
9	60	69	86	27	35
10	60	81	87	37	9
11	44	22	88	13	0
*12	20	5	89	35	41
13	37	43	*90	36	7
14	18	10	91	58	45
15	18	4	92	12	18
16	50	32	93	57	78
17	19	12	94	18	17
18	13	6	95	18	31
19	51	35	96	49	55
20	54	54	97	16	7
21	46	24	*98	12	1
22	47	45	99	18	6
23	29	3	100	10	9
24	31	34	101	12	26
25	79	78	102	32	21
26	25	16	103	56	64
*27	34	20	104	60	45
*28	46	56	105	11	3
29	39	17	106	33	44
30	59	75	*107	66	29
31	24	29	108	56	44
32	16	9	109	40	11
*33	22	5	110	32	12
34	70	50	111	50	57
*35	85	96	112	65	69
36	60	57	113	56	65
37	46	87	114	52	39
38	17	7	*115	40	55
39	48	68	116	26	53
40	38	15	117	18	5
41	23	10	118	23	11
42	30	32	119	23	33

178

PSYCHIATRIC PATIENTS

Question	Broadmoor	Normal	Question	Broadmoor	Normal
43	72	80	120	32	52
44	21	13	121	18	24
*45	9	1	122	73	66
46	26	25	123	11	8
47	35	20	124	12	6
48	9	7	125	59	69
49	32	24	126	17	6
50	66	76	127	34	21
51	10	3	128	20	9
52	25	8	129	24	19
53	34	31	*130	30	38
*54	34	14	131	63	63
55	82	95	132	68	53
56	18	13	133	18	13
57	70	85	134	63	41
58	25	6	135	64	37
59	22	11	*136	24	16
60	37	24	*137	24	16
61	19	6	*138	74	83
*62	48	39	139	18	3
63	59	95	*140	13	5
64	17	7	141	79	90
65	47	34	*142	68	41
*66	52	58	*143	53	26
67	58	69	144	32	36
68	19	22	145	55	55
69	34	6	146	47	15
*70	81	84	147	49	29
71	62	74	*148	65	59
72	40	42	149	30	22
73	73	87	150	33	20
74	70	67	151	77	85
75	26	54	152	74	86
76	74	84	153	38	48
77	35	67			

It will be clear from looking at the figures that the Broadmoor patients are on the whole much more inhibited sexually than are the 'normal' group. Thus they are less easily excited sexually; conditions have to be just right; they think only rarely about sex; they consciously try to keep sex thoughts out of their mind; when they have strong sex feelings they cannot express them; they don't think about sex almost every day; they say that they do not get excited very easily; they look upon sex as being only for reproduction and not for pleasure; sex is not all that important to them; they are not excited by the thought of an illicit relationship; they can take sex or leave it alone. They draw sharp lines between what is right and

179

what is not in sexual conduct: they find it disgusting to see animals
having sexual intercourse; there are some things they would not do
with anyone; they find the thought of a sex orgy disgusting; they
don't think that sometimes a woman should be sexually aggressive;
they prefer intercourse under bedcovers and in the dark; they do
not feel like scratching and biting their sex partners; they object to
four-letter swear words in mixed company; they find wife-swapping
distasteful; and they find some forms of love-making disgusting.
They hold rather conservative views on sexual matters: virginity is
a girl's most valuable possession; seeing a person nude does not interest them; they would protect their children from contact with sex;
they would not take a chance to watch people making love; they are
against pornographic writing being freely published; they believe in a
sexual censorship; they do not uphold the dual standard of morality;
they think that sexual permissiveness undermines society; they do
not consider sex play among young children harmless; and they think
it right that the man should be dominant.

They consider that their lives have not been successful; they
feel they have been deprived sexually; their love life has been
disappointing; they find it hard to talk to people of the opposite
sex; and they feel more comfortable with people of their own sex.
As we have seen, satisfaction with one's love life correlates negatively with personality factors P (psychoticism) and N (neuroticism);
in this psychiatrically abnormal group it is therefore not surprising
to find such dissatisfaction with their sex life.

The personality scale scores of the patients are given in table
5.2, together with the normative scores of a sample of 1,000 normal
males of similar age and social class. The patients are clearly
more introverted, more neurotic and very slightly higher on P.
This slight difference in P may at first seem odd in a sample of
insane persons, but it finds an explanation in the extremely high
L score of this group, which is well over twice as high as that of
the normal standardisation group. It is often found that psychotics
give high L scores, thus showing a tendency to dissimulate which
effectively lowers their P and N scores, sometimes very markedly
(Eysenck and Eysenck 1976). Had answers been honest there is
little doubt that the P and N scores would have been considerably
higher. These high L scores must of course also throw some doubt
on the accuracy and honesty of the answers given to the sex
questionnaires.

Table 5.2 *Personality scale scores of Broadmoor patients and standardisation sample*

	Broadmoor	Standardisation
P	2·69 ± 2·36	2·50 ± 2·71
E	11·45 ± 3·89	12·75 ± 4·11
N	9·52 ± 5·33	7·33 ± 4·37
L	8·03 ± 4·68	3·64 ± 2·34

A factor analysis was undertaken of the sexual attitudes questionnaire, but as in the case of the normal sample it was impossible to use all the questions as the computer could not handle more than 135 items. It was decided to select 131 items, mostly but not entirely identical with those used previously with our normal sample, and to include in the analysis the *P, E, N* and *L* scales. The items omitted from the sex attitude questionnaire are indicated in table 5.1 by asterisks, so as to make identification possible.

Factor analysis of the correlations between the 131 items and the four personality scales gave rise to ten interpretable factors. These are given below; in each case the factor is named, and the items having highest saturations are given, together with the loadings and the item number in the actual questionnaire. This is done to enable readers to check item wording; the wording in the tables below has been paraphrased from the original to avoid too-lengthy statements. The actual factors are very similar to those obtained on our normal group, although the items included in the analysis were not the same in every instance; this may account for the occasional differences. Thus in this analysis items referring to homosexuality were included, giving rise to a factor of homosexuality, while in the analysis of our normal sample these items were for the most part excluded, thus producing no such factor. The naming of the factors is of course somewhat subjective; we have followed the naming procedure of the corresponding factors in the normal group.

Below are set out details concerning factor 1, permissiveness. Statements are worded in the same direction as in the questionnaire; if the loading is preceded by a minus sign, the statement should of course be reversed. Thus people high on the permissiveness factor do *not* think about sex only rarely. It will be seen that high *L* scorers are not permissive, but that high *E* scorers are, as are high *P* scorers.

181

Factor 1 :   Permissiveness

Question	Loading	
6	− 0·44	Think about sex rarely
17	− 0·51	Disturbing to see necking in public
23	− 0·43	Try to keep sex thoughts out of mind
30	− 0·37	Doesn't take much to get sexually excited
37	0·31	Think about sex almost every day
38	− 0·46	Should not experiment with sex before marriage
39	0·36	Get sexually excited very easily
41	− 0·34	Better not to have sex until married
51	− 0·63	Don't like to be kissed
55	0·57	Enjoy petting
58	− 0·59	Seeing a person nude doesn't interest me
63	0·37	Sometimes a woman should be sexually aggressive
82	− 0·30	Dual standards of morality, allowing men greater' freedom, natural
88	− 0·61	Sex should be for reproduction, not pleasure
109	− 0·53	Sex not all that important
110	− 0·38	Most men sex-mad
112	0·42	Enjoy lengthy pre-coital play
116	0·32	Sometimes like scratching and biting partner during intercourse
141	0·41	Naked body is pleasing
154	0·38	Prefer intercourse frequently
P	0·24	
E	0·31	
N	− 0·06	
L	− 0·39	

Factor 2 is connected with satisfaction. This factor correlates positively with E, negatively with P and N. There is no correlation with L.

Factor 2 :   Satisfaction (1)

Question	Loading	
4	0·61	Am satisfied with sex life
11	− 0·68	Have been deprived sexually
14	− 0·33	Sexually rather unattractive
19	− 0·52	Something lacking in sex life
21	− 0·33	Love life has been disappointing
75	− 0·35	Sometimes have felt hostile to partner
111	− 0·34	Good in bed is important in marriage partner
112	0·30	Believe sexual activities are average
126	− 0·36	Can't stand people touching me
P	− 0·14	
E	0·29	
N	− 0·22	
L	− 0·01	

182

Factor 3 deals with neurotic sex. Not surprisingly, N has a high correlation with this factor ($r=0\cdot51$). P, too, is positively correlated with this factor, while E is negatively correlated. The L scale again fails to show any notable relationship with the factor.

Factor 3:   Neurotic sex

Question	Loading	
14	0·35	Am sexually unattractive
18	0·47	Sexual feelings sometimes unpleasant
23	0·32	Consciously try to keep sex thoughts out of mind
24	0·42	Felt guilty about sex experiences
26	0·51	Afraid of what I may do sexually
31	0·35	Parents' influences have inhibited me sexually
32	0·70	Sex thoughts disturb more than should
44	0·70	Conscience bothers me too much
46	0·43	Sexual feelings overpower me
48	0·74	Sex thoughts drive me almost crazy
56	0·66	Worry a lot about sex
59	0·78	Sometimes thinking about sex makes me nervous
60	0·48	Perverted thoughts have sometimes bothered me
68	0·41	Sometimes felt like humiliating sex partner
84	0·42	Had some bad sex experiences when young
111	− 0·48	Being good in bed is important in marriage partner
117	0·33	No one has satisfied me sexually
124	0·51	Am afraid of sexual relationship
139	0·42	Cannot discuss sexual matters with wife
P	0·25	
E	− 0·31	
N	0·51	
L	− 0·10	

Factor 4 deals with impersonal sex. Here L has a high negative loading, while P and E have small positive ones.

Factor 4:   Impersonal sex

Question	Loading	
13	0·39	Do not need respect or love to enjoy petting/intercourse with partner
34	− 0·39	Some things I wouldn't do with anyone
72	0·41	Have been involved with more than one sex affair at same time
77	0·35	If had chance to see people making love, would take it
97	0·47	Prefer to have new partner every night
102	0·38	Sex more exciting with strangers

Question	Loading	
108	− 0·34	Sex partner satisfies all physical needs
119	0·70	Group sex appeals
120	0·49	Thought of illicit relationship excites me
146	− 0·34	Some forms of love-making disgusting
152	0·31	Offered highly pornographic book, would accept
153	0·77	Invitation to an orgy accepted
P	0·18	
E	0·18	
N	0·07	
L	− 0·31	

Factor 5 is clearly concerned with pornography. It is interesting to note that liking for pornography is positively correlated with extraversion and negatively with the L score.

Factor 5: Pornography

Question	Loading	
25	0·39	Wouldn't bother if person married not virgin
36	0·35	Understand homosexuals
43	0·79	Like to look at sexy pictures
61	− 0·32	Embarrassed to talk about sex
64	− 0·40	Sex jokes disgust
73	0·50	Homosexuality normal for some people
76	0·76	Like to look at pictures of nudes
78	0·37	Pornographic writing freely allowed to be published
81	− 0·67	Too many immoral plays on T.V.
82	0·38	Dual standard of morality natural and should be continued
87	− 0·52	Sexual permissiveness undermines civilised society
91	− 0·40	Preoccupation with sex created by media
123	− 0·62	Disturbs me to look at sexy photographs
149	− 0·45	Reading girlie magazines failed adult attitude to sex
151	0·56	Would see blue films
152	0·46	Would accept pornographic book
P	− 0·01	
E	0·31	
N	− 0·11	
L	− 0·34	

Factor 6 deals with sexual nervousness. This factor correlates negatively with extraversion and positively with neuroticism.

Factor 6:   Sexual nervousness

Question	Loading	
4	− 0·44	Am satisfied with sex life
7	0·39	Has been a problem to control sex feelings
16	− 0·41	Sex contacts never a problem
19	0·40	Something lacking in sex life
20	− 0·39	My sex behaviour has never caused me any trouble
21	0·46	Love life been disappointing
22	0·43	Never had many dates
29	0·57	Have strong sex feelings but given a chance can't express myself
47	0·76	Feel nervous with opposite sex
50	− 0·75	Feel at ease with opposite sex
52	0·81	Hard to talk with opposite sex
53	0·41	Didn't learn facts of life until quite old
61	0·38	Am embarrassed to talk about sex
72	− 0·40	Have been involved with more than one sex affair at a time
113	− 0·31	Find it easy to tell partner what I like and dislike about love-making
118	0·33	Feel sexually less competent than friends
P	0·10	
E	− 0·28	
N	0·31	
L	− 0·14	

Factor 7 deals with sexual excitement. This factor has only a slight loading for extraversion.

Factor 7:   Excitement

Question	Loading	
30	0·38	Doesn't take much to get me sexually excited
39	0·32	Get excited sexually very easily
65	0·31	Believe in taking pleasures where find them
80	0·34	Decisions about abortion should be concern of woman only
82	0·37	Dual standards of morality allowing men greater freedom
91	0·32	Present preoccupation with sex created by film, T.V., adverts
99	− 0·38	Prefer partners several years older
132	− 0·43	Tenderness is most important quality
147	0·67	It's right that man should be dominant in sex relationship
P	− 0·07	
E	0·15	
N	0·05	
L	0·06	

Factor 8 is concerned with physical sex. It has positive loadings for psychoticism and neuroticism.

Factor 8: Physical sex

Question	Loading	
39	0·40	Get excited sexually very easily
42	0·36	Coloured sex partner particularly exciting
79	0·56	When excited can think of nothing but satisfaction
86	0·63	Sex is far and away my greatest pleasure
106	0·56	Few things are more important than sex
110	0·57	Most men are sex-mad
127	0·46	Physical sex is most important part of marriage
P	0·25	
E	0·02	
N	0·20	
L	0·01	

Factor 9 deals with sexual aggressiveness. It has positive loadings on psychoticism and negative loadings on L.

Factor 9: Aggressiveness

Question	Loading	
100	0·55	Sexual fancies often involve flogging
101	0·61	Make vocal noises during intercourse
113	0·30	Find it easy to tell partner like/dislike love-making
116	0·52	Feel like biting and scratching partner during intercourse
121	0·55	Usually feel aggressive with partner
123	0·31	Disturbing to look at sexy photographs
132	− 0·38	Tenderness is most important quality
135	− 0·35	'Wife-swapping' is extremely distasteful
P	0·29	
E	0·02	
N	0·08	
L	− 0·24	

Factor 10 is one of homosexuality. Neuroticism loads this factor positively, L loads it negatively.

Factor 10: Homosexuality

Question	Loading	
36	0·41	Understand homosexuals
60	0·31	Perverted thoughts sometimes bother me
73	0·34	Homosexuality is normal for some people
84	0·44	Had bad sex experiences when young
104	0·64	Some things do only to please partner
145	0·33	Men more selfish in love-making than women
P	− 0·12	
E	0·06	
N	0·20	
L	− 0·21	

These factors are not independent of each other, and their correlations can in turn be factored to produce higher-order factors (superfactors). Two of these emerge from the analysis, and are given below in tables 5.3 and 5.4. Table 5.3 shows the loadings on superfactor 1 (sexual libido), while table 5.4 shows the loadings on superfactor 2 (sexual satisfaction). These two factors are very similar to the two superfactors extracted from the analysis of data in our previous work (Eysenck 1971a), and also from the analysis of data collected from normal samples filling in the questionnaire here used. As in our previous work, the correlation between these two superfactors is quite insignificant ($r=-0.03$); in other words, a person's satisfaction with his sexual life is in no way dependent on the degree or strength of his libido.

Table 5.3 *Factor loadings on superfactor 1 (sexual libido)*

Question	Loading	
1	− 0·31	Opposite sex will respect you more if not too familiar
6	− 0·42	Think rarely of sex
9	0·42	Love a person, could do anything
10	0·40	Pleasant feeling from touching sexual parts
17	− 0·44	Disturbing to see necking in public
22	− 0·30	Never had many dates
23	− 0·37	Consciously try to keep sex thoughts out of mind
30	0·39	Doesn't take much to get sexually excited
34	− 0·35	Some things wouldn't do with anyone
36	0·46	Understand homosexuals

Question	Loading	
37	0·32	Think about sex every day
38	−0·47	Should not experiment with sex before marriage
39	0·42	Get sexually excited very easily
40	−0·58	Thought of sex orgy disgusting
41	−0·54	Better not to have sex until married
42	0·43	Thought of a coloured partner particularly exciting
43	0·59	Like to look at sexy pictures
53	−0·35	Didn't learn facts of life until quite old
55	0·49	Enjoy petting
57	0·33	Pill should be universally available
58	−0·41	Seeing a person nude doesn't interest me
61	−0·39	Am embarrassed to talk about sex
63	0·30	Sometimes women should be sexually aggressive
64	−0·48	Sex jokes disgust me
65	0·45	Believe in taking pleasure where I find it
69	−0·40	Would protect children from contacts with sex
72	0·48	Have been involved with more than one affair at time
73	0·41	Homosexuality is normal for some people
74	0·47	All right to seduce a person who is old enough to know what he/she is doing
76	0·58	Like to look at pictures of nudes
77	0·48	If had a chance to see people making love unobserved would take it
78	0·69	Pornography should be freely published
79	0·40	Prostitution should be legally permitted
80	0·38	Decisions about abortion should be concern of no one but woman
81	−0·42	Too many immoral plays on T.V.
85	0·47	No censorship on sexual grounds of plays and films
87	−0·47	Sexual permissiveness threatens to undermine civilised society
88	−0·30	Sex for reproduction, not personal pleasure
89	0·41	Absolute faithfulness to partner as silly as celibacy
93	0·36	Sex play among children harmless
95	0·38	Would vote for a law permitting polygamy
96	0·51	Though having regular intercourse, masturbation good for a change
97	0·36	Prefer new sex partner every night
102	0·39	Sex more exciting with a stranger
103	−0·32	Never discussed sex with parents
109	−0·40	Sex not all that important
112	0·42	Enjoy lengthy pre-coital play
116	0·46	Feel like biting and scratching partner during intercourse
119	0·53	Group sex appeals to me

188

Question	Loading	
120	0·42	Thought of illicit relationship excites me
123	− 0·39	Disturbing to look at sexy photographs
124	− 0·42	Am afraid of sexual relationships
125	0·30	Wish women would be more forthcoming sexually
126	− 0·32	Can't stand people touching me
134	− 0·35	Object to four-letter words in mixed company
135	− 0·47	Idea of 'wife-swapping' extremely distasteful
139	− 0·36	Cannot discuss sexual matters with wife
141	0·37	Naked body a pleasing sight
144	0·37	Would not disturb if partner has sex with someone else, as long as she returned
146	− 0·46	Some forms of love-making disgust
151	0·56	Invitation to blue film accepted
152	0·58	Offer of a pornographic book accepted
153	0·56	Invitation to an orgy accepted
154	0·43	Preference for having intercourse frequently

Table 5.4 *Factor loadings on superfactor 2 (sexual satisfaction)*

Question	Loading	
4	0·41	Am satisfied with sex life
7	− 0·53	Sometimes a problem to control sex feelings
11	− 0·42	Have been deprived sexually
18	0·40	Sexual feelings sometimes unpleasant
19	− 0·44	Something lacking in sex life
20	0·36	My sex behaviour has never caused me trouble
21	− 0·49	Love life has been disappointing
22	− 0·42	Never had many dates
23	− 0·45	Consciously try to keep sex thoughts out of mind
24	− 0·47	Have felt guilty about sex experiences
26	− 0·39	Have been afraid for what I might do sexually
29	− 0·54	Have strong sex feelings but given a chance can't express myself
31	− 0·33	Parents' influence has inhibited sexually
32	− 0·56	Sex thoughts have disturbed more than should
37	− 0·31	Think about sex almost every day
39	− 0·35	Get sexually excited easily
42	− 0·35	Thought of coloured partner particularly exciting
44	− 0·44	Conscience bothers me too much
46	− 0·60	Sexual feelings overpower me
47	− 0·36	Feel nervous with opposite sex
48	− 0·51	Sex thoughts drive me crazy
49	− 0·45	When excited can think of nothing but satisfaction

189

Question	Loading	
50	0·38	Feel at ease with the opposite sex
52	−0·36	Hard to talk with opposite sex
56	−0·52	Worry a lot about sex
59	−0·53	Thinking about sex makes me nervous
60	−0·42	Perverted thoughts sometimes bother
61	−0·49	Am embarrassed to talk about sex
65	−0·30	Believe in taking pleasures where I find them
68	−0·48	Sometimes felt like humiliating partner
75	−0·43	Sometimes felt hostile to partner
84	−0·34	Have had some bad sex experiences when young
86	0·30	Sex is greatest pleasure
92	−0·31	Enjoy partner having intercourse with someone else
97	−0·30	Prefer to have a new partner every night
100	−0·37	Sexual fancies often involve flogging
102	−0·36	Sex more exciting with a stranger
103	−0·32	Never discussed sex with parents
105	−0·44	Don't always know when have had an orgasm
110	−0·35	Most men are sex-mad
114	−0·33	Like partner to be more expert and experienced
117	−0·45	No one has been able to satisfy me sexually
118	−0·47	Feel sexually less competent than my friends
121	−0·38	Usually feel aggressive with partner
122	0·31	My sexual activities are average
124	−0·44	Am afraid of sexual relationships
125	−0·36	Often wish women were more forthcoming
126	−0·35	Can't stand people touching me
128	−0·41	Prefer partner to dictate rules of the game
129	−0·34	Find 'straight sex' unsatisfactory
133	−0·31	Female genitals are aesthetically pleasing
139	−0·43	Cannot discuss sexual matters with wife
150	−0·32	Matters of sex, women always come off second-best

These superfactors are also correlated with personality. Superfactor 1 (libido) correlates positively with E ($r=0·38$) and negatively with L ($r=-0·39$). Superfactor 2 (satisfaction) correlates negatively with P ($r=-0·43$) and N ($r=-0·52$) and positively with E ($r=0·36$). Clearly both the psychiatric factors (P and N) are connected with pronounced dissatisfaction with a person's sex life, while extraversion is connected both with a happy sex life and also with strong libidinal tendencies. High L scorers, while having (or pretending to have) a weak libido, show a mild degree of satisfaction with their sex life ($r=0·12$). These figures on the whole agree well with our previous work, which also tended to show that

P and N interfere with a normal enjoyment of sex while E enhances it. The whole set of correlations is given in table 5.5.

Table 5.5 *Correlations between libido, satisfaction and the four personality variables*

	P	E	N	L	
S.F.1.	0·04	0·38	−0·10	−0·39	Libido
S.F.2.	−0·43	0·36	−0·52	0·10	Satisfaction

Patients were also administered the sexual behaviour questionnaire; their mean scores are shown in table 5.6. This table also gives the correlations with the personality variables. In brackets are given comparison scores with our normal sample of males. It will be seen that the prisoners (if they are to be believed) have on the average been less advanced in their love-making techniques than the normal males by over two steps in the scale; that is quite a large difference. There are more things they would have liked to do, and more things they had done and did not like. These data are in good agreement with the differences already given for the attitudes questionnaire; they emerge as more inhibited and less successful and satisfied. This also agrees with their greater introversion, and their (probably) greater neuroticism and psychoticism (granted that the observed scores should be corrected for dissimulation).

Table 5.6 *Scores on sexual behaviour scales of prisoners and correlation of scales with personality variables*

	Prisoners	Normal Controls	P	E	N	L
Have done and enjoyed	6·75±3·34	8·92±2·16	−0·07	0·39	−0·10	−0·19
Have done and didn't like	0·70±1·33	0·21±0·60	0·00	−0·09	−0·01	−0·01
Would have liked to have done	2·03±2·63	1·37±0·71	0·16	−0·12	·0·15	−0·05

6

Genetic factors in sexual behaviour (1)

N. G. Martin and H. J. Eysenck

There seems to be little doubt that genetic factors are likely to be responsible for many of the individual differences in sexual attitudes and behaviour that we have documented on previous pages; nevertheless, there is very little scientific evidence even for genetic causes of male–female differences other than those directly associated with physical characteristics. Even in animals individual differences have not been widely studied in a genetic context; such a wide-ranging text as that of Scott and Fuller (1965), for instance, makes no mention of such factors, and neither does the textbook on *Behaviour Genetics* by Fuller and Thompson (1960). The present chapter may thus be regarded as a preliminary exploration of uncharted waters, unlikely to provide definitive results but perhaps capable of suggesting likely conclusions. Our main intention here is to explore the possibilities of fitting a relatively simple genetic model to our data; the results may be useful as guidelines to future, more detailed, explorations.

Before turning to our data, it may be necessary to stress certain points that are not always understood by psychologists and psychiatrists who approach the genetic field on the assumption that the major, or even the only, interest of geneticists is the discovery of a single heritability index which could be used to divide the total variance into an 'inherited' portion and another portion due to 'environment'. Such an index might be of interest to stockbreeders, but would have little scientific importance. The well-known debates concerning the inheritance of intelligence have stressed the concept of heritability to the exclusion of other, equally relevant, considerations. It is important to realise the complexity of the task, and the number of variables that enters into any reasonable model of genetic and environmental action and interaction.

If all the genetic and environmental influences acting on a trait are purely additive and independent, then the total variance of the trait in the population can be partitioned into the following four components:

E_1 within-families environmental component
G_1 within-families genetic component
E_2 between-families environmental component
G_2 between-families genetic component.

Notice that we distinguish between E_1, which includes variance due to environmental influences specific to an individual and errors of measurement, and E_2, which includes cultural and social influences common to members of the same family but differing between families. The components of G_1 and G_2 will differ according to the way in which the genes act. For this reason it is usually more instructive to talk directly in terms of the sources of genetic variation. If the genes affecting a trait act in a purely additive way then the only source of variation is D_R, the additive genetic component. However, if some genes are dominant to others then this will create a dominance genetic component H_R, although in practice this is notoriously difficult to detect.

A further complication arises if there is a correlation between spouses for a trait that has some degree of genetic determination. This phenomenon of like marrying like is known as assortative mating and tends to inflate the additive genetic variance between families. For this reason in twin studies it will be automatically confounded with an estimate of E_2 and when we detect such a component, as we do for radicalism below, we cannot tell to what extent it is due to cultural differences between families or assortative mating. If we have independent evidence of a correlation between husband and wife, as we do for radicalism, then this would suggest that at least some part of our apparent E_2 is actually extra additive genetic variance due to assortative mating.

The extent to which E_1, E_2, D_R, H_R and assortative mating contribute to the mean squares from an analysis of variance of M.Z. and D.Z. twin scores is shown in the basic model below.

193

Basic model for mean squares of twins reared together

	E_1*	E_2**	D_R†	H_R‡
M.Z. between	1	2	$1 + \dfrac{A\ \S}{1-A}$	$\frac{1}{2}$
within	1	–	–	–
D.Z. between	1	2	$\frac{3}{4} + \dfrac{A}{1-A}$	$\frac{5}{16}$
within	1	–	$\frac{1}{4}$	$\frac{3}{16}$

* E_1=within-family environmental variance
** E_2=between-families environmental variance
† D_R=additive genetic variance
‡ H_R= dominance variance
§ A=Fisher's assortative mating parameter – correlation between the additive deviations of spouses

We have described the situation in which the different environmental and genetic influences on a trait act additively and independently. However, there are two types of effect that can complicate the simple breakdown of the total phenotypic variance that we have described above, viz. genotype–environment interaction ($G \times E$) and genotype environmental covariation (COV_{GE}).

If a given environmental stimulus has a bigger effect on the behaviour of one genotype than on another then this is known as genotype–environment interaction. For example, glutamic acid. is believed to raise the I.Q. of dull and mentally defective children but not of average or bright ones (Eysenck 1973b). Our twin study provides a simple test of one such type of interaction, described below. However, interaction can be generated as an artefact of the scale of measurement, and in this case it can often be removed by rescaling the data before carrying out a normal additive analysis. This has been done successfully with several factors in this study.

Genotype–environment covariation occurs when genetic and environmental deviations are correlated. Eaves (1976) has distinguished three types of COV_{GE}

1 A genotype seeks out an environment that is most compatible with the advantages and limitations bestowed by the genes. Thus a person inclined to read will seek out libraries and a child predisposed towards music but not to sport will sit and listen to a record rather than go out and play games. It is difficult to think of an experiment

with humans in which this type of COV_{GE} could be distinguished from the genetic effects themselves.

2 Intelligent parents often have bright children who inherit not only their parents' genes but also their environment, well stocked with good books and journals and an atmosphere conducive to learning. These cultural effects (which themselves have a genetic component) will covary with the direct influences of the child's genes. However this type of COV_{GE} produced in the presence of cultural transmission can be detected only by comparing relatives reared together and apart and in the simple twin study we have here will be confounded with E_2 and assortative mating.

3 Brothers and sisters reared together will have different influences on each other according to their genotypes. These influences will covary with the direct influences of the genes on the child himself, and the greater the degree of genetic similarity between two siblings, the greater will be the covariance. Thus the covariance between M.Z. twins will be greater than that between D.Z. twins and this will affect the pattern of mean squares in a way that allows us to detect this source of COV_{GE} as we shall see below in the case of sexual satisfaction in females.

The methods by means of which we can obtain data to fit such a complex model are discussed in detail by Mather and Jinks (1971); worked examples to illustrate the application of such models to human personality data are given by Jinks and Fulker (1970) and by Eaves and Eysenck (1975). The results of applying genetic methods to human personality are summarised in some detail by Eysenck (1975a). Quite briefly, it appears that the major personality factors P, E and N show little evidence of non-additive genetic factors, which in this context means primarily that dominance and assortative mating are both absent or present only to a quite minor extent. A simple model involving additive genetic variance and within-families environmental variance seems sufficient to fit the data. There is no evidence for any between-families environmental variance, which suggests strongly that psychoanalytic and other theories regarding the determination of personality differences by maternal or paternal behaviour are in error. For all three personality traits the value of h^2, when correction is made for the unreliability of the scales, lies between 50 and 80 per cent; no great precision attends these values, of course, but they suggest the region within which the true values are likely to lie. It should also be noted, in view of some of the results reported below, that social attitudes, i.e. radicalism–conservatism, toughmindedness–tendermindedness and emphasis all showed intermediate heritability, on the basis of a similar simple model; in addition it was found that toughmindedness was genetically associated with P and E; emphasis was similarly associated with P (Eaves and Eysenck 1974).

Only one study has been found in the literature that has attempted to investigate the question of genetic determination of sexual behaviour, and this study was self-confessedly a pilot one only, using a very small number of subjects (ten pairs of M.Z. and six pairs of D.Z. same-sexed twins). Equal numbers of twins in each group were male and female, with mean ages of twenty-six and twenty-seven years for M.Z. and D.Z. pairs respectively. Zygosity was established by means of a blood sample test using eight independent blood groups; data were ascertained by means of interviews, personality inventory and body measurement. (The personality inventory used was the E.P.I.) Information was sought on maximum autosexual outlets (maximum number of times masturbation to orgasm had occurred in one day); age at menarche; age at first ejaculation; age when regular masturbation began; age at first orgasm; age at first passive genital stimulation; age at first active genital stimulation; age at first intercourse. Heritabilities were estimated by means of Holzinger's formula:

$$H = (V^{DZ} - V^{MZ})/V^{DZ}$$

and significance by means of the formula $F = V^{DZ}/V^{MZ}$ (Chilton 1972). This formula is of doubtful value for the determination of heritability, but may be used as indicating the significance of the greater similarity of M.Z. as compared with D.Z. twins, for the particular trait investigated. The methodology of this study is clearly faulty from the point of view of modern biometrical genetics, and may with advantage be contrasted with the more adequate methods illustrated in our own research. Jinks and Fulker (1970) have demonstrated the inadequacy of Holzinger's formula and the estimate of F used.

The findings may gain interest by comparing the heritabilities found against certain landmarks. Thus the heritability of height was 0·90; that for weight 0·97; that for body build (the ponderal index) 0·88. Table 6.1 shows the major findings for the various sex behaviour variables. In view of the small number of twins, it is surprising to find that any of the values are statistically significant; it

Table 6.1 *Holzinger heritabilities for sexual behaviours: asterisks indicate statistical significance of* $p < 0.05$ *level*

	H		
	Male	Female	Total
Maximum autosexual outlet	0·89*	0·65	0·80*
Age of menarche	–	0·61	–
Age at first			
ejaculation	0·69	–	–
masturbation	0·80	0·76	0·78*
orgasm	0·70	0·85	0·81*
passive genital stimulation	0·87	0·46	0·80*
active genital stimulation	0·90*	0·00	0·69
sexual intercourse	0·81	0·00	0·61

is less surprising that practically all the values are well above zero. The two exceptions relate to female age at first active genital stimulation and at first intercourse; it is possible that these depend to a large extent on the more active male, whose behaviour is probably more self-determined in sexual matters in our society. The author summarises these results as follows.

The sexual drive is not a uniform one – just as the need and appetite for food varies from one individual to another so does sexual drive and capacity ... The results from this pilot study suggest that genetic factors play a part in determining this variation, that the age at which an individual begins developing and exploring his sexuality is not just a function of environmental experiences but is also, in part, an expression of his genotype.

It is noteworthy that age at menarche, with an H of 0·61, was insignificant in relation to genetic determination; others had previously found this determination fully significant (e.g. Tisserand-Perrier 1953). This suggests that the other almost significant H values are also likely to lack significance simply because of the very small number of cases involved. For the same reason, it seems likely that the personality scale scores also failed of significance. It is interesting, though, that there was a clear association between introversion and neuroticism, on the one hand, and ectomorphic body build on the other;(2) this is very much in line with expectation (Eysenck 1970a, Rees 1973). A high ectomorphic rating was associated with later sexual development; and, in particular, ectomorphs tended to experience first coitus later than either mesomorphs or endomorphs. This finding is supported by McNeill and Livson

197

(1963), who showed that ectomorphs reached menarche later than individuals with a lower ponderal index. These results agree well with our own, as far as personality and its relationship with sexual behaviour are concerned.

The present study was carried out on 153 male twins and 339 female twins from the Institute of Psychiatry Twin Register.(3) Many more pairs of twins were approached, but the sexual nature of the questionnaire put off many twins who had taken part in previous investigations. Roughly one in three of those approached filled in the inventories anonymously. However, the mean personality scale scores of those who did fill in the sex inventories were not very different from those of the total twin sample; it appears that of our total twin sample, the group that constitutes our present sub-sample was not entirely unrepresentative. The questionnaires administered to this sub-sample were the sexual attitudes questionnaire discussed in chapter 3, the social attitudes questionnaire discussed in chapter 4 and the P, E, N and L scales of the E.P.Q. (Eysenck and Eysenck 1975). Only the major sex attitudes scales (satisfaction, libido, masculinity–femininity) were analysed from the sex inventory; R, T and Emphasis were analysed from the social attitudes inventory. Thus we used ten scales in all, namely the above six scales and the four personality scales. Table 6.2 gives the means and standard deviations of the twin groups on these scales.

Table 6.2 *Means and standard deviations for twin sample*

	Female (N=339)	Male (N=153)
Satisfaction	12·40± 3·22	12·45± 3·43
Libido	12·56± 5·95	19·99± 6·27
Masculinity	19·15± 5·02	28·23± 6·16
Radicalism	145·61±21·01	147·08±24·60
Toughmindedness	45·94± 7·85	49·67± 8·20
Emphasis	95·50±18·16	100·53±18·90
Psychoticism	1·05± 1·32	1·77± 1·62
Extraversion	11·59± 4·07	12·61± 4·06
Neuroticism	11·47± 4·61	8·99± 5·00
Lie	8·11± 3·89	6·74± 3·81

Table 6.3 shows the intercorrelations, for males and females separately, of the ten scales in question. It will be seen that the general features of our previous work with different samples are reproduced with a considerable degree of accuracy.

Table 6.3 Twin correlations between sex attitudes, social attitudes and personality scales: males above leading diagonal, females below. Asterisks indicate significance levels (0·05, 0·01 and 0·001)

	Satisfaction	Libido	M-F	Radicalism	Tough-mindedness	Emphasis	P	E	N	L
1 Sexual satisfaction		-0·17*	-0·22**	-0·25**	-0·12	0·09	-0·27**	0·34**	-0·52***	0·19*
2 Sexual libido	-0·01		0·87***	0·30	0·52***	0·10	0·18*	0·23**	0·17*	-0·30**
3 Masculinity–femininity	-0·01	0·81***		0·22**	0·39***	0·08	0·16*	0·16*	0·17*	-0·21**
4 Radicalism	0·03	0·30*	0·23*		0·33***	0·20*	0·28**	-0·10	0·16*	-0·26*
5 Toughmindedness	-0·04	0·56**	0·43*	0·29*		0·19*	0·40**	0·04	0·11	-0·31**
6 Emphasis	-0·14*	0·04	-0·02	0·04	-0·02		0·17*	0·07	0·07	0·05
7 P	-0·21*	0·21*	0·17*	0·17*	0·29*	0·12*		-0·17*	0·15	-0·16*
8 E	0·15*	0·07	0·00	-0·09	-0·05	0·01	-0·14*		-0·24**	-0·06
9 N	-0·30*	0·13*	0·10	-0·10	0·05	0·12*	0·18*	-0·14*		-0·13
10 L	0·10	-0·23*	-0·14*	-0·25*	-0·20*	0·01	-0·21	-0·10	-0·09	

✓ 1 Sexual satisfaction and libido are uncorrelated.

2 Masculinity–femininity correlates with libido, but not with satisfaction.

3 Libido and masculinity correlate with toughmindedness, but satisfaction does not.

4 Sexual satisfaction correlates negatively with the pathological scales, P and N.

5 Sexual satisfaction correlates positively with E.

6 Libido correlates positively with P, E and N, the correlation with E being the highest for the males and the lowest for the females.

7 L correlates positively with satisfaction and negatively with libido and masculinity.

8 P correlates with toughmindedness and emphasis.

9 P, E, N and L show only slight correlations, and are essentially independent.

10 The relationships for males are very similar to those for females, although the different number of subjects in the male and female samples makes the pattern of *significant* correlations differ somewhat.

We may conclude that our sample of twins is essentially similar in all important relationships to the various samples previously studied, so that results on heritability obtained from them may with some confidence be transferred to non-twin samples. (There are differences in *means* between samples, but this is probably less important in the case of genetic analysis where we are mainly concerned with *variances* and *covariances*.)

Analyses of genetic models for our ten scales were made both with the raw data, and also with age-corrected, rescaled data. Raw scales in psychological measurement often produce artefacts in genetic analyses that may take the form of apparent genotype–environment interaction; such artefacts may be detected by means of the sum-difference regression test for M.Z. twins (Jinks and Fulker 1970). It is entirely appropriate to rescale data to minimise this interaction between pair sums which may represent the genotypic value of a pair (G_1) and pair differences which are due to environmental influences specific to the individual (E_1). Bartlett (1947) has given a list of useful transformations to apply when various relationships of mean and variance are found. In many instances it is obvious that these relationships are generated by the distributions of the traits. Thus if individuals are better discriminated at one end of the scale than at the other this will produce a highly skewed distribution of scores which results in a monotonic regression curve with positive slope if the skewness is positive, and negative slope if the skewness is negative. If skewness is positive it can often be removed by taking square roots or logarithms; female radicalism scores show such a distribution. Where skewness is negative, some variant of the antilog transformation may be used. Other transformations that have been used on these data are angles and normal weights; it would be inappropriate here to go into details, particularly as the uncorrected results are strikingly similar to those achieved laboriously with age and scale correction; while recognising the rather low discriminating power we have with this sample, this similarity speaks well for the robust nature of the data and findings.

In generating and fitting genetic models, we usually wish to provide the most parsimonious description of the data, and add parameters only if simpler models fail. We routinely fit the following five models to a set of data:

1 E_1 This model tests whether there is residual variance after removing error and individual environmental (within-family) variance

2 E_1E_2 Simple environmental model

3 E_1D_R Simple genetical model (D_R denotes additive genetic variance)

4 $E_1E_2D_R$

5 $E_1D_RH_R$ (H_R refers to dominance variance).

Eaves and Eysenck (1975) have discussed in detail the assumptions and mechanics of fitting genetic models to win twin data along these lines. We usually resort to interpretation in terms of three parameters only when the simpler models fail. However, if we have external evidence for the importance of a third parameter, if we particularly want to estimate a parameter regardless of its significance or if estimation of a third parameter causes a significant reduction in the residual chi square, then fitting three-parameter models may be worthwhile. In particular, the $E_1E_2D_R$ model can sometimes help elucidate a situation in which both two-parameter models fit.

201

These five models have been fitted to the following combinations of data from the five twin groups (same sex males and females, M.Z. and D.Z. and opposite sex twins). Note, for example, that for females we have between and within-mean squares for both M.Z. and D.Z. twins, giving four statistics in all:

1 Females	4 statistics
2 Males	4 statistics
3 Same-sex pairs	8 statistics
4 Same-sex and opposite-sex pairs	10 statistics

Before fitting a model to all the same-sex pairs jointly, we must decide whether the same set of parameters is appropriate for both males and females. If we sum the residual chi squares obtained after fitting a model to male and female data separately and subtract this from the residual chi square after fitting the model to all eight statistics together we obtain a chi square which tests the heterogeneity of the fit of the model over sexes. If the heterogeneity chi square is suspiciously large, then we must fit different parameters, perhaps even different models, to the sexes separately. If there is some sort of sex limitation or sex linkage, the heterogeneity chi square will not necessarily be significant, but the opposite-sex mean square will be different from the D.Z. same-sex mean squares, and obviously different parameters should be fitted to the two sexes. If neither of these complications is present then we may safely fit the same model to all ten statistics.

Estimates of parameters and heritability, where appropriate, are given for the most illuminating cases in table 6.4. The residual chi squares and the significance of the parameters (one-tail normal deviate) and chi square are also indicated. For the $E_1 D_R$ model the heritability is calculated as:

$$h^2 = \frac{\frac{1}{2}\hat{D}_R}{\frac{1}{2}\hat{D}_R + \hat{E}_1}$$

and for the $E_1 E_2 D_R$ model as:

$$h^2 = \frac{\frac{1}{2}\hat{D}_R}{\frac{1}{2}\hat{D}_R + \hat{E}_1 + \hat{E}_2}$$

and their standard deviations are calculated as the variance of a ratio as shown by Eaves (1970).

Table 6.4 Estimates of parameters from selected cases of model-fitting to different sets of normally scaled, age-corrected data. Heritability estimates given where appropriate ($+ = 0\cdot05 < p\ 0\cdot10$)

Factor	Data set	Model	E_1	E_2	D_R	H_R	x^2	df	h^2
Satisfaction	F	2	189·38***	54·79*	—	—	8·77*	2	
		3	164·29***	—	121·97**	—	5·75+	2	0·27±0·09
		4	148·83***	-103·59+	360·33*	—	1·78	1	
		5	148·83***	—	-261·22	828·73+	1·78	1	
	M	2	139·30***	68·81*	—	—	1·12	2	
		3	124·32***	—	167·72**	—	0·06	2	0·40±0·13
		4	122·67***	-22·42	215·28	—	0·00	1	
Libido	F	2	115·99***	91·20***	—	—	1·18	2	
		3	113·08***	—	182·97***	—	4·63+	2	0·45±0·08
		4	121·83***	-121·26**	-70·78	—	0·71	1	
	M	2	111·91***	122·85**	—	—	2·01	2	0·61±0·10
		3	92·23***	—	282·86***	—	0·02	2	0·53±0·45
		4	92·93***	16·09	250·51	—	0·00	1	
Masculinity	F	2	126·53***	87·42***	—	—	0·61	2	
		3	120·35***	—	185·82***	—	4·50	2	0·44±0·08
		4	130·37***	103·09*	-39·38	—	0·48	1	
	M	2	142·43***	65·92*	—	—	1·75	2	
		3	124·59***	—	169·26**	—	0·34	2	0·40±0·13
		4	121·68***	-15·12	244·54	—	0·18	1	
Radicalism	F	2	75·76***	156·00***	—	—	4·74+	2	0·72±0·05
		3	59·23***	—	299·07***	—	4·03	2	0·33±0·19
		4	62·26***	80·02*	141·21*	—	0·62	1	

Table 6.4—cont.

Factor	Data set	Model	$\hat{E}_1$	$\hat{E}_2$	$\hat{D}_R$	$\hat{H}_R$	x^2	df	h^2
	M	2	59·28***	136·50***	—	—	2·20	2	0·75±0·07
		3	47·36***	—	283·24***	—	0·94	2	0·37±0·31
		4	48·88***	74·21	142·95	—	0·13	1	
	10	4	58·57***	60·73*	189·57*	—	3·26	6	0·44±0·14
Tough-mindedness	F	2	96·03***	119·51***	—	—	6·57*	2	0·64±0·06
		3	76·76***	—	270·66***	—	1·42	2	0·53±0·24
		4	77·70***	22·11	226·74*	—	1·24	1	
	M	2	84·12***	176·21***	—	—	1·47	2	
		3	85·71***	—	332·35***	—	6·65*	2	
		4	94·89***	231·01**	−133·78	—	0·42	1	
Emphasis	F	2	155·77***	55·34**	—	—	4·77+	2	0·36±0·08
		3	135·03***	—	151·03**	—	1·11	2	
		4	130·01***	− 61·02	284·00*	—	0·00	1	
	M	2	156·27***	61·84*	—	—	1·27	2	0·29±0·14
		3	154·21***	—	124·50*	—	1·56	2	
		4	158·89***	83·43	− 47·29	—	1·22	1	
	10	2	168·86***	54·02**	—	—	9·40	7	0·34±0·07
		3	147·32***	—	151·78***	—	5·33	7	
		4	142·63***	− 32·14	224·86*	—	4·77	6	
P	F	2	122·52***	61·07***	—	—	1·51	2	0·39±0·08
		3	112·06***	—	141·67***	—	0·47	2	0·31±0·30
		4	113·08***	12·61	114·82	—	0·42	1	

M	2	120·24***	96·33**	224·39**	–	1·58	2	0·52±0·11
	3	105·48***	–	–	–	1·52	2	0·27±0·46
	4	109·18***	49·06	119·54	–	1·07	1	
E 10	2	124·94***	66·44***	–	–	4·98	7	0·42±0·07
	3	109·72***	–	162·72***	–	4·13	7	0·29±0·22
	4	112·28***	22·99	111·97+	–	3·45	6	
F	2	166·91***	67·16**	–	–	3·07	2	0·34±0·09
	3	154·35***	–	161·34**	–	3·84	2	0·11±0·30
	4	161·22***	43·56	49·55	–	2·92	1	
N M	2	114·10***	127·75**	–	–	1·33	2	0·58±0·10
	3	100·14***	–	275·30**	–	0·61	2	0·38±0·43
	4	102·01***	45·76	182·07	–	0·44	1	
F	2	149·07***	80·26***	–	–	3·09	2	0·35±0·08
	3	141·94***	–	170·66	–	3·27	2	0·11±0·28
	4	145·40***	57·59	51·64	–	2·94	1	
L M	2	101·53***	102·33***	–	–	0·12	2	0·52±0·11
	3	95·54***	–	210·04**	–	1·01	2	0·04±0·40
	4	100·36***	55·17	16·42	–	0·12	1	
F	2	148·17***	58·63**	–	–	2·75	2	0·34±0·08
	3	135·87***	–	140·70**	–	0·99	2	
	4	134·56***	16·95	176·72	–	0·93	1	
	5	134·56***		75·00	135·63	0·93		
M	2	108·85***	92·16**	–	–	3·08	2	0·50±0·12
	3	99·21***	–	195·40**	–	2·81	2	
	4	98·65***	22·59	239·74	–	2·92	1	
	5	98·65***	–	104·18	180·76	2·92	1	

Table 6.4 contains in essence the sum of our results. It may repay detailed study, and it may also be worthwhile to discuss some of the major results as they pertain to the various scales analysed. Note first of all that there is only one case of heterogeneity of fit over sexes (toughmindedness); this will be discussed later. Note next that the E_1 model either fails completely or is a very poor fit in all cases. This indicates that there is significant variation to explain in addition to that caused by errors of measurement and individual (within-family) environmental influences. Our trouble comes in trying to decide whether this residual variation can best be accounted for by between-families environmental variance (E_2), additive genetic variation (D_R) or both.

In most cases, both two-parameter models yield non-significant residual chi squares. Formally, we must accept that either E_2 or D_R is responsible for the residual variation over and above E_1, but in practice we can compare the two chi squares and also fit the $E_1E_2D_R$ model and see which of the extra parameters is significant or takes a nonsense value. Although we have found little significant heterogeneity for any of the traits, it is still instructive to compare the model fitting to male and female data. We shall examine the results of the model fitting for each factor.

1 Sexual satisfaction

Either two-parameter model fits the male data, but the simple genetic model fits slightly but not significantly better and gives a heritability for males of 0·40. For females, the environmental model fails and the genetic model almost does so. The three-parameter models fit, but one gives a large negative $\hat{E}_2$ and the other a significant negative $\hat{D}_R$. Inspection of the mean squares reveals a pattern strongly suggestive of competition between siblings for limited resources. If a particular genotype requires a particular resource in short supply, then competition for that resource will be more intense between M.Z. twins, having the same genotype, than between D.Z. twins, having only half their genes in common.

Eaves (1976) has provided a mathematical model for sibling effects in man and shown how competition or cooperation between individuals of varying degrees of genetic similarity can produce differences in total variance of the groups. If D_R represents the additive genetic variance of a phenotype produced by a set of genes, D_R'' the variance produced by the effect of those genes on a sibling and D_R' the covariance of the additive effect on the individual and the environmental effect on his sibling, then we may write our model for the mean square of twins reared together as follows.

		E_1	D_R	D_R''	D_R'
M.Z.T.	between	1	1	1	2
	within	1	–	–	–
D.Z.T.	between	1	$\frac{3}{4}$	$\frac{3}{4}$	$1\frac{1}{2}$
	within	1	$\frac{1}{4}$	$\frac{1}{4}$	$-\frac{1}{2}$

We see that D_R and D_R'' have the same coefficients and have to be estimated as one parameter. If there is cooperation between twins, then D_R' will be positive, and we expect the total variance of the M.Z. twins to be greater than that of D.Z. twins: $\sigma^2_{TMZ} > \sigma^2_{TDZ}$. If there is competition between twins, then D_R' will be negative, and we expect $\sigma^2_{TMZ} < \sigma^2_{TDZ}$, and furthermore it is possible that the between mean square will actually be less than the within mean square, especially for D.Z. twins. This is what Eaves found for psychoticism in males, and in fact is the pattern we observe in the mean squares for sexual satisfaction in females. Fitting the competition model as shown in table 6.5 gives a remarkably good fit to the data (perhaps reflecting our inspection of the data before fitting the model!). Whether we regard the competition parameter as significant depends on whether we do a one-tail or a two-tail test. In any case, it is clear that there is a large competition effect. Its consequence is that competition is more intense, and so additive genetic variation is less important in the expression of sexual satisfaction in M.Z. twins than in D.Z., and this is reflected in the lower heritability for M.Z. females (0·31) than for D.Z. females (0·45). We can interpret this as meaning that M.Z. females attract the same types of male, and have to compete for his attention to a greater extent than D.Z. females, who will tend to draw companions from populations that do not overlap to the same extent. Males, of course, tend to go out and meet companions outside the home in a way not so characteristic of females; hence the same factors leading to competition are not present to the same extent.

Table 6.5 *Fitting the competition model to the data for sexual satisfaction in females*

		E_1	D_R	$D_R{}'$	df	Observed mean squares	Expected mean squares
M.Z.	b	1	1	2	93	269	270
	w	1	–	–	95	141	141
D.Z.	b	1	$\frac{1}{4}$	$1\frac{1}{2}$	52	241	238
	w	1	$\frac{1}{4}$	$-\frac{1}{2}$	54	275	275

$$\hat{E}_1 \qquad 141\cdot1 \;\pm\; 20\cdot4 \qquad c=6\cdot92\text{***}$$

$$\hat{D}_R \qquad 331\cdot8 \;\pm\; 118\cdot9 \qquad c=2\cdot79\text{**}$$

$$\hat{D}_R{}' \qquad -101\cdot2 \;\pm\; 55\cdot5 \qquad c=1\cdot82$$

$$x^2{}_1 \;=\; 0\cdot005$$

$$\hat{h}^2_{\text{MZ}} = \frac{\frac{1}{2}(\hat{D}_R + 2\hat{D}_R{}')}{\frac{1}{2}(\hat{D}_R + 2\hat{D}_R{}') + \hat{E}_1} = 0\cdot3145 \pm 0\cdot0882$$

$$\hat{h}^2_{\text{DZ}} = \frac{\frac{1}{2}(\hat{D}_R + \hat{D}_R{}')}{\frac{1}{2}(\hat{D}_R + \hat{D}_R{}') + \hat{E}_1} = 0\cdot4497 \pm 0\cdot0983$$

2 Libido and masculinity

In the highly correlated traits of libido and masculinity, the simple environmental model seems more appropriate to the female data than the simple genetic model, while the reverse seems true for the males. It would tally with popular folklore if sexual attitudes on these two scales were determined largely by cultural pressures in females, while men were less inhibited by such pressures (i.e., if there were less in the way of pressures on men!), and variation were an expression of their genotypes.

It may also be noted that there is still significant between-families environmental variance in females (E_2), and this suggests that daughters tend to conform to a set of family standards and attitudes more so than sons. If there were cultural or biological pressures on females to adopt a certain set of sexual attitudes, then we should expect to find between-families variance reduced, relative to that in males. This would be akin to the sex-limited genetic variation found for a trait like baldness, where variation of the major gene effects is largely restricted to males. We should thus expect to find total variance smaller in females than in males, although E_1 should be of the same magnitude in both sexes. The first of these anticipations is fulfilled but the second is not, so that the evidence for coercion to a standard set of attitudes in females is not strong. Nevertheless, it is an hypothesis worthy of more specific formulation and testing in future studies. Of course, if such sex-limited genetic variation for libido were found, it could just as readily be genetic factors that are suppressing the expression of genetic variation in women, as occurs in baldness.

3 Radicalism

For both sexes the simple genetic model gives a better fit than the simple environmental model (which almost fails in females), yielding high heritability in both sexes. However, it is interesting that this is one of the few traits in which the $E_1 E_2 D_R$ model yields positive estimates of both E_2 and D_R that are consistent over sexes indicating the importance of cultural variation or assortative mating (or both) in addition to additive genetic variation and E_1. The heritabilities, taking account of E_2, are similar for the two sexes and indeed the parameter estimates appear consistent over all ten statistics. This is striking confirmation of a similar need for an E_2 or an assortative mating parameter found by Hewitt (1974) in analysing another body of social attitude data in twins, and by Eaves and Eysenck on yet another set of data using an adaptation of the Wilson–Paterson Conservatism Scale (unpublished). (We have already noted that assortative mating is indeed strongly present in our data; cf. chapter 3.)

If cultural effects are important in influencing radicalism throughout life, rather than at a particular formative period, then we should expect these to act increasingly on individuals rather than pairs as twins get older and are separated for longer. This should be reflected in larger within-pair differences in older twins and we should detect these unequivocally as E_1 effects in M.Z. twins. We do indeed find a significant positive regression of pair differences on age in M.Z. females. Although this regression accounts for only about 2 per cent of the radicalism within-pairs variance, or about

1 per cent of the total variance, we may have here further evidence for the action of cultural effects in radicalism scores.

4 Toughmindedness

Here again our results echo Hewitt's (1974) in finding different parameters required for males and females. He found that the simple environmental model failed for both sexes, but that a simple genetic model, while fitting both sexes, yielded a considerably higher heritability for females than males. Perhaps because of poor sampling, our D.Z. within mean square in males is actually smaller than the corresponding M.Z. mean square, and this causes the simple genetic model to fail in males, while the simple environmental model fails in females. We may have here evidence of sex limitation of genetic expression in which sons are more likely to be conditioned into more or less toughminded attitudes that are held by the family than are daughters, of whom no such expectations are held. In contemporary jargon, the large E_2 component for females in libido and masculinity, and for males in toughmindedness, could be evidence of conditioning into 'sexual roles'.

5 Emphasis

Both two-parameter models fit for males, but the simple environmental model almost fails for females, and the simple genetic hypothesis appears to give an adequate fit for all ten statistics, additive genetic variation accounting for about a third of the total, a finding in almost perfect agreement with Hewitt (1974).

6 Personality

We do not propose to say much here about personality variables as these have been studied on much larger samples by Eaves and Eysenck, and will be discussed separately in a forthcoming publication. It is noteworthy, however, that the four personality variables are remarkable in their consistency. No two- or three-parameter model fails with either sex. However, where we estimate that heritability is in the range 0·34—0·39 for females, the male values are all in the range 0·50—0·58. This finding is the more striking since, given equal heritabilities in the male and female populations, we should expect the greater restriction in sampling of male twins to produce *lower* estimates of heritability. Although the difference in heritability is not significant for any trait taken singly, the directional evidence is very strong here. Nichols (1969) too has found higher heritabilities for males than females in almost every personality trait that he measured.

Our heritability estimates from the simple genetic model, fitted to all ten statistics, are 0·43, 0·40, 0·40 and 0·42 for P, E, N and L; they are of the same order as the estimates for P, E and N obtained by Eaves and Eysenck (1974) for much larger samples of same-sex twins (0·35, 0·48 and 0·49). These estimates are of course underestimates of heritability because we have made no attempt to correct for inconsistency of item responses; this is traditionally included with the environmental variance, but strictly speaking should not be so included. The same is true, of course, for all the other estimates of heritability here made; these are lower thresholds rather than firm determinations, even within their fiducial limits.

As an example of the more detailed sort of calculation that might be carried out in this connection, we have selected the libido variable, as being perhaps the most interesting of our factors, for further analysis. By putting both pairs by items interaction and main effects mean squares as a single data set, and estimating genetic and environmental parameters of each, we can estimate the main effects parameters corrected for internal unreliability. This has the effect of altering the heritability upwards or downwards by an amount depending upon the relative size of the genetic and environmental components of the interaction mean square (Eaves and Eysenck 1976, Hewitt 1974). Table 6.6 shows simple genetic models fitted simultaneously to the main effects and interaction mean squares for libido in males. The compound model fits well, and all the parameter estimates are highly significant. The estimate of the heritability of the items interaction is 0·18 + 0·02, identical with a value obtained from a separate analysis of the interaction mean squares. The interaction mean square thus contributes some information to both the genetic and environmental main effects parameters, and making allowance for these contributions we find that the heritability of the libido factor is raised from 0·61 + 0·10

Table 6.6 *Fitting a compound model to the main effects and items interaction mean squares for libido in males*

		Model E_{1_I}	D_{B_I}	E_1	D_B	df	Weight	Observed mean squares	Expected mean squares
M.Z.	b	1	1	36	36	38	5·5752	1·8378	1·8525
	w	1	–	36	–	39	93·4300	0·4622	0·4576
M.Z.I	b	1	1	–	–	1330	22213·8505	0·1719	0·1731
	w	1	–	–	–	1365	47493·4402	0·1201	0·1199
D.Z.	b	1	$\frac{3}{4}$	36	27	16	3·5615	1·5997	1·5038
	w	1	$\frac{1}{4}$	36	9	17	13·1445	0·7532	0·8063
D.Z.I.	b	1	$\frac{1}{4}$	–	–	560	10973·8301	0·1638	0·1598
	w	1	$\frac{1}{4}$	–	–	595	16777·2819	0·1314	0·1332

$$x^2_4 = 0·33 \qquad \hat{E}_{1_I} = 0·1199 \pm 0·0042 \qquad c = 28·54$$

$$h^2_{\text{Interaction}} = 0·18 \pm 0·02 \qquad \hat{D}_{B_I} = 0·0532 \pm 0·0076 \qquad c = 6·96$$

$$h^2_{\text{Main}} = 0·67 \pm 0·11 \qquad \hat{E}_1 = 0·0094 \pm 0·0028 \qquad c = 3·37$$

$$\hat{D}_B = 0·0373 \pm 0·0103 \qquad c = 3·61$$

when our correction is made for items inconsistency to a value of 0.67 ± 0.11 when we make this correction. This would be our best estimate of heritability obtainable from the data in our possession.

It may be useful to recapitulate our main findings, at least in as much as our sex factors are concerned. The discussion so far has been tangled up with technical issues which may have distracted attention from the major conclusions that are suggested by the data and the analysis. The term 'suggested' is used on purpose because the number of twin pairs, although large in comparison with the sort of sample usually employed in studies of this kind, was too small to allow any definitive conclusions, even if problems of selection and other difficulties discussed already could be neglected. We note then that, with respect to libido, additive genetic √ factors play a very strong part for men, but with women cultural influences seem to be far more important. When corrections are made for unreliability in the male sample, the heritability of libido reaches the figure of 67 per cent. Masculinity behaves rather like libido – not surprisingly in view of the high correlation between the two scores.

Sexual satisfaction presents a rather more complex picture, with heritability somewhat lower, and competition likely for M.Z. females. These findings are not perhaps surprising. A person's libido is to some extent independent of others; it can be expressed in different ways depending on circumstances, and genetic factors therefore have a more or less free field. Sexual satisfaction, on the other hand, depends much more on other people – lovers, spouses and the like. Consequently there is more room here for environmental factors to exert an influence, although these in turn are of course in part a reflection of genotypic aspects, such as good looks, intelligence and so forth. Competition, on *a priori* grounds, is not likely to affect libido, but may quite easily arise in connection with satisfaction; there are several treatments of this theme in the world's literature!

We believe that this discussion of our results, brief though it has inevitably been, has succeeded in demonstrating the far-reaching nature of modern biometrical genetic investigations. The stress that has been put on the statistical assessment of 'heritability' has distorted the aims of such research, which are concerned with the construction of a proper model of the influences, genetic and

213

environmental, that go to determine the phenotype. Critics who complained that heritability could not be determined in any meaningful fashion from available data were both right and wrong; they were right when dealing with the usual type of investigation using the simple Holzinger formula, but wrong when dealing with the much more sophisticated model-fitting methods of Mather, Jinks and Eaves. Again, little interest attaches to studies using small numbers of twin pairs with traits of intermediate heritability such as those in the attitudes and personality domain; unfortunately data from such small samples are compatible with almost any model, however unlikely, and cannot be used to differentiate between models in any meaningful manner. Even the number of subjects used in our study, much larger than is usual in this field, is still too small to have complete confidence in the results. We believe that replication is not likely to reverse our major conclusions, but it may well fail to confirm some of our minor ones.

The evidence seems clear that the main factors of sexual attitudes are partly determined by genetic causes, and it seems likely that these effects are mediated through personality traits such as *P*, *E* and *N*, at least in part. However, clearly behaviour is the end product of a chain of chemical reactions which start in the DNA but are mediated through biochemical, endocrine and neurological functions before finally being experienced as behaviour. The question of the biological basis of personality can be answered only by psychophysiological experimentation directly relating personality measures and such factors as cortical arousal (for *E*) and autonomic activation (for *N*), perhaps somewhat along the lines suggested by Eysenck (1967). There is some evidence to suggest that these physiological factors are relevant to extraversion and neuroticism; *P* is too new and unexplored a variable to have any such stable reference. The only suggestion that has come forward for a biological basis for this trait is grounded on the observation that *P* seems to be closely connected with masculinity, a relationship that appears particularly close in the sexual sphere (Eysenck and Eysenck 1976). This links up with the suggestion by Money (1961a, 1961b) that 'in adulthood, androgen is the libido hormone for both men and women. The androgens of eroticism in normal, untreated women may be of adrenal origin or may derive metabolically from the closely related progestins.' However, we shall see that there are some arguments against such an identification (Davidson 1972).

It is known that progestin, usually given as a 'fertility pill', has masculinising effects morphologically (Wilkins 1959, 1960; Young, Gay and Phoenix 1965); it also appears to have such masculinising effects as far as behaviour is concerned (Ehrhardt and Money 1967). These authors studied ten girls whose mothers received progestin while pregnant; nine were born with abnormal genitalia. 'From the sex-role preference tests and the interview material, nine of the ten girls were tomboys. The criteria were play with boys' toys; athletic energy, outdoor pursuits; and minimal concern for feminine frills, doll play, baby care and household chores' (p. 99). These results are in line with similar findings in animal work (Money 1965, Phoenix 1966). These studies suggest strongly a correlation between morphological and behavioural effects of sex hormones.

These studies, while relevant and supportive, nevertheless are only of indirect concern; what is needed is clearly a more direct link between hormones and P+ behaviour, both in the sexual and non-sexual spheres. Unfortunately, there is a dearth of such studies; a review by Eysenck and Eysenck (1976) found the evidence suggestive but certainly not conclusive. The same must be said about the recent work of Daitzman (1976), which should certainly be repeated on larger numbers of subjects, but which constitutes the most direct and relevant study to date of this important problem.

Daitzman (1976) carried out a pilot and a main study, using 25 and 51 male subjects respectively, all of them university students; he also used a very small sample of 7 female students in addition. Measuring level of androgen and estrogen secretion on two occasions (in order to rule out temporary effects and establish the reliability of the hormonal measure), he correlated the results with a variety of questionnaire data. Among his main findings were the following.

1 Androgen secretion is positively correlated with neuroticism, correlations in the two samples being 0·53 and 0·27.

2 Androgen secretion is positively but insignificantly correlated with psychoticism, correlations being 0·10 and 0·07.

3 Correlations with various measures of extraversion tend to be positive (Sensation Seeking disinhibition scale, P.E.N. extraversion, C.P.I. sociability, M.M.P.I. social introversion (negative)).

These results, given the small numbers involved and the pioneering nature of the experiment, tend to fit in quite well with our conceptualisation; high libido is correlated with P, E and N, and all

215

three show (although not always at a significant level) positive correlations with androgen level.

4 However, the heterosexual experience scale used by Daitzman (which resembles our sexual behaviour scale) correlates *negatively* with androgen level (−0·45, −0·49). This is certainly contrary to expectation, and would require replication before being accepted. (Daitzman gives hundreds of correlations in his thesis, and by chance the conventional level of significance would be reached or exceeded by quite a number of these.)

5 Another finding is more in line with expectation, namely that favourable parental attitude to sex in children is positively correlated with androgen secretion (0·31, 0·36).

6 When we turn to estrogen levels, we find that these too show a powerful correlation with neuroticism (0·45).

7 The correlation with psychoticism is positive but quite insignificant, but that with the M.M.P.I. schizophrenia scale is highly significant (0·48).

8 With femininity, using the C.P.I. scale, the correlation is surprisingly negative (−0·33).

9 Estrogen correlates positively with the general Sensation Seeking Scale (0·29) and significantly with the S.S. disinhibition scale (0·37), which is probably the scale most closely related to extraversion in the S.S.S.

10 The correlation of estrogen secretion with heterosexual experience is negative, although quite insignificantly so. With parental attitude towards sex in children it is strongly positive (0·59).

These results suggest, if anything, that estrogen secretion has on the whole *similar* relations with personality and sexual attitudes and behaviours as does androgen secretion; both seem to relate positively to *P, E* and *N* (although these relations are not always clear or significant). Both have negative correlations with sexual experience and positive ones with parental attitudes.

A last set of correlations is offered by Daitzman, using the androgen/estrogen balance.

11 This balance correlates positively with femininity, which is perhaps unexpected.

12 It also correlates positively with extraversion, and negatively with the M.M.P.I. social introversion scale.

13 Correlations with sexual experiences are negative, very significantly so. All the correlations mentioned so far are not changed

significantly by controlling for such variables as weight, age, height, or recency of orgasm.

The sample of girls was, of course, too small to give very meaningful results, but androgen levels were associated significantly with neuroticism, and negatively with masculinity; estrogen levels with the M.M.P.I. schizophrenia scale and the psychopathic deviant scale, the S.S. disinhibition scale, and (negatively) with the C.P.I. socialisation and communality scales, and the ego-strength scale. Thus, in women too there appears to exist a similar relationship between high P, high E and high N on the one hand, and high androgen and estrogen levels on the other. It would almost appear as if high male and female hormone levels both act in a *synergistic* fashion, rather than in an *antagonistic* one, at least as far as personality and sexual behaviour are concerned. The picture would be completely consistent if only the sexual experience scale in this study correlated positively rather than negatively with sex hormone secretions. This failure of prediction constitutes a definite and serious theoretical anomaly which must be left to future research to clear up.

One further set of studies must be mentioned because it suggests a tangible way of measuring an anatomical feature probably determined by antenatal androgen secretion, and in turn correlated with high libido v. low libido behaviour. Schlegel (1969, 1971) has carried out large-scale measurements of the size of the pelvic outlet, using the distance between the ischial tuberosities (*Sitzbeinhöcker*) as his guide. It is well known that the pelvis of the male tends towards a funnel shape, that of the female towards a tube shape, but that intermediate types are frequent in both sexes. Typically, males have a small pelvic outlet, females a large pelvic outlet; this is of course in line with the biological purpose of this particular anatomical feature. Now it appears that, while the size and shape of most parts of the pelvis are properly determined only at puberty, the distance between the ischial tuberosities is already seen to be differentiated between males and females prior to birth (Boucher 1957), suggesting an effect of gonadal excretions at this decisive period.

Schlegel argues that it is possible, using this anthropometric measure, to grade both males and females along a continuum from andromorphic to gynekomorphic; this continuum, he argues (on the basis of some not very convincing familial correlations), is based on a single-gene type of inheritance, located on the x-chromosome, and plentiful mutation. Schlegel's work is of interest because he cites quantitative evidence from very extensive studies of high correlations between size of pelvic outlet and sexual and social behaviour which fits our high P, high libido picture quite well. Thus he finds a correlation of $-0.90(!)$ between the gynekomorph outlet type and preference for active, dominant types of sexual conduct, irrespective of sex. He also quotes a correlation of -0.77 between gynekomorph outlet type and preference for younger, particularly adolescent, sex partners. On the social side, he gives a correlation of -0.43 with social leadership and dominance. It is interesting that these are typically P rather than E behaviours; with E-type social behaviours the correlations are in the opposite direction: 0.38 with sociability, 0.35 with communication, and 0.31 with ability to make social contacts.

The use of the ischial tuberosities' distance as a measure is given support by the fact that the distribution in the population is bimodal, in both men and women. This is very unusual phenomenon, and suggests that some strong biological, sex-linked factor may indeed have been at work here to produce these effects. Another pointer in this direction is the fact that Schlegel found strong correlations between gynekomorph pelvic outlet types and male homosexuality.

Schlegel goes on to argue, on the basis of much animal work, that in the higher mammals there are two quite distinct components of male sexual behaviour: sexual *satisfaction*, and sexual *dominance*, linked with the pecking order. It is the latter that is related to the anatomical and morphological differences in pelvic shape observed, and hence it is not surprising that P-type behaviour is associated with small pelvic outlets. Schlegel has also observed other anatomical correlates of sexual behaviour, e.g. a highly significant correlation of 0.31 between frequency of sexual intercourse and circumference of the hand (this would appear to be a measure of Kretschmer's and Sheldon's athletic-mesomorphic type). These correlations are of less interest because there is no obvious relationship with hormonal secretions of the androgen type, although quite possibly such correlations will be discovered in the future. The area of research opened up by Schlegel promises to be of considerable interest, and it is to be regretted that his work is not better known in the English-speaking countries. At present, however, it would be premature to put too much faith in his results, well though they agree with our own work and theorising, without the necessary replication.

We must conclude this brief discussion of the hormonal effects on sexual and non-sexual behaviour with a question mark. The evidence is suggestive of a causal relation between androgens and $P+$, high libido behaviour,(4) but it seems certain that any theory simply equating androgens with masculinity and estrogens with femininity will run into serious difficulties. It is possible that we may have to discriminate more carefully between the different androgens, attributing different effects to different hormones; it may be that there are synergistic as well as antagonistic interaction effects between androgens, estrogens, progesterons, etc. It would be idle to guess at the complexities that future research may encounter. We seem to have isolated the complex of variables that may be relevant to $P+$ and high libido behaviour, but we have only taken the most preliminary steps to study this relationship in detail.

1. This chapter was jointly authored by N. G. Martin (Department of Genetics, University of Birmingham) and H. J. Eysenck; a more detailed discussion of the results and issues arising will be found in Martin (1976). We wish to thank Mrs J. Kasriel for her invaluable assistance in locating and contacting the twins on whom the research was done; she coordinated the collection of data and managed to keep straight the questionnaire returns that were collected on several different occasions. Without her help this chapter would never have seen the light of day!

2. Ectomorph body-build refers to long, lean physique; mesomorph to squat, powerful physique, and endomorph to large, fat physique.

3. Of the twins, 95 pairs were M.Z. females, 39 were M.Z. males, 54 D.Z. females, 17 D.Z. males, and 41 D.Z. twins pairs of opposite sex. Mean ages ranged from twenty-three (for the unlike sex group) to twenty-eight. Around 60 per cent were middle class.

4. There are two sets of findings that are especially relevant. Ehrenkranz and others (1974), Persky and others (1971), Kreuz and Rose (1972) and others have demonstrated a correlation of plasma testosterone levels with aggressive behaviour and social dominance in man; these are $P+$ activities. Shepherd, Lader and Rodnight (1968) have summarised literature to show that phenothiazines, which have curative powers for schizophrenia, include estrogenic activities; these reported endocrine effects include delayed ovulation and menstruation, oligomenorrhoea and amenorrhoea and breast swelling with lactation, as well as impotence in men and increased libido in women. Drugs which counteract high P are therefore found to have estrogenic properties.

219

7

Sexual attitudes and
social consequences

We have so far been concerned with the trees, rather than the wood; in this final chapter we shall attempt to take stock of what we have found and discuss, at least briefly, the kinds of consequences that might follow from our findings. In summarising our main findings we shall commit two solecisms. In the first place, we shall assume that these findings are genuine and replicable. Now, clearly, our data were collected at a particular place and time, from small though varied samples, in a manner that does not rule out falsification on the part of the respondents; there are many good reasons why errors might have slipped into the experiment, and why the results might not apply in another place or at another time. We acknowledge the difficulties but will not reiterate them each time a finding is mentioned; for the purpose of the discussion we shall assume that the major outlines of our findings are not likely to be disproved in subsequent researches. We are encouraged to believe this because we have found similar results with quite divergent groups (students, normals, adults, prisoners, Broadmoor patients), because the results from many different instruments converge on certain broad generalisations, and because the results largely agree with predictions arrived at from general and experimental psychology, thus forming an attractive example of intergration of theory and fact. Many details of the picture are almost certain to be wrong still, and to require change; much further work will certainly be needed to put this preliminary sketch on an acceptable footing; nevertheless, the broad outlines, we believe, are likely to survive. This belief may not carry conviction for the reader, and we gladly

220

acknowledge that we may be quite wrong; yet for the purpose of this chapter we shall proceed as if the belief were justified.

In the second place, we shall paint this broad picture without paying too much attention to minor anomalies; we shall not enter a detailed discussion of each experiment, carefully setting off the results of one against the other. This we have already done in the major part of this work; it would not be appropriate here. For a more detailed (and consequently more accurate) account the reader must consult the original data; he is of course free to disagree with our summary conclusion. What such a picture loses in detail it gains in intelligibility; scientific work often resembles in its technique the *pointillisme* of the French painters – the resulting picture must be seen at a distance in order to achieve its effect. This distancing is what we are attempting here.

The first finding is that attitudes towards sex fall into groups that have clear-cut psychological meaning. Items denoting sexual satisfaction cluster together; so do items relating to permissiveness, excitement, nervousness, curiosity, repression, experimentation, censorship, promiscuity, hostility, guilt, inhibition, impersonal sex, pornography, dominance, disgust and so forth. Most of these factors can be measured reliably, and would seem to constitute a meaningful way of describing sexual attitudes.

The second finding is perhaps of greater psychological interest. Apparently these factors or clusters of items themselves are correlated, rather than independent; they define two very broad, clearcut, independent factors which we have called Satisfaction v. Pathology, and Libido v. Restraint. These factors emerge equally clearly in men and women, and in students, random samples of adults, Broadmoor patients and other groups; it would appear that they have general significance. Males, as expected, have more libido, but women may, if anything, be more satisfied with their own sex lives; however, the difference for satisfaction is marginal, while that for libido is very marked.

While sexual performance declines with age in both men and women, libido actually increases in men, while it decreases in women; thus libido in women parallels the decline in sexual performance, but goes counter to it in men. The reasons for this curious phenomenon are unknown, and in view of the odd nature of this finding it might be advisable to wait for a replication before taking it too seriously. There is little change in satisfaction with age, except at the very young end of the age scale; at sixteen men and women are less satisfied than at later ages. This is not surprising; society does not make it easy for adolescents to find suitable outlets for their sex drive.

Male–female differences on items and scales are very marked, with men more frequently endorsing items dealing with pornography, orgies, voyeurism, prostitution, impersonal sex, promiscuity, pre- and extra-marital sex, sexual excitement and other indications of libido. Women are more prudish and show more guilt. A special masculinity–femininity scale made up of items giving the largest differences between sexes behaved very much like the libido scale, and indeed featured much the same items.

Personality differences profoundly influenced the views held on the many issues canvassed in the sex inventory. High P scorers endorsed items that featured on the masculinity and libido scales; in particular, they showed lack of concern with virginity, liked impersonal sex, pre- and extra-marital sex and prostitution, and experienced strong sexual excitement. They disliked marriage, censorship and restraint. High P scorers tended to have low scores on satisfaction; they tended to be dissatisfied with their sex lives. There is a definite tendency for high P scorers to indulge in what are commonly called perverted practices, including group sex. Quite generally, high P scorers take a very toughminded, biological attitude to sex, and are opposed to current morality and customs and to idealistic and romantic notions.

Extraverts are similar to high P scorers in their high libido level, but unlike them in their much greater satisfaction. They tended to have intercourse earlier than introverts or ambiverts, have it more frequently, with more partners, in more different positions; they tended to indulge in more varied sexual behaviour outside intercourse, in more prolonged precoital love play, and to habituate more quickly to sexual stimuli, with consequent search for change. A happy philanderer, the extravert has considerable social facility with the opposite sex, likes and enjoys his sexual activity, is contented with it and has no worries or anxieties regarding it. His promiscuity lacks the pathological touches of the high P scorer, or the insistence on perverted forms of satisfaction. The extravert's attitudes seem to derive from hedonism, those of the high P scorer from protest and hostility.

High N scorers have greater libido than low N scorers, but have

222

many hangups which interfere with a peaceful sex life; hence their satisfaction is particularly low. They have strong guilt feelings, worry about sexual activities, have fears and difficulties associated with contact with the opposite sex and often see sex as both troublesome and disgusting. They tend to blame their parents for their inhibitions, and there is an aura of abnormality about their expressed desires. In line with this is the finding that high N scorers show more clearly pathological behaviour, e.g. lack of orgasm and frigidity in women, *ejaculatio praecox* and impotence in men.

Subjects scoring high on the L scale tend to be conformist, as expected from the nature of the scale. They endorse orthodox, socially approved views and attitudes, and deny any thoughts of perverted practices and other socially undesirable habits. They have first intercourse relatively late in life, and they do not approve of pre- or extra-marital sex, the strength of inhibiting influences is high, they take an idealistic rather than a purely biological view of sex, and they approve of censorship, monogamy and faithfulness in marriage and oppose permissiveness. High L scorers are low on the libido factors, but are not dissatisfied with their sex lives. As in the case of P, E and N, here too the pattern of sexual attitudes that applies to men also applies to women; one of the strongest supports for the reliability of our findings comes from the marked agreement of the results obtained for men and women of the various personality types.

Social attitudes in general correlate meaningfully with sex attitudes. Conservatism correlates negatively with permissiveness and stress on physical sex, pornography and libido generally. Toughmindedness correlates with permissiveness, impersonal sex, sexual excitement and quite generally the libido factor and all the items contained in this. It is not surprising that conservatives (with a small c!) endorse orthodox social viewpoints and condemn modern trends, and the established relationship between toughmindedness and P explains the observed relations for T.

Assortative mating is indicated for the sexual attitude factors, and also for the social attitudes factors; in both cases, quite high correlations are found for males and females either married or living together in semi-permanent unions. The correlations are almost as high as those usually found for intelligence, i.e. around 0·5 to 0·6; correlations for personality variables are much lower, and

223

do not deviate significantly from zero in most cases.

Sexual behaviour, as distinguished from sexual attitudes, falls into much the same pattern; several findings, such as the greater indulgence of high P scorers in sexual perversions, have already been mentioned, as has the greater and earlier participation in sexual practices of extraverts, as compared with introverts. Of particular interest to us has been the discovery that, although people may indulge in certain practices, they may actually dislike this participation. Only just over 50 per cent of females who had indulged in fellatio had actually enjoyed doing so; even for such items as manual genital manipulation, male by female, or for mutual genital manipulation, less than 70 per cent of females enjoyed the experience. Males reported enjoyment in almost 100 per cent of all cases. Altogether, we found that females had done things they disliked almost four times as frequently as males. It is not unexpected that dislike of activities indulged in is correlated with sexual shyness, prudishness and disgust; correlations with scales entering into the libido factor are negative – in other words, people high on libido tend to like what they do by way of sexual experimentation. There is little by way of relationship between personality and dislike of sexual activities indulged in. This may be due to the fact that there were too few males in this category to run meaningful correlations, and that women are much more prone to follow the lead of the male in such things, irrespective of their personality configuration almost. This whole area is worthy of much more detailed study than we were able to give it.

Among the abnormal group we tested, Broadmoor patients came out as low on libido and also dissatisfied with their sex lives. The former finding might seem surprising, but it confirms frequent psychiatric observations to this effect. The unhappiness and dissatisfaction of psychiatric patients with their sex lives is not surprising; these results very much bear out expectations based on less systematic research along psychiatric lines done through interviews and other somewhat subjective channels.

Age was found to be an important factor in the sexual attitudes adopted by our subjects. As might have been expected, older subjects tended to be more conservative and less permissive; there was also a general decline of libido for women. This would seem to parallel the decline in the number of times sexual intercourse occurs. Satisfaction however does not seem to decline. It is difficult

224

to say whether these effects are due to actual age-related changes, or whether they merely mirror the social climate in which individuals of a different age grew up.

Social class is another important variable that has perhaps not been studied as much as it deserves; our own findings are incidental, and probably not as trustworthy as those relating to personality. On the whole, the working-class subjects emerge as more 'earthy' and the middle-class groups as more 'moral' in their attitudes; this is not unexpected in view of the greater toughmindedness usually found in working-class groups. Thus working-class people seem to have higher libido, but not greater satisfaction; the former conclusion is perhaps in accord with widespread social beliefs for which hitherto there has not been much empirical support.

The attitudes and behaviours discussed above, as well as the personality traits associated with them, have a clear genetic basis; about half of the variation in attitudes and behaviour that we can observe in our society is due to heredity, the other half to environment. This is a very rough-and-ready summary of our findings; for libido, for example, the males showed a heritability of 67 per cent, which is well above the 50 per cent level. However, such estimates have high fiducial limits, and it would not be realistic to attribute too much accuracy to the actual values found; they can best be used as estimates of the likely region within which the true values may lie. In addition, the genetic models fitted to our data suggest certain complex interactions with within- and between-families environmental influences, as well as competition (as in the case of sexual satisfaction) for limited resources. Our genetic findings are perhaps the most challenging, as well as the most in need of replication, of all our discoveries.

Before turning to a discussion of the social relevance and meaning of these facts, and the consequences that might be thought to flow from them, it may be useful to take a position on a controversy that has for long bedevilled any attempt at reasonable interpretation of psychological data, in this as in any other field. Psychology often seems to be divided into biotropes and sociotropes; into people who stress biological determinants to the exclusion of social ones, and others who reverse this process. Sociologists and social psychologists, as well as psychoanalysts, usually belong with the sociotropes, as do anthropologists. Physiological and experimental psychologists often take the opposite side, as do zoologists and ethologists. Both sides may pay lip-service to the other, but they nevertheless tend to stress one or the other alternative. The position here taken is that so well put by E. O. Wilson in his monumental book on *Sociobiology* (1975); we believe that man is a biosocial organism whose behaviour is determined both by genetic and environmental forces, acting in combination, and that any attempt to understand his behaviour exclusively or even largely in terms of the one determinant or the other is ultimately doomed to futility. At the moment the danger of one-sided interpretation comes much more from the side of the sociologically-minded environmentalists, who often refuse to recognise any biological factors whatever; it would be much more difficult to think of biologically sophisticated writers who would deny the importance of environmental and social factors in human behaviour.

Difficult as it may seem to deny the importance and relevance of hormonal and general physiological differences between the sexes, many modern writers seem to stress overwhelmingly the importance of 'sex roles' and their determination by society – without asking themselves whether perhaps society imposes these roles because nature has so ordained. It cannot be the purpose of this chapter to enter into this controversy, which has generated a huge literature. The reader is referred to Hutt's (1972) book on *Males and Females* for a general introduction and short bibliography; to Ford and Beach's (1952) book on *Patterns of Sexual Behaviour* for a survey of work directly concerned with sex differences in this field; and Levine's (1972) *Hormones and Behavior* for an account of what is known about differential hormonal secretions in the two sexes. Readers interested in the way biological differences between the sexes may determine social behaviour may with advantage study Goldberg's (1973) *The Inevitability of Patriarchy*, subtitled 'Why the biological difference between men and women always produces male domination'. The thesis advanced by the author may not be popular, but the empirical support that it receives would make it very difficult to argue with.

The main difference between men and women, in the sexual field, appears to lie in the area covered by our factor of *libido*, and the differences documented in this book are amusingly illustrated by a recent survey conducted in the United States in which 2,000 men and women, constituting a random sample, were asked to rank the pleasurability of twenty-two everyday activities. Among the men aged between 26 and 39, sex was a clear leader, and among men aged between 40 and 55 it came first or second. But women between the ages of 26 and 39 rated music, nature, family and travel more fun than sex, and among women over 39 even such activities as snoozing, watching television and doing housework came out ahead. Figure 6.1 illustrates this difference very clearly. In this figure we have plotted first of all the decline in actual physical performance for both men and women as they get older; the differences are small and quite insignificant, although pervasive, i.e. apparent of all ages. In so far as they represent a factual difference, they may be due to the existence of prostitutes, none of whom were included among the women questioned, but who might have been used by some of the men, thus swelling the male figures. (The figures are derived from a random national sample questioned in the U.K.) Also given in the figure are data derived from our twin sample; here we have used their factor scores for the libido factor, and drawn regression lines through the resulting scores; only the lines are given in the figure. The ordinate is subdivided only according to the performance data, i.e. in terms of number of times per week that intercourse was had on the average. We have not given the factor scores for the libido data as these have no meaning by themselves; all the data are meant to illustrate is that for women libido declines *pari passu* with performance, while for men there is no decline in libido, and there may be an actual increase. (Actually the decline for women

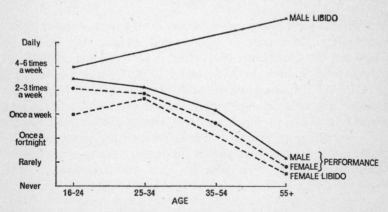

Figure 6.1 *Sexual performance of males and females at various ages;
also degree of libido*

does not set in until after the age of thirty-five; before that there appears to be an actual increase.)

These figures should not be over-interpreted. The number of males in the sample was much smaller than that of females, so that the actual increase in libido must be regarded with suspicion, particularly as in our larger adult sample (see chapter 3) we did not observe such an increase. However, there is a statistical difference between the sexes, not only with respect to libido but also with respect to slope; in other words, women decline in libido with age, while men either actually increase (the 'dirty old man' syndrome), or at least do not decline at anything like the same rate.

Again, there are dangers in interpreting cross-sectional data; as already pointed out in relation to our social attitude data, differences between age groups may not be the effect of ageing as such, but may rather reflect social norms at the time different individuals grew up. That this may have been responsible in part for our findings here is indicated by a series of studies showing that while

... today's adolescents and young adults have a sex-specific view of sexuality which is clearly related to the traditional gender roles: girls behave sexually as if they had less sexual drive than boys; girls show fewer signs of sexual frustration when they abstain sexually; girls behave as if they should show less sexual initiative than their male partners or at least not more than he; girls behave as if their sexuality is more dependent on love, personal relations, and fidelity than do boys. [Schmidt 1975]

Yet during recent years, and especially during the last ten or fifteen years, these differences have decreased considerably (Bell and Chasker 1970, Christensen 1971, Hunt 1974, Israel and others 1970, Sigusch and Schmidt 1973, Sorensen 1973, Schmidt and Sigusch 1971, 1972, Zetterberg 1969). Such changes indicate that social factors have considerable importance; they do not indicate that social factors are all-important. Even among our youngest groups there were large differences in libido between the sexes, and even in the countries that have shown the fastest approach to equality (Denmark, Sweden, West Germany and the metropolitan areas along the East and West Coasts of the United States), differences in attitudes entering our libido factor are still considerable. As Goldberg (1973) points out in his book on *The Inevitability of Patriarchy*, although there may be differences between different societies in the

228

degree of male dominance, yet patriarchy is universal; there is a vital role to be played by social factors, against a backdrop of biologically determined differences.

It seems logical that the most relevant biological factors in this connection should be the sex hormones, with the androgens favouring masculine attitudes and behaviours, high libido and P, while the estrogens might favour feminine attitudes and behaviours, low libido and low P. As regards P (and psychotic behaviour in general) the evidence has been reviewed by Eysenck and Eysenck (1976), and there appears to be some ground for assuming that this rather simple-minded hypothesis is not entirely along the wrong lines. A more general review of the influence of hormones on behaviour is given in Levine (1972); this is more likely to convince the reader of the incredible complexity of the field, and our lack of detailed knowledge (particularly in relation to humans), than to suggest that rash formulations such as that relating androgens and estrogens to male and female behaviours respectively have much empirical support. The true relationship is almost certainly much more complex than this, and it is unfortunately true that there is very little direct evidence in humans on which to build more appropriate hypotheses. We have already discussed Money's (1961a, 1961b, 1965) hypothesis that androgens are the active cause of libidinal behaviour in men and women, and the evidence suggesting that this hypothesis too is probably overly simple, although it may be along the right lines. Male and female hormones almost certainly interact in complex ways, and the time at which they exert their influence seems to be crucial. There almost certainly exists a strong causal relationship between androgens and $P+$ behaviour, and between androgens and high libido; the influence of estrogens is less clear, and the interaction between the two sets of hormones is still a mystery. This area of interdisciplinary research between psychology, biochemistry and medicine promises to be one of the most interesting and fruitful in the immediate future.

We have thus far discussed certain deductions from our general theory, and attempted in various ways to find support or disconfirmation of these deductions. But of course there are very many more deductions that follow from our theoretical framework, and it would be a task of supererogation to list these here. However, in order to give the reader a taste of the sort of detailed prediction that can be made from personality theory on to sexual behaviour, it may be worthwhile to mention *en passant* the fact that extraverts seem to experience their highest state of cortical arousal in the evening, introverts in the morning (Colquhoun 1960, Colqhuoun and Corcoran 1964, Blake 1967). It would be tempting from this well-established fact to make certain predictions which might serve to explain the sad face of Strephon and poor Chloe in Charles Hanbury-Williams' poem, written around 1750:

> Ye famed physicians of this place,
> Hear Strephon's and poor Chloe's case
>   Nor think that I am joking;
> When she would, he cannot comply;
> When he would drink, she's not a-dry.
>   And is this not provoking?
>
> At night, when Strephon comes to rest,
> Chloe receives him on her breast,
>   With fondly folding arms:
> Down, down he hangs his drooping head,
> Falls fast asleep, and lies as dead,
>   Neglecting all her charms.
>
> Reviving when the morn returns,
> With rising flames young Strephon burns,
>   And then would fain be doing:
> But Chloe, now asleep or sick,
> Has no great relish for the trick,
>   And sadly balks his wooing.
>
> O cruel and disastrous case,
> When in the critical embrace
>   That only one is burning!
> Dear doctors, set this matter right;
> Give Strephon spirits over night,
>   Or Chloe in the morning.

The implicit hypothesis that Strephon was introverted, Chloe extraverted, might with advantage be put to a more general test, involving couples where one partner was introverted, the other extraverted; the prediction would be that troubles similar to those afflicting the lovers celebrated in the poem could set the matter right by following the lead given by 1,600 members of the local goldminers' union in Vetikoula (Fiji), who demanded that their present lunchtime be extended to include 'a thirty-minute midday sex break'. According to their secretary, they believed 'that midday is the best time for sex', neatly cutting the Gordian knot of personality differences in circadian rhythms.

If we accept the fact that both social and biological factors produce considerable diversity in the sexual attitudes and behaviours of men and women in our (or any other) society, even though our understanding of either the social or the biological factors is deplorably weak and partial at best, then we may be able to say something about the current (and in fact age-old) debates raging between apostles of permissiveness and protagonists of conservative values, or libertines and puritans, in a short phrase. It will be clear from our general discussion that there are four major groups formed in terms of our factors. First, there are those who have little libido, but considerable satisfaction from their sex lives; on the whole, stable introverts with little evidence of *P*. These people would probably constitute the monogamous section of the population, and their contentment testifies to the fact that this is a viable and perhaps enviable position. Advocates of permissiveness often by implication deny the possibility of achieving this combination, but the facts clearly are against them.

Next we have the happy philanderer, the stable extravert in the high-libido, high-satisfaction group; devoting much of his energy to sexual adventures with many different women, never settling down permanently, or, if apparently settled down, nevertheless always on the lookout for extra-marital experiences. Although puritans might wish to deny the possibility of regarding this as a feasible pattern, nevertheless the evidence suggests that it does occur quite frequently, and does not produce less satisfaction to the person involved than does the first pattern considered. There may be an age shift, in the sense that the high-libido pattern is more appropriate to the young, the low-libido pattern to the old, with the middle-aged in between. The introvert may start out with the sowing of at least some wild oats; the extravert may end up happily married in his dotage. Our samples were not extensive enough to test this hypothesis, and in any case it would probably need follow-up studies to investigate such theories properly.

The other two patterns both show dissatisfaction with the sex lives experienced. The low-libido male or female tends to be the unstable introvert, with strong inhibitions, feelings of guilt, diffi-

culties in meeting people of the opposite sex and generally pre-
cluded from adequate sexual responses. The high-libido male or
female tends to be high on the *P* scale, and may also add the
quasi-hysterical combination of high *N* and high *E* (Eysenck 1971c).
Pseudo-nymphomanic behaviour in the female, Don Juanism in the
male characterises people in this group; they might be said to be
those who give permissiveness a bad name. There is something
attractive about the permissiveness of the extravert; there is little
that is attractive about the permissiveness of the high *P* scorer, who
combines hostility, aggressiveness and impersonal attitudes with
his sexual desires, reducing sex to a biological need, on a level with
eating and defecating. The interesting point, and one that will give
support to the puritans, is that this pattern of sexual behaviour is
self-defeating, leading to low satisfaction.

We thus have two patterns of behaviour that are acceptable
because they lead to personal satisfaction and happiness – the
introvertive traditional one of monogamy and family life, the extraverted one of wine, women and song. Either pattern may lead to
dissatisfaction and unhappiness, however, when there is an admixture in the personality of psychiatric, abnormal, pathological
characteristics, whether of the quasi-neurotic or the quasi-psychotic,
quasi-psychopathic variety. (The term 'quasi-' is used here to make
it clear that none of our subjects were clinically ill, or were in
psychiatric treatment.) In more extreme cases, this pathological
admixture may lead to definite physical symptoms, such as frigidity,
lack of orgasm, *ejaculatio praecox* and impotence. We may thus
distinguish between normal and abnormal patterns of adjustment,
i.e. patterns where men and women receive satisfaction from their
course of conduct and others where they do not, and where they
may suffer from actual physical symptoms of psychiatric disorder
in relation to their sex lives. Within either pattern, we have a permissive–libidinal form and an inhibited–traditional form. Whether
a person falls into one or other of these patterns will depend to
some extent on his personality, and on his genetic makeup; it will
also depend, of course, on myriad other factors, ranging from
accidents of upbringing and physical endowment to peer influences
and unpredictable events of adult life. An inch added to Cleopatra's
nose, it is said, might have altered the course of history; an inch
added to, or taken away from, a girl's breast measurements may
change her destiny in equally marked fashion. Personality factors

232

do not determine a person's fate; they merely nudge it along in certain directions; nevertheless, the nudge can be pretty compelling at times.

The fact that these personality and behaviour differences are so marked, and so firmly established on a genetic basis, makes the task of society very difficult in laying down rules and laws that would lead to the greatest happiness of the greatest number and at the same time safeguard the interests of third parties, such as children and other dependents. Clearly the greatest possible permissiveness on the part of the State, compatible with these safeguards, is most likely to achieve these objectives; our own society still is curiously impermissive and downright vengeful when facing such issues as abortion and prostitution. Religious people and others who judge such matters in terms of prejudged principles derived from putatively divine sources of course can not be expected to share such views; it is still apparently very difficult for most people not to try and impress their own value judgements on others. Yet this is what the principles of freedom demand, and the political forms of democracy are intended to give expression to such principles.

It might be thought that this endorsement of permissiveness on the part of the government in dealing with personal and private matters such as sex could and should be extended to what is customarily called 'permissiveness' in the media, in social life and in society generally. This is not necessarily so. The term 'permissiveness' is probably badly chosen and does not adequately portray what goes on in society; so-called permissiveness can be as dictatorial and non-permissive, in one direction, as was puritanism. To take but one example, Jessor and Jessor (1976) studied 600 adolescents and found that sexual habits had changed so much that now it is the boy or girl who does *not* lose his or her virginity at an early age who is looked upon as psychologically abnormal. There is thus an enormous pressure on young people to behave in a manner that may be contrary to their personality makeup and their value judgements; this is not true permissiveness, which would enable different persons to express in their conduct the outlook and the values that their heredity, their personality and their upbringing have produced in them. So-called permissiveness is not permissive towards traditional values; it is simply a fine-sounding name given to a value system equally irrational, equally dogmatic and equally

233

strictly enforced by peer sanctions as the traditional system. True permissiveness would recognise the relativity involved in such value judgements, and would not put pressure on young people (or their elders), to fall in line with one or the other alternative as the only system worthy of consideration.

By the same token, permissiveness as here understood does not imply agreement with the proposition that there should be no censorship over obscene and pornographic material in the printed word, television, the cinema or the theatre. The argument may perhaps first be stated in a general form, to be followed by a more detailed look at some of the facts. It is fairly universally agreed that freedom of expression is a vital strand in the general fabric of modern democracy, and that censorship is an evil that requires adequate reasoning and potent demonstration of its necessity before it can be tolerated. We do admit the necessity of censorship and the need for interference of the law in the freedom of expression when we deal with such issues as race; incitement to racial hatred and expressions of racial prejudice and discrimination are rightly forbidden by law. Limitations of the freedom of expression may therefore be tolerated in a democratic society, however permissive, in order to safeguard the rights of minority groups.

Now it can be said that much of what passes in modern society as pornography is in fact serving the cause of male chauvinism. Just as Nicolas Chauvin, who became immortal through his boastful, warlike, over-enthusiastic patriotism, abused freedom of expression and turned it into licence to insult and maltreat those of another nationality, so pornographic writings and films incite men to insult and maltreat women. The values expressed in such works, whether intentionally or not, are male values, particularly those of the high-P, high-libido male; women serve only as sex objects in these works, and may be maltreated, raped, beaten and generally humiliated – in short, treated no better than second-class citizens. If we object to seeing blacks as slaves, entertainers and generally servants of the dominant whites, then we should equally object to seeing women as slaves, entertainers and generally servants of the dominant males. Permissiveness, as we have argued, must stop at that point where it interferes with the rights of others; here we would seem to encounter such a limitation to general permissiveness.

Readers who may find that this view exaggerates the dehumanising and downgrading aspects of pornographic films, as far as women are concerned, may like to consider some findings from our own thematic study of a random sample of such films, confiscated by the customs authorities or the police. In the majority of cases, the film ends by the male withdrawing his penis *and ejaculating the sperm all over the face of the female*. This has no erotic appeal (to judge by the comments of our subjects), but simply signifies, in a symbolic form, the subjection of the woman; it recalls the victor in tribal warfare urinating over the face of the vanquished. Sado-masochistic episodes proliferate, always with the woman the first unwilling, then willing victim. Scenes include rape, as in a film showing a burglary; the burglar is discovered by the woman, sleeping alone in her bed. He jumps on her and rapes her, in spite of her struggles, which gradually diminish and end in enthusiastic cooperation. In another film, the boss finds fault with the work of his secretary; he gives her the option of dismissal or being spanked. She choses the latter, is put across his knees, has her panties removed and is spanked; this quickly leads to cooperative fornication. The general moral of these and other films is: 'Treat them rough, and they'll get to like it.' Only the most occasional film showed scenes of tenderness, wooing or feeling of any kind. It is interesting to note that, among our subjects at least, the dehumanising and downgrading parts of the films did not produce a greater physiological reaction, or a higher erotic rating, than did more acceptable scenes; thus the excuse that these aspects of biological sex are emphasised because they produce strong erotic reactions is not valid. The only apparent purpose is to emphasise the superiority of the male and the inferiority of the female.

It is often argued that in fact these objections are immaterial because the evidence does not seem to show that pornographic films have any observable effects. Usually the conclusions of the American Presidential Commission Report on Obscenity and Pornography are cited in this connection, where it is stated that 'in sum, empirical research designed to clarify the question has found no evidence to date that exposure to explicit sexual material plays a significant role in the causation of delinquent and criminal behaviour among youths and adults'. The general conclusion that 'there is no evidence' of the effects of pornography on sexual behaviour is often repeated as if it were true; yet in fact there is a large body of such evidence, so much so in fact that at present there can be very little doubt about the matter. Cline (1974) has brought together both the positive evidence on this point, and also the criticisms of the Commission's Report, and there would be little point here in trying to summarise all the wealth of material referred to by him.

What happened, as Cline (who also assisted in the preparation of the Minority Report appended to the Majority Report) shows clearly, was that the membership of the Commission was determined largely on ideological grounds, with the express aim of justifying the end of censorship. The report itself neglected to mention nearly 90 per cent of the research carried out for the Commission, misrepresented much of what was quoted and over-interpreted restricted data, collected on small and unrepresentative samples. As Cline put it, there was 'a great variety of common errors, omissions and drawing of incorrect conclusions from flawed research, as well as a manifest, systematic bias in marshalling evidence and reporting'. All this is clearly documented, and anyone familiar with the literature, and having read the ten volumes of detailed evidence produced by the research teams of the Commission (and not relying on the biased summaries and potted versions contained in the Commission Report itself), will have no doubt about the determination of the majority of the Commission members to arrive at the conclusion to which they were committed from the beginning. Contrary to popular opinion, then, there is much direct evidence of the enormous power that even quite short snippets of film can have in altering attitudes and behaviours over quite lengthy periods; furthermore, these experimental results are in good agreement with theory regarding the efficacy of 'modelling' (imitation) and desensitisation, and the very large clinical and experimental literature that has been built up around these concepts. To disregard all this evidence is to fly in the face of scientific fact; it is simply not feasible any more to dismiss the view that pornographic and obscene films and publications have an effect on the behaviour of people, or on their attitudes, and it is not even open to anyone to claim that the verdict should be 'not proven'.

It is of course much more difficult to prove beyond the shadow of a doubt that the recent tremendous increases in the incidence of rape, molestation, indecent assault, unlawful intercourse and violence generally are linked causally with the presentation of such activities on the screen, and are caused directly by such presentations. It would seem unreasonable to demand such direct proof; in over fifty years the medical profession has not been able to prove indisputably that cigarettes act as a carcinogenic agent and cause lung cancer in smokers. The correct position to adopt, in my submission, is the one taken by the Government Committees on Drug Safety; new drugs have to be shown to be safe by the manufacturers (within human reason), and it is not required of the Committee to prove them to be lethal! Similarly, grossly pornographic and violent pictures, showing in detail rape and other unlawful activities, should be required to prove their innocence, and not allowed to be shown until they had done so. It is unreasonable to require private persons who suspect (probably rightly) that such pictures have a very destructive influence on society to finance the very time-consuming, expensive and highly technical research that is needed to prove the point. Such research should be financed from the profits of the pornographic industry itself, in order to support, if possible, their plea of harmlessness.

Such financial support should of course be indirect, i.e. be given to an authoritative body (such as the British Psychological Society, or the Medical Research Council), and disbursed through them. The reasons for this are obvious; pornographic film-makers are interested parties, and would do their best to influence the membership and the research activities of any body set up to study these questions. This is what happened, for instance, in the famous case of the U.S. Surgeon General's report on television and social behaviour. The committee set up to carry out the work had some of its proposed members vetoed by the large television companies, on the grounds that they were expected to make the report too realistic and unfriendly to the television companies! The story is told in detail in Cline's book; no wonder that the Committee finally appointed 'misrepresented some of the data, ignored some of it and buried all of it in prose that was obviously meant to be unreadable and unread', as *Newsweek* so admirably put it. Independence of fact-finding and of conclusion-drawing bodies from the practitioners of the arts of pornography and violence is an overriding need in the scientific study of this field.

It is sometimes said that artistic integrity demands the public showing of what is in fact pornography. Psychologically and artistically this is not only not true, but it is exactly the opposite of the

237

truth. Consider the plea recently made that Lady Macbeth should be allowed to sleepwalk in the nude 'because in her time she would not have worn a nightgown'. It is not only that this plea itself is probably untrue and certainly artistically irrelevant (should she also sleepwalk unwashed and evil-smelling?); it should not need a psychologist to point out that the appearance of a well-known actress in the nude would break the spell of the play completely, and invite rude comments on the size of her breasts, and the shape of her behind. Plays and films are meant to create emotional reactions by art and indirection, not by blatant sensory appeals; such direct sensory appeals detract from the message of the medium.

The general argument here put forward is a very simple one. Given that films, plays, television performances and books have a powerful effect on viewers, listeners and readers, a point not now seriously doubted by competent psychologists, then the public showing of scenes of rape, degradation and general abuse of women, and their portrayal as sex objects pure and simple, is likely to have effects on male attitudes and behaviour that go counter to the trend towards greater sexual equality which has been one of the more acceptable and desirable tendencies characteristic of this century. It is not necessary to imagine that all modern pornographers are motivated by a desire to destroy modern civilisation, although some no doubt believe, with Richard Neville, that the weapons of revolution are 'obscenity, blasphemy and drugs'. A far more likely motive is simple greed. But in any case motives are largely irrelevant; effects are the important consideration. Ideally one might like to appeal to all concerned to heed the sentiments expressed so powerfully in Masefield's poem addressed to his mother:

> What have I done, or tried, or said
> In thanks to that dear woman dead?
> Men triumph over women still,
> Men trample women's rights at will,
> and man's lust roams the world untamed.
>
> . . .
>
> O grave, keep shut lest I be ashamed!

The probability of such an appeal being heeded is not high, and in consequence one must seek more powerful help in the form of censorship, however agonising the choice may be. It is interesting to note, in this connection, that although it is usually men of the left who demand 'pornographers' licence', it is the communist countries, from the U.S.S.R. to China, that are least tainted by the pornographer's trade, and which uphold old-fashioned virtues of virginity and marriage. Perhaps Richard Neville had a point, after all.

It will be seen that I have been dealing largely with pornographic products, which would be related particularly to our fourth quadrant, i.e. the high-libido–high-satisfaction, pathological one. It is possible to produce light-hearted, gay (in the proper meaning of the word!) and amusing pornography which would be suitable for the first quadrant, i.e. the extraverted, high-libido–high-satisfaction one, and which would give expression to healthy male and female sensuality. Contrary to some anti-pornographers, I do not feel that the same objections apply to works of this nature, particularly if produced in a tasteful and artistic fashion. Clearly, in the words used by Cline (1974) in the title of his book, the question is: Where do you draw the line? Arguments range all the way from the completely puritan and censorious to the completely libertarian, but in practice every society draws the line somewhere, and the position here suggested is determined by the general thrust of our experimental results; that which is pathological, and likely to promote pathological activities, is out, while anything that does not fall into this category is in. It is not suggested that all potential viewers of pathological material are likely to be tempted to indulge in pathological practices; there is good evidence that some at least, usually already psychiatrically ill to some extent, will be so tempted, and it seems likely, on the existing evidence, that for many people, if not the majority, there will be a profound impact in the direction of devaluation of female sexuality, feminity and female ideals. In the same way, racialist propaganda and incitement to racial violence are ruled out by law, not because everyone who is exposed to such propaganda will become a racist, but because some, usually already psychologically flawed in certain ways, will be encouraged to live out their phantasies. (The concept of the 'marginal viewer', corresponding to the notion of marginal utility of the economist, might be useful here.)

Our results may also carry a message to those who would enforce sex education on often unwilling schoolchildren, and to those who would teach everyone to 'do sex by numbers', and assiduously read the many sex manuals now available. Such an approach clearly mirrors attitudes characteristic of the 'high-libido' group, but is antagonistic to the views of the 'low-libido' group. To the tough-minded person, sex is largely a biological activity, impersonal and designed to produce a maximum of sensuous pleasure; like any other sport, it demands competence, training and competitive excellence. What more appropriate than to teach sex at school, like football, and to publish manuals teaching people the various positions which past experience has found to be useful and profit-able? In the same way, the gourmet 'lives to eat'; both worship at the shrine of old-fashioned hedonism, of a particularly simple-minded kind.

To the tenderminded sex is only in part a biological fact; they would rather see it in terms of Plato's beautiful parable of the circle cut in two, and reconstituted when the male and female half are again united. Sex to them has a spiritual, value-laden, com-panionate side which may be far more important than biological factors such as number of orgasms achieved, or variety of positions mastered. It is wrong to impose the sexual teaching appropriate to the toughminded child on the tenderminded; this is propaganda at its worst, directed at defenceless children, often against the wishes of their parents. It would be equally wrong, of course, to make illegal the sale of sex manuals; they serve a useful function for those who feel in need (although the factual information given in many of these manuals must be said to be of very doubtful value, and often downright wrong in terms of our present-day physiological knowledge). But there is an important difference. Sex manuals are bought only by those who wish to read them; sex education is enforced on children who may not wish for it, and whose parents may be opposed to such teaching. When it is realised that most teachers are even less equipped for this task than are the writers of sex manuals for theirs, one must conclude that the good that may be achieved is probably cancelled out by the bad.

Although it is doubtful if the vaunted liberation from Victorian repression that modern society has achieved is entirely to the good, the disturbing increase in male impotence (difficult to prove beyond doubt, yet attested to by many experts working in this field) may be a direct consequence of modern stress on performance. Many men not up to Wimbledon standards feel inferior, and such feelings only make matters worse, and may produce impotence. Similarly, many women believe that failure to achieve instant orgasm reflects adversely on them, making the achievement of orgasm even more difficult. Or else they may blame their unfortunate husbands, inflicting guilt feeling on them which impede their performance in turn. There is a double bind involved in sexual relations which is not solved by the added stresses of modern insistence on 'performance'. So-called permissiveness in fact imposes rules and standards that are as strident and compelling as were the entirely different ones imposed by puritanism and Victorian orthodoxy; neither set of standards is suitable for everyone. True permissiveness involves an all-embracing tolerance for human diversity, and a recognition that toughminded and tenderminded males and females have different ideals, different standards, different ways of reaching happiness. These differences are only in part susceptible to social influence and manipulation; in large part they are anchored in heredity, in personality, in the very physiology of the person concerned. We should allow maximum freedom to all to develop along the lines of their biological programming, provided only that the rights of others are protected. Permissiveness in this sense is clearly the essence of democratic society; its achievement can be advanced only by gaining a much better understanding of sexual behaviour than we possess at the moment, and in particular a better understanding of the relation between sex and the mysterious processes of personality.

References *and*
Author index

BARTLETT, M. S. (1947) 'The use of transformations', *Biometrics* 3, 39-52 *200*

BELL, R. R. and CHASKER, J. B. (1970) 'Premarital sexual experience among coeds: 1958 and 1968', *Journal of Marriage and the Family* 32, 81-4 *228*

BENTLER, P. M. (1968) 'Heterosexual behaviour assessment – 1: males', *Behaviour Research and Therapy* 6, 21-5 *77*

BLAKE, M. J. F. (1967) 'Relationship between circadian rhythms of body temperature and introversion–extraversion', *Nature* 215, 896-7 *230*.

BONEAU, C. A (1959) 'The effects of violations of assumptions underlying the *t* test', *Psychological Bulletin* 57, 49-64 *140*

BOUSCHER, B. J. (1957) 'Sex differences in the foetal pelvis', *American Journal of Physiology and Anthropology* 15, 581-600 *217*

BOWERMAN, C. and DAY, B. (1956) 'A test of the theory of complementary needs as applied to couples during courtship', *American Sociological Research* 21, 602-5 *109*

BRADY, J. P. and LEVITT, E. E. (1965) 'The scalability of sexual experiences', *Psychological Record* 25, 275-81 *77*

BRAGANÇA, G. (1972) 'A comparative study of attitudes to sex of a sample of sexual offenders, arsonists and non-sexual offenders, resident at Broadmoor Hospital' (Southampton: unpublished B.Sc. dissertation) *177*

BURGESS, E. W. and WALLIS, P. (1944) 'Homogamy in personality characteristics', *Journal of Abnormal and Social Psychology* 39, 475-81 *109*

BYNNER, J. M. (1969) 'The association between adolescent behaviour and attitudes as revealed by a new social attitude inventory' (London: unpublished Ph.D. thesis) *14, 69*

BYRNE, D. (1971) *The Attraction Paradigm* (New York: Academic Press) *139*

BYRNE, D., CHERRY, F., LAMBERTH, J. and MITCHELL, H. E. (1973) 'Husband–wife similarity in response to erotic stimuli', *Journal of Personality* 41, 385-94 *139, 140*

243

SEX AND PERSONALITY

CATTELL, R. B. (1952) *Factor Analysis* (New York: Harper) *87*
CATTELL, R. B. and NESSELROADE, J. R. (1967) 'Likeness and completeness theories examined by sixteen personality factor measures in stably and unstably married couples', *Journal of Personality and Social Psychology* 7, 351-61 *109*
CHILTON, B. (1972) 'Psychosexual development in twins', *Journal of Biosocial Science* 4, 277-86 *196*
CHRISTENSEN, H. T. (1971) *Sexualverhalten und Moralishe Reinbeck* (Hamburg: Rowohlt) *228*
CLINE, V. B. (1974) *Where do you draw the line?* (Provo, Utah: Brigham Young University Press) *236, 237, 239*
COCHRANE, R. and DUFFY, J. (1974) 'Psychology of scientific method', *Bulletin of the British Psychological Society* 27, 117-21 *22-7*
COHEN, M. L. and others (1971) 'The psychology of rapists', *Seminars in Psychiatry* 3 no 3
COLQUHOUN, W. P. (1960) 'Temperament, inspection efficiency and time of day', *Ergonomics* 3, 377-88 *230*
COLQUHOUN, W. P. and CORCORAN, D. W. J. (1964) 'The effects of time of day and social isolation on the relationship between temperament and performance', *British Journal of Social and Clinical Psychology* 3, 226-31 *230*
COMREY, A. L. and LEVONIAN, E. (1958) 'A comparison of three paired coefficients in factor analysis of MMPI items', *Educational Psychological Measurement* 18, 739-48 *87*
CONNER, R. L. (1972) 'Hormones, biogenic amines and aggression', in Levine (1972) *77*
COOPER, A. J. (1969) 'Some personality factors in frigidity', *Journal of Psychosomatic Research* 13, 149-55 *17*
COPPEN, A. (1965) 'The prevalence of menstrual disorders in psychiatric patients', *British Journal of Psychiatry* 111, 155-67 *17*
DAITZMAN, R. J. (1976) 'Personality correlates of androgens and estrogens' (Delaware: unpublished Ph.D. thesis) *215-16*
DAVIDSON, J. M. (1972) 'Hormones and reproductive behavior', in Levine (1972) *77, 214*
EAVES, L. J. (1970) 'The genetic analysis of continuous variation', *British Journal of Mathematical and Statistical Psychology* 23, 189-98 *202*
EAVES, L. J. (1976) 'A model for sibling effects in man', *Heredity* 36, 205-14 *194, 206*
EAVES, L. J. *214*
EAVES, L. J. and EYSENCK, H. J. (1974) 'Genetics and the development of social attitudes', *Nature* 249, 288-9 *150, 171, 196*
EAVES, L. J. and EYSENCK, H. J. (1975) 'The nature of extraversion: a genetical analysis', *Journal of Personality and Social Psychology* 32, 102-12 *195, 201*
EAVES, L. J. and EYSENCK, H. J. (1976) 'Genetic and environmental components of inconsistency and unrepeatability in twins' responses to a neuroticism questionnaire', *Behaviour Genetics* 6, 145-60 *211*
EAVES, L. J. and EYSENCK, H. J. *209, 210*

REFERENCES *and* AUTHOR INDEX

EHRENKRANZ, J., BLISS, E. and SHEARD, M. H. (1974) 'Plasma testosterone: correlations with aggressive behavior and social dominance in man', *Psychosomatic Medicine* 36, 469-75 *219*

EHRHARDT, A. A. and MONEY, J. (1967) 'Progestin-induced hermaphroditism: IQ and psychosexual identity in a study of ten girls', *Journal of Sexual Research* 3, 83-100 *215*

ELLIS, A. and BRANCALE, R. (1956) *The Psychology of Sex Offenders* (Springfield, Mass.: C. C. Thomas)

EYSENCK, H. J. (1947) *Dimensions of Personality* (London: Routledge and Kegan Paul) *18*

EYSENCK, H. J. (1954) *The Psychology of Politics* (London: Routledge and Kegan Paul) *24, 130, 150, 151, 156, 171, 173*

EYSENCK, H. J. (1964) (ed.), *Experiments with Drugs* (New York: Pergamon Press)

EYSENCK, H. J. (1967) *The Biological Basis of Personality* (Springfield, Mass.: C. C. Thomas) *9-13, 23, 24, 214*

EYSENCK, H. J. (1970a) *The Structure of Human Personality*, 3rd ed. (London: Methuen) *10, 18, 197*

EYSENCK, H. J. (1970b) *Crime and Personality* (London: Paladin) *12*

EYSENCK, H. J. (1970c) 'Personality and attitudes to sex: a factorial study', *Personality* 1, 355-76

EYSENCK, H. J. (1971a) 'Personality and sexual adjustment', *British Journal of Psychiatry* 118, 553-608 *12, 69, 75, 104, 187*

EYSENCK, H. J. (1971b) 'Masculinity femininity, personality and sexual attitudes', *Journal of Sexual Research* 7, 83-8 *61, 104, 130*

EYSENCK, H. J. (1971c) 'Hysterical personality and sexual adjustment, attitudes and behaviour', *Journal of Sexual Research* 7, 274-81 *16, 65, 74, 232*

EYSENCK, H. J. (1972) 'Personality and sexual behaviour', *Journal of Psychosomatic Research* 16, 141-52 *68, 70, 133*

EYSENCK, H. J. (1973a) 'Personality and attitudes to sex in criminals', *Journal of Sexual Research* 9, 295-306 *73*

EYSENCK, H. J. (1973b) *The Measurement of Intelligence* (Lancaster: Medical and Technical Publishers) *194*

EYSENCK, H. J. (1974) 'Personality, premarital sexual permissiveness, and assortative mating', *Journal of Sexual Research* 10, 47-51 *109*

EYSENCK, H. J. (1975a) 'Genetic factors in personality development', in A. R. Kaplan (ed.), *Human Behaviour Genetics* (Springfield, Mass.: C. C. Thomas) *18, 133, 195*

EYSENCK, H. J. (1975b) 'The structure of social attitudes', *British Journal of Social and Clinical Psychology* 14, 323-32 *151, 167*

EYSENCK, H. J. (1976) 'Personality and participation in group sex: an empirical study', *Revista Latinoamericana de psicologia* (to appear) *139*

EYSENCK, H. J. and COULTER, T. (1972) 'The personality and attitudes of working-class British communists and fascists', *Journal of Social Psychology* 87, 59-73 *174*

EYSENCK, H. J. and EYSENCK, S. B. G. (1964) *Manual of the EPI* London: University of London Press) *20, 74*

EYSENCK, H. J. and EYSENCK, S. B. G. (1969) *Personality Structure and Measurement* (London: Routledge and Kegan Paul) *10, 18, 31, 47, 87*

EYSENCK, H. J. and EYSENCK, S. B. G. (1975) *Manual of the E.P.Q. (Eysenck Personality Questionnaire)* (London: University of London Press) *18, 19, 30, 127, 167, 198*

EYSENCK, H. J. and EYSENCK, S. B. G. (1976) *Psychoticism as a Dimension of Personality* (London: University of London Press) *18, 21, 30, 76, 180, 214, 215 229*

EYSENCK, H. J. and WILSON, G. (1974) *The Experimental Study of Freudian Theories* (London: Methuen) *8*

EYSENCK, S. B. G. (1961) 'Personality of pain assessment in childbirth of married and unmarried mothers', *Journal of Mental Science* 108, 417-30 *69*

EYSENCK, S. B. G. and EYSENCK, H. J. (1970a) 'Crime and personality: an empirical study of the three-factor theory', *British Journal of Criminology* 10, 225-39 *19*

EYSENCK, S. B. G. and EYSENCK, H. J. (1970b) 'A factor-analytic study of the lie scale of the Junior Eysenck Personality Inventory', *Personality* 1, 3-10 *20*

EYSENCK, S. B. G. and EYSENCK, H. J. (1971a) 'Crime and personality: item analysis of questionnaire responses', *British Journal of Criminology* 11, 49-62 *19*

EYSENCK, S. B. G. and EYSENCK, H. J. (1971b) 'A comparative study of criminals and matched controls on three dimensions of personality', *British Journal of Social and Clinical Psychology* 10, 362-6 *19*

EYSENCK, S. B. G. and EYSENCK, H. J. (1971c) 'Attitudes to sex, personality and lie scale scores', *Perceptual and Motor Skills* 33, 216-18 *74*

EYSENCK, S. B. G., NIAS, D. K. B. and EYSENCK, H. J. (1971) 'The interpretation of children's lie scale scores', *British Journal of Educational Psychology* 41, 23-31 *20*

FERGUSON, G. A. (1941) 'The factorial interpretations of test difficulty', *Psychometrika* 6, 323-9 *87*

FISHER, S. (1973) *The Female Orgasm* (London: Allen Lane) *17, 18, 29*

FORD, C. S. and BEACH, F. A. (1952) *Patterns of Sexual Behavior* (London: Eyre and Spottiswoode) *226*

FOSS, G. L. (1951) 'The influence of endogens on sexuality in women', *Lancet* 1, 667-9 *77*

FULLER, J. L. and THOMPSON, W. R. (1960) *Behavior Genetics* (New York: Wiley) *192*

GIESE, H. and SCHMIDT, A. (1968) *Studenten Sexualität* (Hamburg: Rowohlt) *14, 15, 16, 110*

GIESE, H. and SCHIMDT, A. *69*

GOLDBERG, S. (1973) *The Inevitability of Patriarchy* (New York: Morrow) *226, 228*

GOTTESMAN, I. I. (1965) 'Personality and natural selection', in S. G. Vandenberg (ed.), *Methods and Goals in Human Behaviour Genetics* (London: Academic Press) *109*

GRAY, H. (1949) 'Psychological types in married people', *Journal of Social Psychology* 29, 189-200 *109*

GUILFORD, J. P. (1975) 'Factors and factors of personality', *Psychological Bulletin* 82, 802-14 *139*

HACKETT, T. P. (1971) 'The psychotherapy of exhibitionists in a court clinic setting', *Seminars in Psychiatry* 3 no 3

HAVLICEK, L. L. and PETERSON, N. L. (1974) 'Robustness of the *t* test: a guide for researchers on effect of violations of assumptions', *Psychological Reports* 34, 1095-114 *140*

HENDRICKSON, A. and WHITE, P. O. (1964) 'Promax: a quick method for rotation to oblique simple structure', *British Journal of Statistical Psychology* 17, 65-70 *31, 87*

HEWITT, J. H. (1974) 'An analysis of data from a twin study of social attitudes' (Birmingham: unpublished Ph.D. thesis) *209, 210, 211*

HILL, M. (1968) unpublished Ph.D. thesis quoted by H. J. Eysenck, 'Genetic factors in personality development', in A. R. Kaplan (ed.), *Human Behaviour Genetics* (Springfield, Mass., 1974: C. C. Thomas) *109*

HUNT, M. (1974) *Sexual Behavior in the 1970s* (Chicago: Playboy Press) *228*

HUTT, C. (1972) *Males and Females* (Harmondsworth: Penguin Books) *226*

INGLL, P. M. (1971) 'Family similarities in personality, intelligence and social attitudes' (London: unpublished Ph.D. thesis) *110*

ISRAEL, J., GUSTAVSSON, J., ELIASSON, R. M. and LINDBERG, G. (1970) 'Sexuelle Verhaltensformen der schwedischen Grosstadtjugend', in M. B. Bergstrom-Walan (ed.), *Modellfall Skandinavien?* (Reinbeck: Rowohlt) *228*

JAFFE, Y., MALAMUTH, N., FEINGOLD, J. and FESHBACH, S. (1974) 'Sexual arousal and behavioral aggression', *Journal of Personality and Social Psychology* 30, 759-64 *175*

JENSEN, A. R. (1973) *Educability and Group Differences* (London: Methuen) *23*

JESSOR, S. and JESSOR, R. (1976) 'Sex: the first time', *Journal of Personality and Social Psychology* (in press) *233*

JINKS, J. L. *214*

JINKS, J. L. and FULKER, D. W. (1970) 'A comparison of the biometrical genetical MAVA and classical approaches to the analysis of human behaviour', *Psychological Bulletin* 73, 311-49 *195, 196, 200*

JOE, V. C. (1976) 'Social attitudes and sexual behaviors of college students', *Journal of Consulting and Clinical Psychology* (to appear) *76*

KAGAN, J. (1964) 'Acquisition and significance of sex typing and sex role identity', in M. L. Hoffman and Lois W. Hoffman (eds), *Review of Child Development Research* (New York: Russell Sage Foundation), 137-68 *28*

KALLMAN, F. J. and MICKEY, J. S. (1946) 'Genetic concepts and Folie à Deux', *Journal of Heredity* 37, 298-305 *109*

KINSEY, A. C. *5-8, 22, 25, 28, 130*

KIRKPATRICK, C. and STONE, S. (1935) 'Attitude measurement and the comparison of generations', *Journal of Applied Psychology* 19, 569-82 *175*

KOLASZYNSKA-CARR, *65*

KREITMAN, N. (1964) 'The patient's spouse', *British Journal of Psychiatry* 110, 159-73 *109*

KREITMAN, N. (1968) 'Married couples admitted to mental hospital', *British Journal of Psychiatry* 114, 699-718 *109*

KREUZ, L. E. and ROSE, R. M. (1972) 'Assessment of aggressive behavior and plasma testosterone in a young criminal population', *Psychosomatic Medicine* 34, 331-6 *219*

KTSANES, T. (1955) 'Mate selection on the basis of personality type: a study utilising our empirical typology of personality', *American Sociological Reports* 20, 547-57

LANDIS, C., BOLLES, M. and D'ESOPO, D. A. (1940) 'Psychological and physical concomitants of adjustment in marriage', *Human Biology* 12, 559-65 *17*

LEVINE, S. (1972) *Hormones and Behavior* (London: Academic Press) *226, 229*

LEWIS, N. D. C. and YARNELL, H. (1951) 'Pathological firesetting', *Journal of Nervous and Mental Disease*, monogr. no 82 (New York)

McCLOSKEY, H. (1967) 'Survey research in political science', in G. Y. Glolk (ed.), *Survey Research in the Social Sciences* (New York: Russell Sage Foundation) *28*

McKERRACHER, D. W. and DACRE, A. J. I. (1966) 'A study of arsonists in a special security hospital', *British Journal of Psychiatry* 112, 1151-4

McNEILL, D. and LIVSON, J. (1963) 'Maturation rate and body build in women', *Child Development* 34, 25-32 *197*

MARTIN, N. G. (1976) Unpublished Ph.D. thesis, Department of Genetics, University of Birmingham *219*

MATHER, K. and JINKS, J. (1971) *Biometrical Genetics* (London: Chapman Hall) *195*

MATHER, K. *214*

MICHAELIS, W. and EYSENCK, H. J. (1971) 'The determination of personality inventory factor patterns and intercorrelations by changes in real life motivation', *Journal of Genetical Psychology* 118, 223-34 *20, 21, 76, 173*

MILGRAM, S. (1974) *Obedience to Authority* (London: Tavistock) *25-7*

MISCHEL, W. (1968) *Personality and Assessment* (New York: Wiley) *10*

REFERENCES *and* AUTHOR INDEX

MONEY, J. (1961a) 'Components of eroticism in man: 1. The hormones in relation to sexual morphology and sexual desire', *Journal of Nervous and Mental Disease* 132, 239-48 *77, 214, 229*

MONEY, J. (1961b) 'Sex hormones and other variables in human eroticism', in W. C. Young (ed.), *Sex and Internal Secretions* (Baltimore: Williams and Wilkins) *77, 214, 229*

MONEY, J. (1965) 'Influence of hormones in sexual behavior', *Annual Review of Medicine* 16, 67-82 *77, 215, 229*

MORGAN, C. L. and REMMERS, H. H. (1935) 'Liberalism and conservatism of college students as affected by the depression', *School and Society* 41, 780-4 *175*

MURSTEIN, B. I. (1971) (ed.) *Theories of Attraction and Love* (New York: Springer) *109*

NELSON, E. *13*

NEWCOMB, T. and SVEHLA, G. (1937) 'Intra-family relationships in attitude', *Sociometry* 1, 180-205 *175*

NIAS, D. (1975) 'Personality and other factors determining the recreational interests of children and adults' (London: unpublished Ph.D. thesis) *110*

NICHOLS, R. C. (1969) 'The resemblance of twins in personality and interests', in Manosewitz, G., Lindzey, G. and Thiessen, G. (eds), *Behavioral Genetics: Method and Research* (New York: Appleton-Century-Crofts) *211*

PERSKY, H., SMITH, K. D. and BASU, G. K. (1971) 'Relation of psychologic measures of aggression and hostility to testosterone production in man', *Psychosomatic Medicine* 33, 265-71 *219*

PHOENIX, C. (1966) 'Psychosexual organization in nonhuman primates', paper delivered to conference on 'Endocrine and neural control of sex and related behaviour', Puerto Rico, Dorado Beach, Kray *215*

PICKFORD, J. H., SIGNORI, E. I. and REMPEL, H. (1967) 'Husband–wife difference in personality traits as a factor in marital happiness', *Psychological Reports* 20, 1087-90 *109*

POPPER, K. R. (1959) *The Logic of Scientific Discovery* (London: Routledge and Kegan Paul) *23*

POPPER, K. R. (1972) *Objective Knowledge* (Oxford: Clarendon Press) *23*

PURTELL, J. J., ROBINS, E. and COHEN, M. E. (1951) 'Observations on clinical aspects of hysteria', *Journal of American Medical Association* 146, 902-9 *17*

QUIRION, N. F. (1970) 'Extraversion, neuroticism and habituation of the orienting reaction' (University of Ottawa: unpublished Ph.D. thesis) *13*

REES, L. (1973) 'Constitutional factors and abnormal behaviour', in H. J. Eysenck (ed.), *Handbook of Abnormal Psychology* (London: Pitman), 487-539 *197*

REISS, I. L. (1967) *The Social Context of Premarital Sexual Permissiveness* (New York: Holt, Rinehart and Winston) *131*

REITER, H. (1970) 'Similarities and differences in scores on certain personality scales among engaged couples', *Psychological Reports* 26, 465-6 *109*

ROBERTS, R. C. (1967) 'Some concepts and methods in qualitative genetics', in J. Hirsch (ed.), *Behavior-Genetic Analysis* (New York: McGraw-Hill)

ROOS, D. E. (1956) *Complementary Needs in Mate Selection* (Northwestern University: unpublished Ph.D. thesis) *109*

SCHELLENBERG, J. A. and BEE, L. S. (1960) 'A re-examination of the theory of complementary needs in mate selection', *Marriage and Family Living* 22, 227-32 *109*

SCHILLER, B. (1932) 'A quantitative analysis of marriage selection in a small group', *Journal of Social Psychology* 3, 297-319 *175*

SCHLEGEL, W. S. (1969) 'Konstitutionsbiologie und Verhaltensforschung im Menschen', in F. Keiter (ed.), *Verhaltensforschung im Rahmen der Wissenschaften vom Meuschen* (Gottingen: Musterschmidt) 228-32 *217*

SCHLEGEL, W. S. (1975) 'Parameter Beckenskelett', *Sexualmedizin* 4, 228-32 *217*

SCHMIDT, G. (1975) 'Male–female differences in sexual arousal and behaviour during and after exposure to sexually explicit stimuli', *Archives of Sexual Behavior* 4, 353-65 *228*

SCHMIDT, G. and SIGUSCH, V. (1971) *Arbeitersexualitä* (Berlin: Luchterhand) *228*

SCHMIDT, G. and SIGUSCH, V. (1972) 'Changes in sexual behavior among males and females between 1960-70', *Archives of Sexual Behavior* 2, 27-45 *228*

SCHOFIELD, M. (1968) *The Sexual Behaviour of Young People* (Harmondsworth: Penguin Books) *14, 61, 69*

SCHOOLEY, M. (1936) 'Personality resemblances among married couples', *Journal of Abnormal and Social Psychology* 31, 340-7 *175*

SCHUSTER, E., and ELDERTON, E. M. (1906) 'The inheritance of psychical characters', *Biometrika* 5, 460-9 *175*

SCOTT, J. P. and FULLER, J. L. (1965) *Genetics and the Social Behavior of the Dog* (Chicago: University of Chicago Press) *192*

SHEPHERD, M., LADER, M. and RODNIGHT, R. (1968) *Clinical Psychopharmacology* (London: English Universities Press) *219*

SHOPE, D. F. (1966) 'A comparison of selected college females on sexual responsiveness and non-responsiveness' (Pennsylvania State University: unpublished Ph.D. thesis), quoted by Fisher (1973) *17*

SIGURT, V., SCHMIDT, G., RHEINFELD, S., and WEIDEMAUN-SUTOR, I. (1970) 'Psycho-sexual stimulation: sex differences', *Journal of Sexual Research* 6, 10-24 *69*

SIGUSCH, V. and SCHMIDT, G. (1973) *Jugendsexualität* (Stuttgart: Enke) *228*

SIMON, P. (1972) *Rapport sur le comportement sexuel des Français* (Paris: Julliard et Charron) *28, 136*

SORENSEN, R. C. (1973) *Adolescent Sexuality in Contemporary America* (New York: Ward Publishing Co.) *228*

TENNENT, T. G. and others (1971) 'Female arsonists', *British Journal of Psychiatry* 119, 497-502

TENNENT, G., LOUCAS, K., FENTON, G. and FENWICK, P. (1974) 'Male admissions to Broadmoor Hospital', *British Journal of Psychiatry* 125, 44-50 *177*

TERMAN, L. M. (1938) *Psychological Factors in Marital Happiness* (New York: McGraw-Hill) *17*

TERMAN, L. M. (1951) 'Correlates of orgasm adequacy in a group of 556 wives', *Journal of Psychology* 32, 115-72 *17*

THARP, R. G (1963) 'Psychological patterning in marriage', *Psychological Bulletin* 60, 97-117 *109*

THOMAS, D. R. (1975) 'Conservatism and premarital sexual experience', *British Journal of Social and Clinical Psychology* 14, 195-6 *175*

THOMASON, D. B. (1951) 'Differential non-sexual and sexual behavior in the marital adjustment of Penn State alumni' (Pennsylvania State College: unpublished Ph.D. thesis), quoted by Fisher (1973) *17*

THORNE, F. C. (1966) 'The Sex Inventory', *Journal of Clinical Psychology Monograph Supplement* no 21 *30*

TISSERAND-PERRIER, M. (1953) 'Etude comparative de certains processes de croissance chez les jumeaux', *Journal génétique humain* 2, 82-98 *197*

UDRY, J. (1967) 'Personality match and interpersonal perception as predictors of marriage', *Journal of Marriage and the Family* 29, 122-3 *109*

WELCH, B. L. (1937) 'The significance of the difference between two means when the population variances are unequal', *Biometrika* 29, 350-62 *140*

WELLS, B. W. P. (1969) 'Personality characteristics of VD patients', *British Journal of Social and Clinical Psychology* 8, 246-52 *69*

WHERRY, R. J. and GAYLORD, R. H. (1944) 'Factor patterns of test items and tests as a function of the correlation coefficient; content difficulty, and constant error factors', *Psychometrika* 9, 237-45 *87*

WHITE, O. *77*

WILKINS, I. (1959) 'Masculinization of the female fetus due to the use of certain synthetic oral progestins during pregnancy', *Archives d'Anatomie Microscopique et de Morphologie Experimentale* 48, 313-30 *215*

WILKINS, I. (1960) 'Masculinization of female fetus due to use of orally given progestin', *Journal of the American Medical Association* 172, 1028-32 *215*

WILSON, G. (1973) (ed.), *The Psychology of Conservatism* (London: Academic Press) *76, 124, 130, 150, 173*

WILSON, G. D. and BRAZENDALE, A. H. (1973) 'Social attitude correlates of Eysenck's personality dimensions', *Social Behavior and Personality* 1, 115-18 *173*

WILSON, E. O. (1975) *Sociobiology* (Cambridge: Belknap Press) *226*

REFERENCES *and* AUTHOR INDEX

WINCH, R. F. (1958) *Mate Selection: A Study of Complementary Needs* (New York: Harper Bros) *109*

WINOKUR, G., GUZE, S. B. and PFEIFFER, E. (1958) 'Developmental and sexual factors in women: a comparison between control, neurotic and psychotic groups', *American Journal of Psychiatry* 115, 1097-100 *17*

YOM, B. L., BRADLEY, P. E., WAKEFIELD, J. S., KRAFT, I. A., DOUGHTIE, E. B. and COX, J. S. (1976) 'A common factor in the MMPI scales of married couples', *British Journal of Social and Clinical Psychology* (to appear) *109*

YOUNG, W. C., GAY, R. W. and PHOENIX, C. N. (1965) 'Hormones and sexual behavior', in J. Money (ed.), *Sex Research: New Developments* (New York: Holt, Rinehart and Winston) *215*

ZETTERBERG, H. L. (1969) *Om Sexuallivet i Sverige* (Stockholm: Statens offentliga utredninger) *228*

ZUCKERMAN, M. (1973) 'Scales for sex experience for males and females', *Journal of Consulting and Clinical Psychology* 41, 27-9

ZUCKERMAN, M. (1974) 'The sensation-seeking motive', in B. Maher (ed.), *Progress in Experimental Personality Research* vol. 7 (New York: Academic Press) *15*

ZUCKERMAN, M., BONE, R. N., NEARY, R., MANGELSDURFF, P., and BRUSTMAN, B. (1972) 'What is the sensation seeker? Personality trait and experience correlates of the sensation-seeking scales', *Journal of Consulting and Clinical Psychology* 39, 308-21 *14*

Index